MEDALS OF THE RENAISSANCE

SIR GEORGE HILL

FELLOW OF THE BRITISH ACADEMY

MEDALS OF THE RENAISSANCE

Revised and enlarged by

GRAHAM POLLARD

KEEPER OF COINS AND MEDALS
FITZWILLIAM MUSEUM, CAMBRIDGE

A COLONNADE BOOK

PUBLISHED BY
BRITISH MUSEUM PUBLICATIONS LIMITED

© 1978, Estate of Sir George Hill and J. G. Pollard

First published 1920
Revised and enlarged edition published 1978

ISBN 0 7141 0843 X

Published by British Museum Publications Ltd.,
6 Bedford Square, London, WC1B 3RA

Colonnade Books
are published by British Museum Publications Ltd
and are offered as contributions to the enjoyment, study,
and understanding of art, archaeology and history.

The same publishers also produce the official publications
of the British Museum

Designed by Bernard Crossland
Set in 'Monophoto' Apollo 14/15pt
by Filmtype Services Limited, Scarborough
Printed in Great Britain at the University Press, Oxford
by Vivian Ridler, Printer to the University

Le sonnet . . . sans se refuser à un souffle romantique, est essentiellement classique parceque, comme la médaille de bronze, il enferme dans un étroit espace un tableau achevé, une impression définie ou suggérée, un tout qui, parfois, est peu de chose, mais qui se donne tout entier et dont l'expression est adéquate.

AUGUSTIN FILON, *Journal des Débats*, 25 mars 1914

Contents

CONTENTS

Editor's Preface

This book by Sir George Hill was his only extensive essay on medals, and being based on lectures bears the stamp of his personality, for there is warmth and wit in the printed version. It has remained for so long the best survey of the European Renaissance Medal that for this re-issue the text remains hardly touched by editorial interferences. It has been reset and supported by a new Bibliography and a series of new notes added (incorporated with the earlier ones for ease of reference) in the hope that it will remain both a remarkable essay and a standard work of reference. Hill wrote so extensively on Italian medals that a separate bibliography of all of his writings on medals is appended, accompanied by a Biographical Note. The Key to the Plates and the Index have been carefully revised.

The publisher expresses thanks for permission to reproduce medals in the British Museum, the National Portrait Gallery, the Museo Nazionale (Bargello), Florence, the Birmingham City Museum and Art Gallery, the Fitzwilliam Museum, and Jacques Schulman B.V., Amsterdam.

J.G.P.

Fitzwilliam Museum,
Cambridge, 1977

Preface

In the autumn of 1915, at the invitation of the Council of the Society of Antiquaries of Scotland, I had the honour of delivering in Edinburgh the Rhind Lectures, of which this book is the outcome. In preparing it for the press, the matter of the lectures has been revised, partly re-arranged, and occasionally re-written with large additions, while footnotes have been supplied throughout with the object of making the book of some use as a work of reference. There are many volumes on separate portions of the subject, but none, I believe, that can be regarded as an attempt to give a general summary of the whole.

Illustrations have been a serious difficulty. In delivering the lectures, every medal that was mentioned was also illustrated. Was the same plan to be followed in the printed book? That would have meant either an unusually lavish amount of illustration or else the cutting out of a great number of links in the argument. I have preferred to leave many of the pieces unillustrated, in the hope that those who take a real interest in the subject will refer to the illustrations which are to be found elsewhere, and to which references are supplied.

The arrangement of the medals on the plates will, I fear, prove irksome. Thus, medals by the same artist are illustrated on different plates, and not in the order in which they are mentioned in the text, an inconvenience which is due to the fact that some of the plates are from borrowed negatives, while others are newly photographed. Again, the scale on which the reproductions are made has inevitably varied with the size of the original. Reproduction is now so costly that it was absolutely necessary to borrow negatives and, further, to reduce the scale of reproduction of many pieces; the result is a distribution of the medals which is anything but scientific.

Two works on Italian medals which are seldom mentioned in the footnotes—simply because the only alternative would have been to mention them on every page—are Alfred Armand's *Médailleurs de la Renaissance*, which, with all its faults, remains and will long remain the standard book on the subject, and

Cornelius von Fabriczy's clever though rather ill-proportioned sketch, which I have cited by Mrs. Hamilton's translation, entitled *Italian Medals*. Any references give in my notes for details about an Italian medallist should be supplemented by reference to these books, which are fully indexed. The leading works on other branches of the art are, I believe, fairly indicated in the footnotes and in the bibliography. Perhaps I should apologize for the frequency of the references to books and articles of my own. My excuse must be that, since I have now for many years been trying to fill up the gaps necessarily left in their work by the pioneers, these references are required to complete the bibliographical apparatus, until the time comes for a book which will gather up all the scattered material. The materials for such a book have for over fifteen years been accumulating in my hands; but since 1914 some of the most fruitful sources have been cut off, so far as men of my generation are concerned, and what I had hoped would be a *corpus* will, if it appears at all, be but an imperfect *torso*.

One of the tragedies of the war has been the death, fighting for his country, of Jean de Foville, an enthusiastic student of Italian medals, of whom great things were hoped. There are still many collectors and connoisseurs, and able compilers of sale-catalogues; but of serious systematic students of the subject, if one may judge from the periodical literature, there are sadly few left on the Continent.

My thanks are due to the Trustees of the British Museum for the loan of the negatives from which Plates 1, 4, 8 and 15, as well as portions of a number of other plates, are printed; to the Directors of the *Burlington Magazine* for permission to reprint in the Introduction the substance of two articles; to the owners of the medals which are illustrated, more especially to my friend Mr. Maurice Rosenheim; to Miss Helen Farquhar for certain suggestions in connexion with Chapter VIII; and to Mr. George Macdonald for reading the whole of the proofs and making many helpful criticisms.

G. F. HILL

Introduction

Obvious as may seem the meaning of the words which form the title of this book, it is necessary to give some sort of consideration to the connexion between the period that has to be covered and the particular form of art with which we are concerned. Were our subject the Painting or the Sculpture of the Renaissance, it would be superfluous to enter into generalities about painting or sculpture. But the medal, as we know it now, was in fact one of the creations of the Renaissance; a minor creation, doubtless, and one on which some critics suspect the specialist of laying too much stress; nevertheless, as we shall see, a very characteristic creation. It follows that the medallic art, in relation to this period, is on a different footing from arts that had flourished before the Renaissance began. There must be some intimate connexion between the art and the genius of the age, or why did it come into being? The conditions must have been especially favourable, or why has it never since flourished, if we may not say so luxuriantly (for there is no lack of bad medals of a later date), yet with so sound and beautiful a growth? The problem of this relationship has not, perhaps, been solved conclusively; indeed, what problem of artistic origins has been satisfactorily answered? But we can, with a little thought, discern certain facts which make it clear why the conditions were favourable for the development of the medal in the fifteenth century.

But, first, it is desirable to have a clear idea of what sort of thing a medal[1] is, and to consider how it is related to and distinguished from its congeners. Modern dictionaries define a medal as a 'piece of metal, usually in the form of a coin, struck or cast with inscription and device to commemorate an event, etc.' In older writers, ancient coins are all spoken of as 'medals', and the names of the Medal Room at the British Museum and the Cabinet des Médailles in the Bibliothèque Nationale at Paris preserve the old tradition. But the medals with which we are concerned are of the commemorative sort.

Notes to this chapter begin on p. 168

From the coin, which was its chief if not its only begetter, the medal has certain points of distinction, growing out of the fact that it was not, like the coin, a medium of exchange. First, then, the metal of which it is composed is inessential; and indeed, from an artistic standpoint, the baser metals, bronze and lead, afford by far the most satisfactory medallic material. On the other hand, like the coin, it affects a circular shape; there are indeed oval or rectangular or otherwise shaped medals, as there are also coins of eccentric fashions; but for the most part medals are circular, because the medal is essentially a portable thing, to be passed from hand to hand, and the circular shape was found to be most convenient for this purpose. Any one who has experience of handling a large number of rectangular plaques will see that there is reason in this. Further, the medal, like the coin, is almost invariably in relief; since, however, it does not circulate incessantly, but is usually preserved with some care, the relief need not be limited in depth in order to avoid abrasion. Nevertheless it is limited by the practical consideration that if a medal is laid down on the table, and the relief on the under side is too high, it does not rest comfortably. Therefore, if a medal has a reverse—and the best medallists seldom failed to realize that a medal is not complete without a reverse—it is desirable that it should not be in excessively high relief. But, even if it has no reverse, there is the aesthetic consideration—perhaps only a translation into another form of the practical one—that the depth of a relief should bear some proportion to its area. The area, again, is limited by the essentially portable nature of the medal. A great medallion, like Andrea Spinelli's medallion of Bernardo Soranzo, which measures 31 centimetres, or $12\frac{1}{4}$ inches, is only fit to be fastened to a wall; a better artist than Spinelli would accordingly have cast it without any inscription on the reverse. But in size the medal is on the average much larger than the coin; and this affects the technique. For, owing to the mechanical difficulty of striking a large piece of metal with a large die, the process of casting is more suitable than that of striking for the production of large medals. In the best period the greatest masters realized this; it is only in the days when the art of the medal was at its lowest ebb that the use of dies was supreme. But of the technical processes it will be convenient to speak in detail later.

If the coin is one of the neighbours of the medal, another is the plaquette. A plaquette may be briefly defined[2] as any small flat piece of metal decorated in relief on one face only, for application as ornament; normally, too, the plaquette is cast, at any rate in the age of the Renaissance. As its object is mainly decorative (though some plaquettes were used for religious purposes) and as it finds its place in a setting, is not independent, and has not to pass by itself from hand to hand, its shape may be anything you please. And its subject is, for the same reason, frequently insignificant; all that the artist required was a pleasant piece of relief. The Italian plaquette, often exquisite in composition and modelling, is too often at the same time uninteresting in content, since, unlike the reverse of a medal, it has no relation to any particular person.

This word *person* is the key to the significance of the medal and its place in Italian art. It is a mistake to think of medals in their too frequent modern association with institutions or learned societies. The medals with which this book is concerned are essentially personal documents. The definition quoted at the outset spoke of the medal as 'commemorating events, etc.' The Italian conceived it rather as commemorating 'persons, etc.'; and since it was in Italy that the medal, in its proper sense, was first developed, we must regard that conception as the governing one.

And so we come to the other word in our title. This is not the place for a lengthy disquisition on the genius of the Italian Renaissance, or for an estimate of its moral character. There will always be some to believe, in the words ascribed to Dean Milan, that 'perhaps in no period of the civilized world, since Christ, was the moral condition of mankind, in some respects, in a lower and more degraded state; never were the two great enemies of human happiness—ferocity and sensuality—so dominant over all classes; and in those vices Italy, in one sense the model and teacher of the world, enjoyed, and almost boasted, a fatal pre-eminence'. In spite of such outbursts—and they are not confined to clerical or Protestant writers—it is to be suspected that some other ages may have been not more moral but only less articulate than the Renaissance. We need say nothing about our own times. The Middle Ages have long served as a foil to the iridescent wickedness of the Renaissance, but something of their monotony has been chequered by the light thrown upon them by recent studies. Were the seventeenth and eighteenth centuries so much more respectable than those which preceded them, or were they only less brilliant? And, if Italy was so very bad, let us not forget that one of the most savage of the leaders of bands who ravaged Italy in the fourteenth century was John Hawkwood, an Englishman; that it was Werner, a German, who claimed to be the Enemy of God, of Pity, and of Mercy; and that the worst excesses in Italy in the wars at the end of the fifteenth century and at the sack of Rome in 1527, were committed not by Italians, but by Frenchmen, Spaniards, and Teutons.

But the fact we have to bear in mind is that, if the Renaissance was an excessively wicked time, it had the force to be so, and that its alleged excessive wickedness was only one revelation of the moving spirit of the age—an extraordinary, an unexampled development of personal character, and of the power of self-expression, in the individuals of the race.[3] The Italian name for this realisation of individuality was simply *virtù*. It was the same force that produced Nicolò d'Este, Sigismondo Malatesta, Alexander VI, and Cesare Borgia on the one hand, and Alfonso V of Aragon, Federigo of Urbino, San Bernardino of Siena, Savonarola, or Vittorino da Feltre on the other. In a picture of too vivid contrasts, the eye can only find rest by dwelling on the shadows and ignoring the lights, or vice versa. But the historian has to find out why the contrasts are so strong.

There was, however, more than one way of expressing personality. The most obvious, the portrait, was employed for the front or obverse of the medal, almost without exception. But a medal, strictly speaking, is not complete unless it has a reverse; and for this some kind of design is necessary, except in those medals which commemorate pairs of people. The design could be historical, or strictly heraldic—as it almost always was in Germany—but the Italians specially favoured the personal device or, as they called it, *impresa*.

These *imprese*, which developed into a sort of bastard heraldry, have quite a literature of their own; the most famous book on the subject, Paolo Giovio's *Dialogue of Warlike and Amorous Devices*, first published in 1555, went into many editions in a few years.[4] He gives five conditions that a good device should fulfil: first, it should show a just proportion between soul (*anima*) and body (*corpo*), that is, between motto and design; second, it should not be so obscure as to require a Sibyl to interpret it, not so plain that all the vulgar crowd can understand it; third, it should be decorative and attractive in appearance; fourth, it should not contain the human figure (a condition, by the way, which is constantly violated); fifth, it should have a motto, if possible in a foreign language, so as to disguise the meaning somewhat more, but not so much as to make it doubtful. Other writers, such as Lodovico Dolce, lay stress on the necessity of obscurity, that the device should not be understood of the people. Another authority on the subject, Sertorio Quattromani, in a letter of 1564 to yet another inventor of devices, Annibal Caro,[5] remarks that the rules do not permit that the motto should actually name the thing which is represented; thus, if you have the motto *Chirone magistro*, you must not give a picture of the centaur Chiron, but only of his lyre and bow. In fact, towards the end of the sixteenth century it becomes impossible to defend the whole business of the *impresa* from the charge of childishness and ineptitude. Any such accusation in the case of Pisanello, however, and of the greater medallists, is irrelevant; they are only producing suitable reverses for their medals; and there is still a freshness about the fifteenth-century *impresa* which often redeems it from any possibility of frigidity. It must be confessed that at all times most of the devices err on the side of obscurity, and if one solves the riddle it is more often by accident than not. A good instance of this is afforded by the device on the medal of the humanist Florio Maresio of Belluno, made about 1545: a bird perched on the crupper of a horse, pecking at it. One might guess for ever, and be no wiser, unless turning over the pages of the *Hieroglyphica* of Florio's friend, Pierio Valeriano Bolzani, one chanced to come across the identical design. The bird is the *anthos*, Latinized into *florus*, of which the Greek naturalists related that it was an enemy of the horse, whom it would attack and even drive out of its meadow. So Florio Maresio took it for his device, with the motto *Ferox a mansueto superatus*, which occurs both on the medal and in the woodcut. No doubt Bolzani devised it for him.[6]

We shall see many instances of all kinds of *imprese*—those which are based on old bestiaries, like the unicorn purifying a spring by dipping his horn into it; mere punning devices, like the *florus* just described; elaborate allegories, classical allusions, and so on.

Given the moral conditions which we know prevailed during the Renaissance, and the tendency of the Italian mind to express itself in plastic form, it is obvious that the artist was ready to pick up from the remains of ancient plastic art a suggestion as to the particular forms which might be employed. All that ferment of life, so characteristic of the period, in which good and bad, but always clad in distinct, clear-cut forms, come so prominently to the top, may or may not have been caused by the rediscovery of antiquity[7] which has given its name to the age. If not the chief cause, that rediscovery was at least an encouraging condition. Now one of the most constant agents in familiarizing the inquirers of the age with antiquity was the ancient coin. Coins are small, insignificant looking things, but of all classes of antiques, if we except potsherds, which are not complete in themselves, they are the most numerous. The soil of Italy is thickly sown with Roman coins, a seed which bore considerable fruit. Turned up by vine-dressers and ploughmen, examples were brought, we know, to Petrarch, who became an enthusiastic student—the first modern collector of coins. His object in collecting, be it noted, was a purely ethical one. These little gold and silver images of the ancient emperors, inscribed in tiny

letters with their names, were to him memorials of persons from whose lives moral lessons were to be learned. That was the text on which he preached to the Emperor Charles IV when he had audience of him at Mantua in 1355. And the first modern epigraphist, Cyriac of Ancona, when in audience with Sigismund at Siena in 1433, drew from some gold coin of Trajan an argument for a crusade against the Turk. Alfonso the Magnanimous, King of Naples, was a famous collector in his day, and was especially fond of coins of Caesar. Such coins, he used to say, since no other portraits of these men existed, did marvellously delight him and in a manner inflame him with a passion for virtue and glory. A gold piece of Nero, recording the closing of the temple of Janus, inspired him with the remark that the emperor was to be condemned for arrogating to himself a glory to which he had no right. Always, we observe, the ethical point of view is the one that matters: the application of these relics of antiquity as guides to conduct. Something of the same kind, of course, has inspired many collectors down to the present time. Goethe's object in collecting medals—his collection is still at Weimar—was to bring the great men of the past vividly before us. But such an object, admirable as it is, is largely overshadowed nowadays by the purely scientific aim, or by the collector's desire to possess a complete series, or by the love of coins for their own beauty. It is impossible to suppose that the old Italian collectors did not appreciate the beauty of coins; yet that their taste was not necessarily highly cultivated we may gather from a remark of Ambrogio Traversari. He writes to the collector Nicolò Nicoli that he had seen some gold coins of Constantine and Constans, beautiful indeed, but in no way equal in beauty to one of Berenice. Now the gold coins of Berenice are of a class, the Ptolemaic, in which the Hellenistic die-engraver comes nearer than anywhere else to pretentious vulgarity. One would have liked those old collectors to have had some better standard of comparison.

This passion for the moral estimation of the coin or medal produced some strange results. An instance is the well-known *Promptuaire des Médailles*, published by Rouille at Lyons in 1553. The ethical object was dominant in the author's mind. He felt justified, therefore, when no extant coin or medal was to hand, in inventing a picture of one, to the best of his ability. After all, was this more of a lie than writing a character of the man? When a nation is apt to think plastically or graphically with as much ease as we think in words, is a graphical representation less likely to be true than a literary one? Rouille, therefore, had a free hand and used it for the vast majority of his subjects, at any rate for the earliest period. He begins with Adam and Eve. All the famous characters of antiquity, including the Minotaur, are figured. For Eve he apparently made free use of Albrecht Dürer's medal, dated 1508, of the supposed Agnes Dürer. For the Minotaur he borrowed the human-headed bull, the river-god, from the coins of ancient Gela. For many of his heroes of classical antiquity he drew on certain 'coins' or little medals made by the medallist Valerio Belli of Vicenza, who died only seven years before the book was published. Doubtless these passed among the public as genuine coins, and Rouille was himself deceived; but he would not have shrunk from his high moral purpose even if he had known them to be what they were, the creation of Belli's fancy. To suppose that he would have hesitated is to misunderstand the spirit of the age.

Is it incorrect to speak of the medal as the creation of the Renaissance? Some may object that what are known as Roman medallions are an anticipation of the Renaissance medal. That objection must be granted; but it is necessary to distinguish. What would have happened, let us imagine, if under the Roman Empire a private person had had a medal made with his own portrait? No reader of Tacitus can hesitate for an answer; the offender would have had short shrift. The Roman medallions, though they were in the main commemorative, were strictly official; none but members of the imperial family figure on them, whereas the Italian medal may represent any one from the head of the Holy Roman Empire or the Pope down to the most insignificant private person.

Yet, after all, the Roman medallion it was that gave the impetus to the man who was to make the first modern medal, in the proper sense of the term. One or two other slight anticipations apart, there is much probability that Pisanello was originally inspired by the sight of some Roman medallions. Those anticipations are worth dwelling on for a moment.[8] In the inventories of the collections of the French Maecenas, Jean Duc de Berry, we find described, in 1401, a leaden impression of a medal with the portrait of Francesco of Carrara on one side and the badge of Padua on the other. This was one of two pieces which represent Francesco and his son, and were struck to commemorate the recovery of Padua from Milanese hands on June 19, 1390. The imitation of Roman imperial coins on the obverse of these medals is so close that they used to be attributed to the sixteenth century, when such imitation was more in fashion. Had we not the Duc de Berry's inventory, we should still have a reproduction of the medal in a fifteenth-century manuscript of Livy at Paris[9] to prove the early origin of this piece and its fellow. It is possible that they were made by one of the Sesto family, who are known to have been working for the Venetian mint at the end of the fourteenth century, and to have struck other little pieces showing classical influence. However that may be, the connexion of the first attempt at a modern commemorative medal with Padua, where the tradition of classical learning was so strong, is significant.

The Carrara[10] medals were struck from engraved dies, although most of the existing specimens are cast. The other pre-Renaissance pieces were cast and chased; indeed, some if not all of them were perhaps made in two hollow pieces, and joined together to make what is called a shell. Specimens of these medals were also in the Duc de Berry's collection, and they were probably made about the end of the fourteenth century. Of some that he possessed we can only guess at the appearance; but old copies of the medals of the Emperors Constantine (Plate 24.1) and Heraclius have been preserved. These are distinctly neither Italian nor Byzantine in style; they belong to the art of Northern France or of Flanders. Evidently part of a series representing important persons in the history of Christianity, they are packed with mediaeval symbolism. But they stand at the very end of the Middle Ages, looking backward, not forward. The Carrara medals are different; their reverses are thoroughly mediaeval in style, but their obverses point forward to the revival of art. Yet the Carrara examples had, fortunately, no influence on the general development of the medal, which, had it proceeded on the same lines of slavish imitation of the antique, would soon have become quite negligible in the history of art.

Before proceeding to the historical sketch which is the main theme of this volume, we shall consider the nature of medallic technique; but a word may be in place here about the order of arrangement adopted, and about a certain question of method. Italy naturally comes first, as the founder of the art. France and the Low Countries might seem to have most claim to be treated next, as being closely dependent on Italy in style and technique. But, on the other hand, the very independence of the German school gives it a claim to priority. The short chapter devoted to the medals of England and Scotland comes last, and will not perhaps be considered disproportionate in a book intended primarily for English readers. The extension of the period so as to include the French and English medallists of the first half of the seventeenth century is justified by the high development which the art achieved in that period.

Within Italy itself it seems convenient to deal with the Florentine school of the fifteenth century after the schools of the North and Centre, because the latter were intimately connected with each other, whereas the Florentine stood apart and provides a good transition to the sixteenth century.

The reader may find in this book a tendency to indulge in the game and play of attribution. It was, I think, a Quarterly Reviewer who remarked that the least important thing about a picture is the question who painted it. That is perfectly true from the purely aesthetic point of view, and valuable as a protest against the natural tendency in all of us to bow to great names. All progress, however, in a scientific sense, depends on classification; and the process of attribution of pictures or medals to particular artists is necessary quite apart from their aesthetic value. If the artist is a great artist, as a few of the Italian medallists were we get from the sifting of attributions something better than a mere barren classification. This or that work may be in itself beautiful, but when it is brought into relation with others by the same man, the combination reveals something more; it reveals, in some degree, the mind of the artist. If that is of no interest to the Quarterly Reviewer, so much the worse for him. To many minds, in a series of portraits by Titian it is in Titian, and not in the sitters, that the supreme interest lies. 'A great portrait', wrote Samuel Butler,[11] 'is always more a portrait of the painter than of the painted. When we look at a portrait by Holbein or Rembrandt it is of Holbein or Rembrandt that we think more than of the subject of their picture. Even a portrait of Shakespeare by Holbein or Rembrandt could tell us very little about Shakespeare. It would, however, tell us a great deal about Holbein or Rembrandt.' Butler is right in the main, although it is odd how often portraits of artists by themselves are failures. However, apart from this there is a scientific joy in settling attributions; and when we have allowed for the absurdities into which the too confident critic will from time to time be led, there is no doubt that the total result, not of any one man's work perhaps, but of a generation of labour, is the clearing of our ideas about artistic values and development, without spoiling our aesthetic appreciation. Even the botanist has been known to take pleasure in flowers apart from their identification. The method which the critic who is studying medals—or indeed any other class of works of art—should adopt seems to me to be that he should begin with the general impression and end with the details. That is to say, if a certain medal strikes him at first sight as being in the same manner as an identified group which goes by the name of an artist, he may then set to work to examine it, to see whether the details, such as lettering, stops, treatment of hair, border, and the like confirm the general impression. Even if they do, he must still be ready to admit, on necessity, that these resemblances may be due to imitation—a question of which the general spirit of the work will perhaps afford the only criterion. And always, failing documentary proof—since signatures may be forged, they are not enough—he should remember when talking of 'medals by N.M.' that this phrase is really only an abbreviation of: 'medals of a group associated in their style and content, of which the majority or the most characteristic may with as much certainty as is possible in such matters be regarded as the work of N.M.'

I

Medallic Technique

The process of striking with dies, by which, as we have seen, the Carrara medals were produced at the end of the fourteenth century, was not to find favour with medallists for some generations to come; and the medals of Constantine and Heraclius, with their approximation to jeweller's technique, make quite a different impression from the ordinary cast medals of the Renaissance.[12] To produce these latter, the artist took a flat disk of some material—most usually, to judge from the few examples that have come down to us, black slate. Benvenuto Cellini mentions also bone and black glass; and wood was sometimes used. This was the basis of the model, and also provided the actual field or background surrounding the type. On this the craftsman modelled the type, building it up in wax. Doubtless every medallist had his favourite recipe for wax.

Vasari in his introduction says that the wax for modelling was generally mixed with a little tallow (to make it more supple), turpentine (to make it tenacious), and black pitch (to give it a black hue, and also a certain firmness after it is worked, so that it becomes hard). Other colouring matter could be added in powder, when the wax was molten. If, as was usual for small works in relief, like medals, you wanted it white, you used powdered white lead. Benvenuto Cellini gives a somewhat similar recipe: pure white wax, mixed with half its quantity of well-ground white lead and a little clear turpentine. Cellini also describes an elaborate composition with which he coated the wax model of a statue, but it is improbable that anything of the kind was used for small objects. Gypsum and resin were mixed with the wax which was used, by people like Capocaccia, for the so-called stucco-reliefs and portraits which became popular in the second half of the sixteenth century, and from which medals could be cast, though the reliefs were valued for themselves. This produced an extremely durable material.

Notes to this chapter begin on p. 169

But, whatever the material, the artist built up with it obverse and reverse of his model either on two separate disks, or on the two sides of a single disk. The Negroboni model,[13] belonging to Mr. Henry Oppenheimer, shows the extraordinary care with which the lettering was executed by some artists (Plate 2.*1*). On this a strip of parchment has been laid down round the edge of the disk of wood. Radii have been drawn with a blind point from the centre of the disk to the circumference, in order to fix the axes of the letters accurately. Then the letters have been drawn in ink on the parchment, and the wax built up on these drawings. But no other wax model that I have seen shows so elaborate a process. The beautiful little model for the medal of Barbara Romana, by an unknown artist, in Mr. Maurice Rosenheim's collection, shows the ordinary method (Plate 2.*2*).

It was quite usual to draw with compasses a couple of incised concentric circles, as a guide for the lettering; such incised lines reproduced themselves more or less plainly on the final casting. These incised lines, in one instance, attain the dignity of a mark of authorship. Kenner, in his study of the medals made by Leone Leoni for the imperial court,[14] has shown that a certain number of the large cast medals by this artist, representing chiefly imperial personages, have not merely the usual couple of incised circles, between which the letters of the inscription are placed, but a third, inmost one, drawn very close to its neighbour. In the narrow space between the two latter circles Leone was accustomed to place his signature, as on the medal of Ippolita Gonzaga. But this actual signature seems to have been confined to his medals of private persons. The medals of Charles V, of the Empress Isabella, of Don Philip, of the Emperor Ferdinand I, all have the double inner circle, but no signature. Kenner's suggestion, which seems plausible, is that the artist was not allowed to place his signature in such close proximity to the portraits of these exalted personages,[15] but that he nevertheless drew the extra inmost circle as a sort of artist's mark. This third circle is certainly, so far as I know, not found on the medals of any other artist. It is of course only visible on the finest specimens, like those in the Vienna collection.

On certain medals, though not on any of an early period, the bust appears to encroach on the inscription; for instance, on the medal of Nicolò Madruzzo by Antonio Abondio (Plate 18.*10*),[16] portions of the lettering are actually covered by the head and left shoulder of the portrait; and again on the medal of Cardinal Cristoforo Madruzzo by Pier Paolo Romano[17] some of the letters are partially covered in the same way, while others have been placed actually over the bust.

What happened was doubtless this: the artist modelled his inscription on the disk, leaving room, as he supposed, for the bust within it. He then modelled the bust separately and transferred it to the disk; but now he found that the bust was so large that it covered part of the inscription. Where the letters were not so much covered up that they could not be read, he left them alone; but when they were entirely covered, he remodelled them, as he has done in this medal of Cristoforo Madruzzo, actually on the top of the bust.

There is evidence of another kind which shows that inscriptions and bust were sometimes modelled separately, the former being worked on a ring fitting round the latter.[18] It can be demonstrated that Amadeo da Milano, a jeweller turned medallist, made his inscription on a separate ring, probably even cut it on a ring of metal. This was fitted round the disk on which was the model of the portrait, and the two were impressed into the mould together (Plate 5.3). In different specimens of the same medal the ring is not always in exactly the same position, as is proved by the fact that the inscription does not always begin at exactly the same point in the circumference. Clearly therefore the inscription-ring must have been movable. The same process was employed by some of the medallists who worked for Pope Paul II, by Enzola, and doubtless by others. But it was fortunately only the exception; for every process which disintegrates the execution of a design into independent parts tends to destroy the unity of composition.

When the artist desired to give a border to his design he could, of course, model the border in wax. But he could also impress the border, cut or modelled in relief in some hard substance, separately in the mould, as in the process just described for the separate inscription-band; and it is not improbable that this was frequently done, as in the style of border of large pearls on a raised band which was introduced by Pastorino of Siena. Or he could carve or turn the border in the actual disk of wood or bone or metal on which he worked his model. This is almost certainly the method by which medals with what we call moulded borders were produced. Thus a fine medal of Fernando I of Naples[19] shows marks of turning in the moulded border on the obverse, and over the whole of the plain back; indeed it may have been entirely carved in wood. Two large, rather coarse, but very vigorous medals, one of Giuliano II de' Medici, Duc de Nemours, the other of Leo X,[20] plainly show the turning marks on the field. These were all built up on disks of wood.[21]

In Germany the medal originated in two crafts, sculpture and goldsmithery. Normally, therefore, the models for German medals were made in wood or in fine stone, the materials natural to these crafts. The predominance of the wax model in Germany dates from the decline of the art, and was presumably due to Italian influence. The result of the use of more durable material was that a far greater proportion of the original models was preserved than is the case with the Italian branch. One may add that the number of forgeries is also large.

Many of the German models, in fact the majority of the earlier ones, bear no inscription, or, if they do, it is incised, and was probably cut after the casts had been made from the model. The fact is that the letters were impressed in the mould after the model had been impressed and taken out. Hagenauer, for instance, seems to have used type for this purpose.[22] Christoph Weiditz, on the other hand, carved his lettering on the wood model. Obviously the latter was the process more likely to produce a good result—on the principle, already stated, that anything in the way of separate punches in the preparation of a design is liable to destroy its unity.

I have said nothing of the actual tools used in building up the wax model; they have probably been more or less the same from the earliest times. The extraordinary precision secured by the old modellers seems to indicate the use of quite sharp-edged instruments; or else, as Mr. Henry Wilson suggests to me, it may have been obtained by working on the design *in the reverse* in some fairly hard material, such as plaster. That is a method still employed by some medallists. The stages of the process would be these: you first build up a wax model; then you make a plaster mould from this; you work on this mould to obtain definition; and then you press your wax for a new model into this mould, and when it has taken the sharper impression remove it. This model could then be used for the *cire perdue* process, though, as is said below, it is improbable that this process was much employed by the early medallists. If a sand mould was used, a new plaster positive would be taken from the retouched mould; this positive, having been retouched, would be used to make the impressions in the sand mould. (No such plaster models of an early date have survived.) Mr. Wilson adds:

> I strongly suspect that some of the finely finished wax impressions which remain have been made in sulphur moulds taken from a chased and highly finished original in metal. The surface of the sulphur is so velvety and precious, besides being hard, that when very slightly oiled the wax impression seems almost to receive some of the bloom of the sulphur. In Italy of course sulphur was much used.

And now, how was the mould made?

In the last chapter of the *Book of the Art*, by Cennino Cennini[23]—which was finished in 1437—is a recipe for taking impressions of seals or coins for moulding purposes. Cennini knew nothing about medals, but the material he describes would serve equally well for them. It was made by mixing fine ashes in water, drying the precipitate in the sun, and pounding it into a paste with salt and water; the impression made in this paste was allowed to dry without fire or sun, and would serve for casting in any metal—silver, lead or what you will. It was strong and would stand any strain. Benvenuto Cellini, from whom we should expect similar information, was unfortunately so proud of his achievements in the art of striking medals that he gives much more attention to that than to casting. The moulding material which was used in his day was either a tufa or other sand—the best he knew was found on the shore of the island in the Seine at Paris, near the Sainte-Chapelle—or else a mixture of gesso, pith of sheep's horn, tripoli, and pumice ground up with water. The medal was cast in moulds of some material of this sort; we shall see later that, even if it were to be a struck medal, the blank was first cast in the desired form, so that the dies in striking should suffer the less strain.

The two sides of the model having been impressed in the moulding material and removed, these two moulds were joined together, and the molten metal poured in. It is improbable that the *cire perdue* or waste-wax process was employed by early medallists—the process, that is, in which the complete model was enclosed in moulding material, and the mould then heated so that the wax was melted and ran out.

Although hollow shells, made by casting the two sides of a medal separately and joining them together by their edges, are exceptional before the seventeenth century, it is quite common in the sixteenth century to find such hollow castings of single sides. They are often so fine that nearly every detail is as plain on the back as on the front; that side of the mould which produced the hollow back was evidently an exact positive reproduction of the model of the front.

The most skilful bronze casters attained such extraordinary efficiency that it is not infrequently very difficult to say whether a medal is cast or struck. The Germans, admirable craftsmen as they were, generally surpassed the Italians in this particular branch of their art, if in no other. The ideal medal, from the technical point of view, is surely one which is so well cast that it is unnecessary to retouch the surface with the graver in order to remove flaws caused by air-bubbles or grains of sand in the wrong place. For the more such re-touching or chasing is done, the less is preserved of the delightful warm surface due to direct contact of the metal with the smooth surface of the mould, which in its turn reproduces the surface of the original wax model. There is an extraordinary difference between the work of different medallists in this respect. Sperandio, for instance, or Laurana or Pietro da Milano produced such rough castings that they usually required chasing over every square millimetre to make them at all presentable. Even when the work was done by the medallist himself, and not by some other person, it did not increase the truth to model of the finished product.

From a metal casting made from the original wax model, whether this casting were made as a complete medal or with the two sides separate, another mould could be made. It is probable that the wax model could seldom be used more than once, and that the medallist would keep casts, say in lead, of the two sides of his medals, ready for use to make new moulds when occasion required. He might, like the Florentines of the end of the fifteenth century, want to use the same reverse for different obverses. He would take, say, his cast of the Three Graces from his medal of Giovanna Albizzi, work out the inscription in the mould, work in another one and fit this new reverse to his portrait of Raphael Martin.[24] And it is not unreasonable to suppose that he would have little scruple in borrowing not merely his own but somebody else's design in this way. Still, though combinations of obverses by one man with reverses by another are of course innumerable, most of them are late, belonging to a time when both the artists concerned were dead.

These late casts, whether representing legitimate or illegitimate combinations, are the bane of collectors. It is safe to say that at least seventy-five per cent. of the medals in any old collection are not contemporary. Only in some modern private collections, formed with connoisseurship, where bad casts have been weeded out, is the percentage of good ones higher; and every collector who is also a student of medals, though he may not show any but his best casts, has a number which he preserves for lack of better specimens. Experience is of course the only master that can train the eye to detect the late from the early casting. But it is necessary to discount the pretensions of those connoisseurs who profess to be able to decide off-hand on the age of a piece and, if it is a reproduction of a fifteenth-century medal, to say whether it dates from the sixteenth, seventeenth, eighteenth, or nineteenth century. A well-known craftsman has made, from the Victoria and Albert Museum specimen of Pisanello's medal of Sigismondo Malatesta, a cast in bronze, of which I defy any one to prove the modernity, apart from the maker's own testimony.

One method of testing late casts is by their dimensions.[25] If an original medal (A) is reproduced by casting, the metal of which the reproduction (B) is made shrinks very slightly in cooling. If a third piece (C) is cast, not from A but from B, its shrinkage will make it still smaller. Thus the more stages there are between a medal and its original, the smaller it will be. But it is not sufficient to take the diameter from edge to edge, for accidental inequalities, or the more or less extensive trimming of the edges, will mislead. The only satisfactory method is to take the same points in the interior of the field of two medals, one of which is admittedly early, and measure them with a micrometer. If a falling-off in the dimensions is accompanied by a weakness and slurring of details, we may be assured that the smaller medal is the later. But only the cumulative evidence of dimensions and of clearness of details not due to chasing can count as conclusive. All metals do not shrink equally; a quite modern cast may have been made from a fine original of the fifteenth century, and therefore be much nearer in quality to the artist's work than a sixteenth-century casting from a less fine specimen of the same medal; a rough cast of late date may have been skilfully chased. There are in fact a dozen pitfalls for the unwary.

In the second half of the fifteenth century one or two medallists, notably Gianfrancesco Enzola, began to make experiments in the art of producing medals by striking them from engraved dies. Bramante is said to have invented new machinery for impressing Papal *bullae*, but nothing definite is known about it; nor can any clear idea of Leonardo da Vinci's experiments with coining presses be obtained from the fragmentary notes and drawings which have survived. But the process of striking medals is described in considerable detail by Cellini and Vasari. It was practically the same as that used for striking coins; the differences were due to the greater size of the medal, which necessitated the making of the dies all of pure steel, whereas for coins only the heads of the dies, to about the thickness of a finger, were made of steel, the main part being made of iron. The dies[26] or *tasselli* of the medal were blocks, usually square. The surfaces having been carefully polished, the positions of the pearled border or *granitura* and of the inscription were marked on them with compasses. The medallist could then cut with a grave direct into the metal, guiding himself by his models. The letters were also cut with gravers or burins. Some medallists used the gem-cutter's wheel for engraving the dies. Cellini himself, however, for his medals of Clement VII, employed puncheons or *madri*,[27] as for his coins. That is to say, for the portrait-head, and for various details, Cellini carved steel punches in relief; these were driven into the die, which had been softened in the fire, and left impressions in reverse. Similarly he had an alphabet of punches for the inscriptions, and a punch with dots or pearls to make the pearled border or *granitura*. While the work of engraving, however it was done, was proceeding impressions would be taken in wax, to see what it looked like in relief; and before the dies were finally tempered a complete trial piece would be struck off in lead. The use of punches, which meant a great saving of labour (since for one thing—or at any rate, for many craftsmen—it is easier to carve in relief than intaglio), became very general in the sixteenth century, and, since most labour-saving appliances are the enemies of beauty, it had not a little to do with the decay of the medallic art. Cellini, who is quite unabashed and is clear in his own mind that his work was much better than that of the ancients, says that he could not possibly have worked so well or so quickly had he cut his dies direct. One one occasion, when working for Pope Clement, he had to turn out thirty *pile* and *torselli* in one day; this was possible, working with punches; but had he had to cut his dies direct, he could not, he says, have produced two in the same time, nor would they have been so good. He admits, however, that the ancients made 'medals' (that is, presumably, their larger coins and medallions) superlatively well. But he does not seem to know that they used the same method of direct engraving for both large and small pieces.

Such a leaden impression as I have mentioned, or even one made in wax from the dies, when they were finally complete, was then used to make a mould in fine clay. In this mould was cast the blank of the medal which was to be struck, in gold, silver, brass or bronze, as the case might be. The cast was then placed between the dies and struck. As Vasari neatly puts it, the blank receives from the die the skin which it did not receive from the mould. This preliminary casting of the blank in the exact form of the medal saved the dies from a great deal of strain. The most primitive method of striking was with the sledge-hammer, the dies being placed in a collar to prevent their moving. If the medal was of brass, it has to be heated between the blows. Or the dies could be placed in a frame, and forced together by wedges driven between the edge of the frame and the dies; this, of course, lessened the danger of fracture of the dies, which were not struck directly with the hammer.[28] More elaborate was the screw. The collar in which the dies were placed had a female screw inside it; in this fitted a male screw, which, by a strong lever passing through its head and handled by four men, worked down upon the upper die. It was so powerful that by its means Cellini struck for Clement VII, as he tells us, about a hundred medals in bronze without even casting the blanks first in the requisite shape.

Two turns of the screw sufficed where a hundred blows of the hammer would have been necessary. It is possible that the press, which Bramante is said to have invented for impressing Papal *bullae*, and Caradosso Foppa to have used for striking medals, may have been something of this kind. But in any case the screw, of which Cellini describes the simplest form, is the essential principle of the mill, which was known in most of the chief European mints in or soon after the middle of the sixteenth century. The mill was first used in England in 1561,[29] but the conservatism of our mint authorities prevented its being fully established for quite a century. In Scotland, however, Briot succeeded in inaugurating it about 1636–7, while efforts to impose it upon the Tower authorities were still without avail. But into the later development of the various methods of engraving dies and striking this is not the place to enter.[30] It seems fairly obvious that if you design a medal and then work it out in separate little bits, carving a punch for each separate portion, and subsequently combining them, you must be a very great artist if your design does not go all to pieces. The artists of the older school must have felt towards the new art of striking medals much as calligraphers and lovers of fine manuscripts felt towards printers, although printing was a new invention, and the striking of medals was only a transference to medals of an art that had already been employed for coins for over 2,000 years. Some of the older artists may have viewed with dismay the base mechanical ease with which, the die once made, the product could be multiplied. It certainly cheapened the work; but that in itself need not have affected its artistic quality. The mischief was in the use of punches and other labour-saving devices, though the Renaissance was spared the crowning disaster of the reducing machine. The best artists of the sixteenth century continued, some of them exclusively, to use the casting process.

The artist, in cutting his dies, may have worked merely from drawings; but it was not unusual to make models in relief. A certain number of such models, most of them for coins and not for medals, have come down to us; but I know of none earlier than the last years of the sixteenth century. To this and later dates belong the two most important sets of such models with which I have met. The best known, the Bessborough set of models for Florentine coins of Francesco Maria (1574–87) and Fernando (1587–1600), now in the collection of Mr. Henry Oppenheimer, has already been illustrated elsewhere.[31] In Mr. Whitcombe Greene's possession there are a large number of models, the remains of a collection which once belonged to L. C. Wyon,[32] and which was evidently brought together in Italy. It contains models of various kinds, dating from the

end of the sixteenth century to the middle of the eighteenth. A few are models
for cast medals, as for instance the medal of Leo XI with a bouquet of flowers and
the motto SIC FLORVI on the reverse. There are a number of minute models for
oval pendants with religious subjects. But the models for coins are in the great
majority.[33] Of the Florentine models the earliest seems to be that with the
Decollation of St. John Baptist, dated 1599. More numerous are the designs for
Papal coinage. Among these the earliest seem to be a fine design for a scudo of
Ferrara, with St. George and the Dragon, probably of the time of Paul V, and a
design for the testone of the same Pope with St. Paul on the reverse. The
Mantuan mint is represented by the model, dated 1612, of St. Andrew giving
the pyx to St. Longinus; this appears on a ducatone of that year, which seems
to be the work of Gaspare Mola.[34] Before leaving this subject I must mention
two interesting, if late, models on lead for medals. The lead disks seem to have
been struck from dies, one of which had already had the inscription cut in it.[35]
Inside the circle of the inscription the design is modelled in wax in the usual
way. The other model is within a few years of the same date.[36] It is treated in
the same way, save that the inscription has not been added to the die before
striking the disk. Taking such a lead impression from a die was a quicker and
more convenient way of producing the necessary disk than cutting down a
piece of slate.

The metals which were employed by medallists were chiefly gold, silver,
bronze or other alloys of copper, and lead or pewter. The first two are rarely
found in original examples before the sixteenth century. The great majority of
medals in any collection will probably be found to be of bronze (alloy of copper
with tin). A larger proportion of tin in this alloy than usual gives the pale metal
which is known as bell-metal; this was occasionally, though not frequently,
used by medallists. Brass (copper alloyed with zinc) was not uncommonly used,
especially in the sixteenth century. As to lead, it was a favourite material in the
fifteenth century for making trial proofs owing to the ease with which it was
melted. It would seem that pewter (the grey alloy of lead with tin) was little if
at all used by medallists before the sixteenth century.[37]

The bronze which results from casting, and even that produced by striking,
has a raw surface which is not pleasant to the sight. But it is rarely that medals
are to be found in that unfinished condition. The surface has been modified in
various ways,[38] which are popularly spoken of as patination, although *patina*,
strictly speaking, should be limited to an *incrustation* of verdigris (green carbonate of copper or other compounds of copper) brought about by natural

chemical action, and giving to the metal a green, blue, or black surface. These incrustations may be produced in various ways; the copper alloys become gradually decomposed and a crust is formed, owing to the presence of favourable elements in the earth in which the specimen may be buried, or in the mixture of which the specimen itself is made, or in the atmosphere to which it is exposed.

But there are other methods of giving a finish to the surface of medals, which may be divided roughly into two classes, viz. *varnishes* or *varnish-enamels* (popularly called lacquers), and forms of *bronzing* or *colouring*.

The varnishes of the old medallists were doubtless identical with those which were used by armourers to finish and preserve the hilts of swords, etc. One which was recommended in an Italian manuscript of 1520 for arquebuses, iron armour, etc., was compounded of linseed oil (2 lbs.), sandarac gum (1 lb.), and Greek pitch (2 oz.).[39] Another 'excellent common varnish, good for varnishing anything you wish' is described in the same manuscript as made of linseed oil (2 oz.), Greek pitch (1 oz.), and a little rock alum; if black pitch were used it was good for pommels of swords, spurs, etc. Gauricus also recommends varnishing with liquid pitch for giving a black tone to bronze. The gum mentioned is the Mogador sandarac, produced by the *Thuja articulata*, not as usually supposed by the juniper.

For 'bronzing' or colouring, as distinct from varnishing, the following processes (among many which are known) might be used.

(1) Pomponius Gauricus says that a yellow colour can be produced by cleaning the figure[40] thoroughly and placing it on a white-hot plate, until it appears to have acquired the same colour as the plate, and then cooling gradually.[41]

(2) 'Crocus', i.e. oxide of iron, which in its finer form is known as jeweller's rouge. This red powder is made into a paste with water and spread upon the face to be bronzed; the object is subjected to a moderate heat—the primitive method was apparently to heat it on an iron plate over a charcoal fire. The paste having dried to powder is brushed off, and a second coating applied and baked at an increased heat, and so on, repeating with an increase of temperature from three to four times according to the tone required. Result: a tone ranging from golden to deep brown.

(3) Black lead, in a similar way; the result is not so good as with crocus.[42]

In this class of bronzing, brushing the surface with unctuous haematitic ore after the final heating produces a beautiful lustre, and a tone varying according to the amount used.

(4) Nitric acid. An old manuscript recipe read as follows: Take of water a wine-glass and add to it from four to five drops of acid azoticum, and with the solution wet the medal (which ought to have been well and properly cleaned from all grease and dirt) and allow it to dry, and when dry impart to it a gradual heat of equable character, by which if properly carried out a darkening of a golden hue should be made in proportion to the heat imparted.

(5) Exposure to the elements, more especially during winter. A London fog is the best agent in the world for the purpose. The medal should not be handled during the exposure, which may sometimes last for weeks before a good tone is produced.

(6) Black-bronzing, by a solution of sulphur in dilute ammonia (the early method) or, as now, by sulphuretted hydrogen or ammonium sulphide. The medal is subjected to the fumes of sulphuretted hydrogen, or washed over with a weak solution of ammonium sulphide and dried at a gentle heat. In the latter case a precipitate is left of a whitish-green permanent powder, which collects in the hollows, and to which waxing gives a brownish-yellow tone.

(7) According to Gauricus, black colour can be produced by the fumes of (burning) chaff, the object being first wetted.[43]

(8) Green bronze is produced by the very simple process of steeping the specimen in a solution of sodium chloride (common salt) for a few days.[44] A partial bronzing is brought about, which after the medal has been well washed and slowly dried is very permanent. Sal ammoniac (ammonium chloride) was often used in place of common salt; also a strong solution of sugar, or sugar acidified with acetic acid.

There are of course numerous other methods known to modern chemists; the amateur will find plenty of opportunity for experiment with the above, and will perhaps be wise, until he becomes expert, in avoiding those which necessitate the use of strong acids. After bronzing, some metal-workers plunge the medal into boiling paraffin-wax;[45] but a better method is merely to brush it with a soft brush upon which beeswax has been spread lightly. Common grease of any sort should be avoided, since the fatty acids contained therein are deleterious to the metal.[46] The German experts[47] recommend zapon, but any clear celluloid varnish will serve to protect the surface from noxious influences.

Finally there are the various methods of gilding or silvering; and bronze medals are occasionally found coated with baser metals such as tin. These are obviously processes for the professional.[48] Gauricus's account of them (in Maclagan's translation) is as follows:

The finest white colour is got with silver thus: the best silver is beaten into very thin foils and amalgamated with quicksilver, and then laid on with nitre and alum solution, using an iron-pointed tool. Next the object is plunged into boiling oil to heat it through and set on glowing coals, then quenched in vinegar, salt, urine and tartar, and finally polished again with the burnisher. The finest golden colour is got with real gold by the same method as white from silver, except that it does not need to be cooled down[49] in oil; but this only if there is no tin mixed in, for the method is different with foil made of the two metals.

Medals that have not been well cared for may be found covered with dirt, or with a decayed and ugly varnish or coat of colouring matter, or with an unsatisfactory 'bronzing'. The offending surface may be removed, if the medal is of bronze (lead had better be left to the professional), by soaking in a not too strong solution of ammonia. Some of the harder coating-materials may require to be treated with caustic potash. When the raw surface of the metal has been reached, the tone may be restored by one of the processes above described.

The lead of which medals are made is frequently impure, and susceptible to change of atmosphere. A piece which has seemed perfectly healthy may, when moved to new quarters or subjected to changes of temperature, suddenly develop spots of white efflorescence—lead carbonate. This tends to spread and may in time reduce the whole piece to powder. The piece, according to the usual recipe (which is not always successful), should be brushed and thoroughly boiled in water; then well dried, by soaking in pure alcohol for some hours; and then coated with the zapon or other varnish, as above mentioned.

Old lead medals are frequently found covered with a dull yellowish coat, which obscures details. This is the remains of a so-called 'gold paint', which probably contains no gold but powdered bronze. To remove it without damage to the lead is the work of an expert.

II

Northern Italy
in the Fifteenth Century

If it was to the ancient Roman medallion that Pisanello owed the suggestion which was to bear such remarkable fruit under his cultivation, it would be interesting to know how that suggestion was first made.

Probably it came about in this way. In the year 1438, Antonio Pisano,[50] conveniently called Pisanello, a Veronese of Pisan origin, already highly distinguished as a fresco and panel-portrait painter and also as an animal artist, was at work at the court of Nicolò III d'Este, at Ferrara. He was about 40 to 45 years of age. To Ferrara there came, to attend a Council for the reconciliation of the Eastern and Western Churches, the handsome if weak emperor, John VIII Palaeologus, the last but one of the Western rulers of Constantinople (Plate 3.*1*). We can well imagine that Pisanello should have been called upon to paint his portrait. But suppose that he had seen the mediaeval medal of Constantine described above—whether he thought it ancient or modern matters not—or such a piece as the gold medallion of Justinian,[51] on both of which we have striking equestrian figures of the emperors. What more natural, if he had in him, as the event proved, the genius of a sculptor, than that he should propose to this latest representative of the long line of Roman emperors that he also should be portrayed in 'brass eternal'? Everything tends to suggest that the older medallions, Roman or pseudo-Roman, were the source of Pisanello's inspiration. The combination of a bust on the obverse with an equestrian figure on the reverse is common to the Palaeologus, the Constantine, the Justinian, and many other Roman medallions. What is more, the reverse of the Constantine, with the figures of the two Churches or the Old and the New Dispensations, supporting the Fountain of Life, may well have suggested the reverse of a second medal of Palaeologus, which is only known to have existed from Paolo Giovio's description: on this the cross was supported by two hands, representing the Latin and Greek Churches.

Notes to this chapter begin on p. 171

But whatever the origin, there is no doubt about the result. The success of the attempt was immediate, complete. We shall see later medals of Pisanello's in which the reverse is more finely composed, but none which renders more successfully the character of the sitter—in this case the handsome, half oriental, somewhat effeminate, picturesque but always dignified emperor. On the reverse[52] the huge, long-barrelled, stiffly-moving horse—a masterpiece for its time, in spite of certain anatomical faults, as in the junction of the near foreleg with the forehand—is clearly, as some critics have seen, a portrait. In the arrangement of the subsidiary foreshortened figure and of the rocky landscape towering behind, in the summary rendering of the ground, in the finely proportioned and balanced lettering, we have indications of the leading counts in Pisanello's claim to be the greatest of all medallists and one of the truest of all artists.

From 1438 until 1449 medal after medal came from Pisanello's workshop. They form an astonishing series of masterpieces which, fine as his extant paintings are, and glowing as are the eulogies which his contemporaries poured out on his work as painter of portraits and landscapes, rank much higher in the history of art than his extant panels or frescoes. Yet he never forgot that he was a painter; he signs his medals always as 'the work of Pisano the Painter'. He doubtless considered them as secondary to his paintings, possibly indeed as reproductions thereof. In the age before the invention of engraving, the medal was the only way of making speedily a number of replicas of a portrait. Such replicas could be sent about, as we know they were, as presents with infinitely less trouble than paintings.

Pisanello's second medal was probably that of Gianfrancesco I, Marquis of Mantua, which may have been made in 1439.[53] The reverse, which comes very close to the Palaeologus, took Rembrandt's fancy, and the figure of the marquis on horseback is reproduced exactly (but reversed) in the etching of the Three Crosses. The obverse is curiously stiff, undoubtedly the least successful of his portraits, and betraying, in all the specimens that I have seen, some difficulty in the modelling of the face, which may have been due to an idiosyncrasy of the sitter. There is an interesting little sketch of the profile among Pisanello's drawings in the Louvre.[54] To about the year 1441 belongs a group of three medals, representing Filippo Maria Visconti,[55] Duke of Milan, and the two famous condottieri Francesco Sforza and Nicolò Piccinino. It was said that the Duke of Milan objected strongly to his repulsive looks being represented in painting; but many portraits of him came into existence, and Pisanello's medal

at any rate was done from the life. In it there is nothing repulsive, though suspicion and lack of refinement are written large upon the features. On the reverse
the artist is still experimenting with equestrian figures in a rocky landscape;
the effect of the great lances is finely decorative. But we feel that he has not yet
got into his swing; the composition is stiff. In the medals of the two condottieri
he has been less ambitious, and quite successful. That of Francesco Sforza,[56]
the future Duke of Milan, is at once the earliest and the finest medallic portrait
of the man. A good critic, Weizsäcker, thinks to recognize a Spanish breed in
the horse's head on the reverse; however that may be, that this charger is a
beast full of mettle is shown by the modelling of its bony head and its small ears.
Nicolò Piccinino, that mighty warrior of little stature who commanded Visconti's forces against Venice, is represented in another noble portrait.[57] On
the reverse, in a scheme based on the Roman she-wolf and twins, the griffin of
Perugia suckles the two great condottieri whom that city produced, Braccio da
Montone and Piccinino himself.

From 1441 to 1448 Pisanello was chiefly engaged at Ferrara, though in the
last half of this period he contrived to make medals of the rulers of Mantua and
Rimini, as well as of various private persons. There is a remarkable series of
pieces representing Leonello d'Este, Marquis of Ferrara, culminating in point of
art, if not of time, in the medal commemorating his marriage in 1444 with
Maria of Aragon, the natural daughter of Alfonso of Naples (Plate 3.3). In these
medals Leonello (Plate 4), the enlightened patron of art and letters, the lover
of peace and domestic virtue, looks cruel and sensual; no attempt is made to
soften the extraordinary outline of his cranium; the ugly fashion, as it seems to
us, of cutting the hair in a straight line from forehead to nape is faithfully
reproduced. In spite of such drawbacks the never-failing note of Pisanello is
dominant; the portraits are wholly dignified. Apart from the marriage-medal
and a small piece by another artist on which Pisanello's signature has been
forged, there are five different reverses combined with more than one obverse.

Of only one of them can we be assured of the meaning. The blindfolded
lynx (Plate 4.3) is a symbol of statecraft; on another medal by one 'Nicholaus',
the motto *Quod vides ne vide* explains it for us: the statesman must be blind to
much that he sees. In many of these Estensian devices both on the medals and
elsewhere there seems to be some sort of contrast expressed. Thus we have
(Plate 4.1) the old man and the young seated at the foot of the sail, which,
bellied by the wind, while the mast or rather column to which it is attached
remains immovable, seems to indicate the unshaken firmness which guides the

ship of state or of his life safely on its way. In the beautiful device (Plate 4.2) of the young man, Michelangelesque in his recumbent pose, with a vase on rocks above him, note that one of the chains of the anchors attached to the vase is broken, the other intact. On other medals, the triple-faced head between two knee-pieces seems to indicate prudence combined with self-protection; and the nude men holding baskets full of the fruits of the earth, while the rain falls from the clouds on vases, may indicate prosperity in combination with justice, with a reference to Isaiah xlv. 8: 'Drop down, ye heavens, from above, and let the skies pour down righteousness.' But it is tedious to speculate on such riddles, whereas we may wholeheartedly admire the beauty of their representation.

Entirely delightful, and as a composition one of the artist's finest works, is the marriage-medal of 1444 (Plate 3.3). That Pisanello had a sense of humour not a few of his drawings as well as this medal give certain proof. The Marquis Leonello, whose musical taste was well known, here appears as a lion, learning to sing from a scroll which the little god of love holds before him. Above, on a column, is the *impresa* of the mast and sail. The Este eagle, perched on a tree, seems scornfully to turn its back on the scene. In this beautiful design Pisanello shows complete mastery of the principles of his art. Analysed, the composition resolves itself into vertical and horizontal stresses. In some of the best Greek reliefs, such as the tombstone of Hegeso, we may observe exactly the same principle informing the composition. Note at the same time the extraordinary severity of the obverse; this felicitous combination of stern dignity on the one side, with genial humanity on the other, is quite inimitable. Note, too, the bold disregard of the generally accepted rule that unnecessary elements should not be introduced to help the composition; the vertical lines of the column are required, so they are introduced, and adorned with the *impresa*. Other characteristics of the artist are seen in the conventional rendering of the ground, with its round stones, just enough to break up the heaviness of the rocky foreground; and in the leafless tree. Being a true painter, Pisanello was content to be picturesque in his medals; but he was never pictorial, and he never attempted to do more in the way of detail than his material allowed. His trees are always leafless.

In the church of Sa. Maria della Scala at Verona, in a chapel to the right of the high altar, are the remains of some frescoes by Giovanni Badile, which were commissioned in 1443. In these the artist has reproduced the medal of John Palaeologus, the medal of Leonello of the type which has the triple-faced head on the reverse, and a portrait of Pisanello himself, of which later.[58] The date of the Palaeologus needed nothing external to fix it; but we learn from this that the two others were in existence by 1443.

The portrait of Leonello on these medals should be compared with the wonderful panel painting by Pisanello at Bergmano, which shows what a great colourist as well as modeller the artist was.

Pisanello's relations with the Malatesta family are recorded in three magnificent medals, two of Sigismondo and one of Domenico, known generally as Malatesta Novello. The bust of Sigismondo on the smaller of his two medals (Plate 3.2) is one of the most powerful pieces of portraiture that can be found anywhere on a medal, perhaps even in the whole domain of sculpture in relief. The whole character of the man, his keen culture, his passionate and brutal lust, his fierce courage and determination, are there. The reverse, however, with its wonderfully live figure in armour, lacks repose. The larger medal,[59] dated 1445, with an almost equally remarkable obverse, combines a reverse which reminds us of the earlier medals with equestrian figures.

Probably about the same time as these two medals, and at any rate not later than 1448, was made the beautiful medal (Plate 3.4) of Domenico Malatesta, Lord of Cesena, a singular contrast to the two of the Lord of Rimini. Gabriele d'Annunzio, in *Il Fuoco*, has described in glowing words this 'effigy of a youth, with beautiful waving hair, imperial profile, Apolline throat, sovran type of elegance and vigour, so perfect that imagination could not figure him in life save as immune from all decadence, and unchangeable, even as the artist had shut him for eternity in the circle of metal—Dux equitum praestans Malatesta Novellus Cesenae dominus'. The reverse, recording a vow made by Domenico when hard pressed in battle, a vow to which the Saviour inclines his head, is infinitely touching in its lyrical simplicity. Technically, too, it shows the artist's greatest success in that foreshortening of the horse at which he was constantly aiming.

About 1447 or 1448 we may date the medal of Lodovico Gonzaga, Marquis of Mantua; that of his sister Cecilia bears the date 1447. The medal of the marquis,[60] with its reverse showing him on his charger with his emblems, the sun and the sunflower, is nobly sculpturesque, blocked out in massive proportions, with a simplicity quite Greek. The sun and flower are placed in the field of the medal, just to fill the space, with the same absence of pretence as a Greek vase painter shows when he puts ornaments on his background. The allegory of Innocence—only the spotless maiden could tame the unicorn—on the reverse of Cecilia's medal (Plate 3.5) is again among the finest existing compositions in the round. It is designs like this that justify Gabriele d'Annunzio's description of the master as 'one of the greatest stylists the world has ever seen: the most purely Greek mind of all the Renaissance'. We note—quite apart from the deep poetic charm of the whole—the application of exactly the same principles of composition as we observed in the medal of Leonello d'Este. The personification of Innocence is seated in the romantic desolation of the mountains lit by the crescent moon, her slight lovely figure contrasting with the great hairy monster whom her touch has subdued. There is charm, too, in spite of her lack of good looks, in the virginal bust of the accomplished and devout Cecilia. It is as characteristic of the artist as his panel painting of the unfortunate Ginevra d'Este in the Louvre. Cecilia was a pupil of the famous teacher Vittorino da Feltre, of whom Pisanello made a fine medal about the same time (Plate 3.8). Of this, and of the medals of Belloto Cumano[61] a young scholar, and of the humanist Pier Candido Decembrio, Secretary to the Milanese Republic, we can only make passing mention; though the last[62] is a fine instance of the way in which an apparently dull subject, an open book, can be transformed into a work of art. It was made in 1448.

Some years earlier Pisanello had been invited to Naples, but had not found it possible to escape from his engagements in the north of Italy. Now, towards the end of 1448, Alfonso succeeded in capturing him. Three splendid medals of the king, and one of Don Iñigo d'Avalos, Marquis of Pescara and Vast, with several drawings, remain as records of this period. One of the drawings[63] is particularly interesting as indicating the way in which the artist selected from his material. The finished medal (illustrated Plate 1) shows the helmet much simplified; the bat which served as crest has disappeared, and so has the device on the king's shoulder-piece; the crown is less elaborate; and there are various other changes, all improving the balance of the composition. The superb group of birds of prey on the reverse illustrates the mediaeval *exemplum* of magnanimity; the king of birds, it was said, always left part of his prey to the lesser birds, who waited around until his meal was over. It is difficult to say which is the finer, this design or that of the *Venator Intrepidus* medal (Plate 3.6), on which the young king slays a mighty boar. The bust on the obverse of the second piece is an equally dignified portrait; but the curious fancy of placing the crown below the bust is a little disconcerting. In the third medal,[64] where it appears further below, forming as it were an element in the border of inscription, it is less puzzling. The reverse of this medal seems to refer to the king's triumphal entry into Naples in 1443. Sometimes the piece is unsigned; when the signature is found, it is weak and undecided. I am inclined to think it never was signed by the artist himself, though there can be no doubt that it is Pisanello's work.

The list of Pisanello's medals closes with the exquisitely beautiful portrait of the young Spaniard, Don Iñigo d'Avalos (Plate 5.*1*). In it the whole art of Pisanello, as portrait-painter and medallist, is expressed in its quintessence. It needs little imagination, if one recalls, for instance, Pisanello's picture of St. Eustace, to read the colour into this composition, to imagine how the warm golden brown of the man's face would be set off by the grey of his hat or the bright blue of the scarf which descends in so fine a sweep on his shoulders. The reverse, with the earliest modern attempt to render plastically Homer's Shield of Achilles, is less happy; in fact it is perhaps the only instance among all Pisanello's medals in which he verges on the commonplace. But for the consummate achievement of the portrait, one would think that the master's hand was beginning to lose its cunning. He was, it is true, no longer young, having been born at latest in 1395. From 1449 onwards we lose trace of him, until we learn of his death in 1455. These last six years are a blank; it would appear, at any rate, that he made no more medals.

Pisanello left no school, in the ordinary sense. There is indeed a curious reminiscence of his medals in a marble relief attributed to the Tuscan sculptor Matteo Civitali; this is a portrait of Gianpietro d'Avenza at Lucca,[65] which seems clearly to be inspired directly or indirectly by a medallist's work, and by Pisanello's rather than by any other's. But there are no medals of which we can say that, while they are in his style, they cannot be attributed to any known artist. No other medallist approaches him in his own art. The man who recalls him most, Matteo de' Pasti, was strongly under his influence, but his work can never be mistaken for Pisanello's. Other younger contemporaries serve for the most part as foils to his distinction. The court of Ferrara supported a crowd of artists, many of them quite mediocre. Among these was Amadeo da Milano, a goldsmith, who signed two medals of Leonello and Borso d'Este (Plate 5.*3*), made probably during the lifetime of their father Nicolò III, i.e. before 1441; and he, too, is possibly responsible for the uncompromising portraits of Nicolò himself, which have sometimes been rashly attributed to Pisanello.[66] Another Ferrarese medallist has already been mentioned in connexion with the lynx-device of Leonello; he calls himself 'Nicholaus' on his only signed piece.[67] It is extremely probable that another small medal of Leonello, with the vase *impresa* on the reverse, is also his.[68] The signature 'Pisanus F.'—a form which Pisanello did not use on his medals—has been very clumsily inserted over the border of the reverse. Border, stops, and general treatment of this mediocre little piece show distinct analogies to the large medal signed 'Nicholaus'. Whether this medallist is identical with the sculptor Nicolò Baroncelli, does not seem to be quite made out.

A better and more interesting artist than either Amadeo or Nicholaus is Antonio Marescotti[69] who was working from 1446 to 1462. One of his best-known medals represents San Bernardino of Siena, and was probably made immediately after the saint's death in 1444. Rays surround his head, but it does not follow that the medal must be subsequent to his beatification in 1450; such honours were often accorded by popular consent before the official machinery got to work. The same is true of another medal of Marescotti's, representing the Bishop of Ferrara, John of Tossignano (Plate 3.7), who died in 1446. Both these pieces breathe a deep spirit of devotion, not surpassed in sincerity by the Florentine medals of that great preacher of Ferrarese origin, Savonarola. And this sincerity does much to atone for the crabbed uncouthness of Marescotti's style, which reminds one of his younger contemporary the painter Cosimo Tura, and is perhaps characteristic of Ferrarese art at the time.

Besides these two medals, Marescotti made portraits of a number of persons, dated from 1448 to 1460. They are all extremely rare, but comparatively insignificant. It is possible that Marescotti made the terracotta bust of John of Tossignano in the Hospital of St. Anne at Ferrara. But nothing is known of him save what the medals tell us.

It is to one of these medallists, Nicholaus, or more probably Marescotti, that I would assign the responsibility for the two medals which portray Pisanello himself.[70] It is quite incredible to me that either of them should be from the master's own hand; they have a certain vigour, but the complete lack of distinction, the poverty of invention, are sufficient to exclude them from his work; and the handling of the relief distinctly suggests Marescotti. The letters F.S.K.I.P.F.T. on the reverse are the initials of the seven virtues. Nothing but the quite illogical tendency to attribute all portraits of artists to the artists themselves can account for the fact that Pisanello has been credited with these works.

Before passing on to the major line of development, it is convenient to mention the remaining Ferrarese medallists, especially as they are of small importance. Giacomo Lixignolo of Ferrara and Petrecini of Florence[71] both made medals, very close to each other in style, of Duke Borso d'Este (Plate 3.9). They give a good idea of the vain but amiable ruler; the unicorn purifying the spring with his horn, and a baptismal font (if that is what it is[72]), symbols of purity, are his devices. Both are dated 1460, and Petrecini also made in the same year a strange-looking medal of Count Gianfrancesco Pico della Mirandola, which has nothing but rarity to recommend it. Yet another medal, of Lorenzo Strozzi, is only known now from an old description. Petrecini seems to have worked at Ferrara from 1447 to 1480 at least; but it is curious that all his medals are dated in one and the same year.

Another indifferent artist is Baldassare d'Este, one of the innumerable illegitimate sons of the old Marquis Nicolò III, and therefore a half-brother of Leonello and Borso; he was better known as a painter than as a medallist. His medals represent Ercole I, Borso's brother and successor, and are dated 1472; as a painter he worked for the Milanese court as early as 1461, but from 1469 more especially for his brothers Borso and Ercole I. He died about the same time as the latter, in 1504. His medals, though weak in themselves, show an appreciation of good models; the equestrian figure of the duke is evidently inspired by Pisanello. But there is little more to be said for him as a medallist, although as a painter he has recently excited considerable attention, and has been credited with portraits formerly assigned to more famous artists, such as Ercole de' Roberti and Francesco Cossa.[73]

Lodovico Corradini of Modena was a medallist and a worker in majolica and terracotta; his one signed medal, like Baldassare's, was made in 1472 and represented the duke.[74] A rather attractive medal of Rinaldo d'Este, dated 1469,[75] in some ways recalls his style, but it is safer to leave it among the un-attributed Ferrarese medals of the period. Of these there are a goodly number made in the second half of the fifteenth century, representing members, some of them legendary, of the house of Este. One of the most pitiful and notorious tragedies of the Italian Renaissance finds an echo in a quaint rectangular medal or plaque, with the heads of a man and woman confronted, in true Ferrarese style.[76] The original medal, I believe, had no inscription; but some one engraved on a specimen names identifying the persons as Ugo d'Este and Parisina Mala-testa. From this engraved specimen the example in the British Museum derives. The original is undoubtedly of the quattrocento; but it may be doubted whether the tragedy of these two persons, brother and step-mother of the reigning dukes, would have been commemorated in this way at Ferrara before the century was out. The engraving of the names was probably done in the sixteenth century at the earliest. To say, however, with Alfred Armand, that the two heads were first combined and the inscription engraved by some one who had read Byron, is to suppose that Byron invented a story which rang through the whole of Italy some three and a half centuries before he was born.

We may now return to the main line of descent, so to speak, in the accomplished Veronese artist Matteo de' Pasti,[77] architect, sculptor, painter, miniaturist, and diplomatist; though, as far as concerns diplomacy, he seems to have bungled sadly in his only recorded attempt at the art, when he was arrested on a voyage to Constantinople in 1461 by the Venetian authorities. He is first heard of in 1441; in 1446, and doubtless earlier, he was working for the Ferrarese court, though living at Verona. It was doubtless about this time that he made his wonderfully vigorous portrait of the fine old humanist Guarino of Verona (Plate 3.*10*), who had been tutor to Leonello d'Este, and had been for a long time settled at Ferrara. And probably all Matteo's medals, other than those which he made at Rimini, belong to this period, which closes in 1446. Such are the medal of his brother Benedetto (who died in 1445), and the rather weak head of Jesus Christ—the first Renaissance medal of that subject. In 1446 he settled at Rimini, having married Lisa Baldegara; it is evident that he soon won high favour at court, for by 1454 he is called *nobile*, and in 1461 Sigismondo entrusted him with the already mentioned mission to Constantinople, which proved abortive. He died in 1467 or early in 1468. His medals of Sigismondo Pandolfo Malatesta and of that remarkable woman Isotta degli Atti, who was first the mistress and then the wife of Sigismondo, were made from 1446 to 1450, to judge by the dates on them. But there are a great many specimens on which his signature has been taken out in the process of casting, and various slight modifications introduced into the inscriptions. These may have been made from his models after 1450, but not necessarily always under his supervision. Also there are many, undoubtedly his work in origin at least, which never bore his signature.

As Pasti assisted Leone Battista Alberti at Rimini, it was doubtless there that he made the medal of that famous architect between 1446 and 1450, when Alberti left Rimini for good. All the other medals which we can definitely associate with the artist's Riminese period represent either Sigismondo or Isotta; in all, there are, counting small varieties and different combinations of obverse and reverse, nineteen different medals of these two, of which only four actually bear the artist's signature. The portrait of Sigismondo (Plate 5.5) will hardly bear comparison in respect of virility and character with Pisanello's;

but the castle of Rimini on the reverse must rank as almost if not quite the finest representation of a building on any medal. In the portrait of Isotta (Plate 5.4)[78] it is not difficult to recognize the shrewd capacity for management which enabled her to retain her hold over Sigismondo for so many years. These medals of Isotta grow upon one, although at first the fashion of plucking the hair off the forehead repels our modern taste, which prefers other methods of deformation. The elephant—not a very naturalistic rendering of the beast—is one of the Malatesta devices, as a symbol of superiority to small misfortunes. 'Elephas Indus culices non timet,' said the family motto. It occurs again on a medal of the younger Pandolfo Malatesta.[79] A beautiful medal in Mr. Henry Oppenheimer's collection combines the portraits of Sigismondo and Isotta as obverse and reverse.[80] The most vigorous of Pasti's portraits of Sigismondo is on a large medal (90 mm.) on which he is represented wearing a laurel wreath.[81]

The smaller medals of the pair are comparatively insignificant; but one of Sigismondo[82] is interesting as showing Alberti's never-realized idea for the façade of the church of San Francesco, the so-called Tempio Malatestiano; the piece was cast in 1450, when the still unfinished church was inaugurated.

As we have spoken of Pasti's medal of Leone Battista Alberti, it is opportune to mention here two remarkable oval plaque portraits, not, strictly speaking, medals, of the great architect;[83] the larger, in the late Monsieur Gustave Dreyfus's collection (Plate 6.1), is, it seems to me, easily the finer of the two; the smaller, in the Louvre, would seem fine if we had not its fellow. Neither appears to me to be the work of a trained medallist; and both betray a certain amateurishness, though it is the amateurishness of genius. Seeing that Alberti confessed to dabbling in sculpture, I see no reason why one, if not both, should not be from his own hand. The attribution of these pieces to Pisanello and Pasti need not be considered seriously. Judging from Alberti's age, they may date from an earlier period than Pisanello's first medal, being possibly as early as the year 1435.

It is usual to regard two artists, Pietro da Milano and the Dalmatian Francesco Laurana,[84] as taking up the mantle of Pisanello in Naples. But since it does not appear that Pietro was in Naples before 1458, when Pisanello was dead, and since the influence of the Veronese master on them seems to have been very shadowy, we may mention them here not as his disciples, but on their own merits—which, from the medallic point of view, are small. Their medals fall between 1461 and 1466, and were executed not at Naples at all, but in Provence, whither they were summoned by René d'Anjou after the death of

Alfonso. Most of the medals are concerned with members of that strange court, of which Scott has given us an entertaining glimpse in *Anne of Geierstein*. The work of these two artists is marred by great and obvious technical defects; in fact, Pietro's medals are mere curiosities, even if, architect as he was, he did succeed in making the architectural setting of the Judgement of Solomon, which forms the reverse of one of his medals of René and Jeanne de Laval,[85] comparatively interesting. More remarkable than beautiful, and typical of his clumsy and ineffectual modelling and casting, is the unique piece (Plate 6.4) which is supposed, on good grounds, to represent our unfortunate queen, Margaret of Anjou, and to have been cast when she took refuge with her father from 1461 to 1463. The portrait hardly bears out her reputation for beauty. As clumsy as his artistic style are the halting, often unintelligible Latin verses with which he and Laurana inscribe their medals. But Laurana, an accomplished sculptor, is a more capable medallist. His portrait of Louis XI[86] hits off that cunning diplomatist admirably; and the portrait of Giovanni Cossa (Plate 6.2) is equally full of character. Perhaps his best achievement, however, is the medal—the unique specimen of which is possessed by the Hunterian Museum at Glasgow—of Ferry II of Lorraine, Count of Vaudemont.[87] The equestrian reverse with the finely subordinated architectural background is in the best Pisanello tradition, although it does not, perhaps, show great originality. It is the only reverse among Laurana's medals that shows any power of design; and he usually takes refuge in copying the antique. These two artists had little influence on the origins of the medallic art in France, although it is possible that Candida, the Italian founder of the French school, knew their work.

The Ferrarese school, as I have hinted, came to a close with a number of minor medallists, whose originality was not equal to bearing up against the forcefulness of an imported rival, Sperandio. But I may mention here, a little out of chronological order, one medallist of Ferrarese origin, Costanzo[88] who stands head and shoulders above the rest, in virtue of his one signal performance, the medal of the Sultan Mohammad II, which he cast in 1481 at Constantinople. The other medals of the Sultan, by Bellini and Bertoldo, look mean beside its powerfully conceived portrait and the dignified equestrian figure on the reverse (Plate 6.6), in composition and details strongly reminiscent of Pisanello. Costanzo seems to have worked as a painter in Naples; but this medal is the only remaining work that can with certainty be assigned to him.

The close connexion between Ferrara and Naples makes it convenient to mention here a remarkable medal of Fernando I of Aragon (King of Naples

1458–94), represented by a unique specimen in the British Museum.[89] Not a work of the first rank, it is interesting as being possibly an example of the method, very rarely employed in Italy, of casting medals from a model carved in wood. The whole treatment of the relief and border points to this, and there are traces of the tooling visible which seem to place such a view of its origin beyond doubt. The piece has been attributed to one Bernardino de Bove, and it has also been suggested that it represents not Fernando I but Federigo his son;[90] but the older identification seems to me undoubtedly correct. There are one or two very attractive medals of the latter prince, but they must not detain us here.

In Verona, though it boasted Pisanello and Pasti as its citizens, there arose in the fifteenth century no school of medallists; but it must be remembered that the political condition of the city was not likely to favour the growth of a school there at the time. Faction and war seem, in the Italian Renaissance, to have been a rather good soil for the plant of art; but subjection to the domination of another city meant depression of vitality and personality.

In Mantua, however, which, next to Ferrara, had enjoyed the greatest share of Pisanello's attention, a distinct school of medallists did flourish. It had its own special artists, such as Talpa, Melioli, L'Antico; it adopted Isabella d'Este's pet medallist, Giancristoforo Romano; it produced Sperandio, whose fame spread over all the north of Italy; its influence radiated even to Rome, through artists like Cristoforo di Geremia and his nephew Lysippus, who, Mantuans in origin, worked for the Papal court. And it produced some unsigned medals which have presented to those who enjoy the game of attribution, very pretty problems, likely to remain unsolved.

Early in the series of Mantuan medals comes one by a certain Pietro of Fano, representing the Marquis Lodovico III. But this artist may more fitly be classed with the Venetian school.

Bartolommeo Melioli,[91] a Mantuan goldsmith and coin-engraver, as well as medallist, signed six medals, of which five portray members of the Mantuan court. The young Gianfrancesco II, as represented on what is perhaps Melioli's best known piece (Plate 7.*1*), is much more attractive than he became with years. The goldsmith comes out in the elaborately decorated bust; an elaboration which is carried to excess in the medal of Gianfrancesco's grandfather Lodovico III. Two of the artist's medals bear the date 1475; another, of Christiern of Denmark,[92] must have been made in 1474, when the king passed through

Mantua: 'talis Romam petiit' in the fourth year of Sixtus IV, says the inscription. In this medal Melioli was evidently inspired by a medal of Alfonso V made a few years before by another Mantuan, Cristoforo di Geremia. Another of his reverses, that of the Marquis Lodovico III, of the same year, shows the influence of Mantegna. In fact he was more a craftsman than an original artist. Of unsigned medals, an attempt has been made to attribute to him not only the portrait of Clara Gonzaga, Comtesse de Montpensier, which may well be his work, but a group of other medals which have just that touch of originality and grace which his signed medals lack. They are the medals with a captive Cupid on the reverse, of which more presently.

A somewhat conventional, if accomplished, medallist of Mantua in this period is Bartolo Talpa, who is probably identical with one Bartolino Topina, a pupil of Mantegna who painted for the Mantuan court.[93] He has left two medals.[94] One is of Gianfrancesco Gonzaga as the liberator of all Italy, with a reverse representing him like Curtius leaping into the fiery gulf. This obviously refers to the battle of Fornovo, when Gonzaga sought to bar the way to Charles VIII of France, and Charles won through with the loss of his baggage, in the face of heavy odds. Both sides claimed the victory, and Gonzaga was acclaimed as the saviour of his country.

The other medal (Plate 6.3), representing the third marquis, Federigo, if made during his reign, must date between 1478 and 1484. But the two pieces have so much the appearance of being a pair, that Friedländer[95] is probably right in his view that the medal of Federigo is posthumous.

It is strange that one of the most fresh and charming medals in the whole Italian series has been associated by nearly all recent writers with this somewhat dry artist. One of the novels of Bandello tells the story of a girl called Giulia, who was outraged by a servant of the Bishop of Mantua, and drowned herself in despair. The bishop commemorated the tragedy by a monument. Now we have a Mantuan medal (Plate 7.2) of a girl called Giulia Astallia; that she is called Diva does not indeed prove that the medal is posthumous, but it is not against that assumption. On the reverse is a phoenix, and an inscription describing her as 'a unique example of chastity and courage'. There is thus considerable probability in the identification of the Giulia of the medal with the poor girl of Bandello's story. The portrait is one of inexpressible charm; there is nothing quite like it on any other medal, and it comes nearest to some of the Florentine painted profiles of girls of the last quarter of the century. But, in handling of the relief and in pose, it should be compared with the medal of

Maddalena of Mantua which most authorities agree in ascribing to L'Antico, an artist to whom we shall presently come. It is in him, or very near him, that the author of the medal must be sought. The prevailing attribution to Talpa is an illustration of the unintelligent way in which critics follow each other through a gap in the hedge. Friedländer happened to remark that the medal was of Mantuan origin and contemporary with Talpa, adding that the style was not very like his, and the portrait much better and more characteristic than those on his signed medals. Armand, coming next, catalogues the medal under Talpa, and claims Friedländer as the author of the attribution! Having found its way into the standard list, of course the absurd attribution has become consecrated by use, although one or two protests have been made against it.[96]

Two medallists of the Mantuan school, one born in the neighbourhood, the other in Rome, illustrate the transition from the fifteenth to the sixteenth century. Jacopo Alari Bonacolsi,[97] called L'Antico (born at Gazzuolo or Mantua about 1460, died 1528), was a goldsmith and bronze-worker; and indeed his claim to remembrance is much better founded on his statuettes than on his medals, which, though neat and skilfully executed, are not great works of art, unless we may count as his the Giulia Astallia above described. He was probably first employed by Federigo Gonzaga in Mantua; then by Gianfrancesco Gonzaga in Bozzolo; and then after 1496 also in Mantua and Gazzuolo. His medals represent for the most part Gianfrancesco Gonzaga of Bozzolo and his wife Antonia del Balzo; but there are pretty little portraits of one Julia (Plate 7.3) and an unknown Maddalena of Mantua; the latter unsigned, but dated 1504. His statuettes, while they are all inspired by the antique, have a crisp quattrocento artlessness, and none of the academic tediousness which imitations of the same subjects were soon to acquire. Mrs. Ady has with great probability identified the 'Diva Iulia primum felix', as the medallist calls her, with Giulia Gonzaga, daughter of Lodovico of Bozzolo, said to be the most beautiful woman of her time. Since she was born in 1497 at the earliest, and is no longer in her 'teens, the medal must belong to the latest years of L'Antico. It is unfortunate that the medallist has left us no portrait of his patroness, the famous Marchesa Isabella d'Este. For this we have to look to his contemporary Giancristoforo Romano (about 1465 to 1512).

This artist,[98] though born at Rome, came of a Pisan family of sculptors, and worked as sculptor, architect, and medallist in Milan, Mantua, Rome, Naples, Urbino, and Loreto. A number of medals can, on documentary evidence, be attributed to him; one of these, first made in 1498, and then perhaps reissued in a modified form in or before 1505,[99] represents Isabella d'Este, for whom he worked in Mantua. On the reverse is a figure of Astrology, standing under the sign Sagittarius. Isabella, like most cultivated people of her time, dabbled in the so-called science. There is something peculiarly attractive and genial about this medal, as about those of Julius II[100] and Isabella of Aragon which the same artist made in 1506 and 1507. His medals relating to various Papal buildings are of less importance.

The Mantuan school at this period produced another small group of unsigned but quite charming medals, and attempts have naturally been made to attribute some of them to Giancristoforo, since he was so great a favourite at the court. As the relations between the Este and the Gonzaga, between Ferrara and Mantua, were so close just then, if he made medals for one court he doubtless made them for the other. There is a fascinating group of pieces with allied reverses representing a captive Cupid. They represent the Italian medal in its most intense form, so to speak. That does not mean that as works of art they are the greatest among medals; far from it. But they have qualities which will be sought in vain outside the Italian medal, especially an intimate charm which you will not find in works of a grander style. Take for instance the medal of Jacoba Correggia (Plate 7.4); you may at first think it overladen with ornament, but you will come back to it with unalloyed pleasure, and find after all that the little details of ornament, and the graceful flower behind the bust, are really quite well subordinated to the general design. And how delicious is the little captive love-god on the reverse!

A captive Cupid also occurs on the reverse of a curiously attractive medal of Lucrezia Borgia,[101] the probably much maligned daughter of the most notorious of Popes, and the wife of Alfonso I d'Este. It is somewhat heavy in its treatment, especially of the bust, which is in very high relief. Those who have studied her enigmatic career will probably admit that the bust is a wonderful presentation of a sensuous and non-moral, rather than immoral, character, and that it renders something of the charm with which she fascinated the people of Ferrara over whom she came to rule.

The same bust of Lucrezia occurs attached to a portrait of her husband Alfonso which is utterly different in treatment, and must come from another hand. Because they occur attached together, it does not follow that one man originated them. When Alfonso was married in 1502 some one made a marriage medal by joining these two busts together; in doing so he provided a new inscription, so that the lettering of the two sides is by the same hand.[102]

I confess I can see absolutely no ground for the attribution of this group of medals to Giancristoforo Romano, proposed by Bode and accepted and amplified by Fabriczy.[103] Nor can I accept the rather more plausible suggestion of Melioli, made by de Foville.[104] Melioli is an uninspired, ungraceful artist. No, these Mantuan medals, like that other beautiful one of Giulia Astallia, must remain anonymous until documentary evidence is found for an attribution.

One more medallist and coin-engraver, goldsmith and sculptor in bronze, must be mentioned before we leave Mantua. This is Gian Marco Cavalli,[105] who worked from 1481 to 1506 or later. The only work that can with probability be ascribed to him was done outside of Mantua, and consists of coins of the Emperor Maximilian I and Bianca Maria his consort,[106] and a series of pretty little medals representing Maximilian (Plate 11.2) and his father Frederick III in various combinations.[107] These were made in 1506. There is little ground for accepting the theory that he made the medal of the poet Spagnoli; but if he did, then the poet's bust in Berlin, and the famous bust of Mantegna at Mantua are probably also his; and they carry with them the bust of Gianfrancesco Gonzaga at Mantua, and a medal of Girolamo Andreasi. These works of art have all been attributed to the Venetian Gambello by M. de Foville, on grounds which seem to me somewhat inadequate.[108]

The Mantuan artists have brought us to the threshold of the sixteenth century, and incidentally Cavalli has illustrated the way in which Italian influence set in a current across the Alps. It is difficult to keep to any settled order of procedure, now that the various artistic centres in Italy all begin to produce medals. But it is convenient to deal next with certain medallists of other northern towns, such as Bologna, Parma, Padua, Verona, and especially Venice. In these places we must trace the development of the art down to about 1540, since it is quite impossible to draw a hard and fast line at 1500.

Sperandio Savelli[109] was the son of a goldsmith, and was probably born about 1425 at Mantua; but he must have received his artistic education at Ferrara, where his father went in 1437. His activity dates from about 1466 to 1504. During these nearly forty years he was undoubtedly the most popular medallist in Italy. That is a singular thing. It is not for us, whose taste has been formed on Italian models, to accuse the patrons of the time of bad judgement in artistic matters. Yet how it is that this medallist, whose drawing and composition are alike faulty, whose artistic conscience seems to have been non-existent, whose ideas, when not borrowed, are skimble-skamble, whose execution is hopelessly slovenly, how is it that he attained so high a reputation? The answer must be that his undoubted forcefulness and vigour—one may think of him as playing Cleon to the Pericles of Pisanello—and his power of imparting the true Renaissance 'swagger' to his portraits, appealed effectively to his patrons. For it is undoubtedly true that in art the Italians were too often ready to mistake rant for eloquence, and hysterics for pathos. Rant and hysterics were new weapons in the hands of the Italian artists of the Renaissance, as a critic has reminded us that rhetoric was in the hands of the Elizabethan dramatists;[110] and many of them cannot be acquitted from the charge of playing to the gallery.

That this is not too harsh a view of Sperandio may be judged from a few of his very large series of medals. He worked mainly at Ferrara, especially from youth down to about 1477, when he settled at Faenza for about a year. From 1478 to 1490 or later is his Bolognese period. Thereafter he seems to have wandered about a good deal, and to have visited Padua and Venice. One of his latest medals commemorates the battle of Fornovo in 1495; after that he seems to have settled at Venice, where he worked chiefly as a cannon-founder until his death in or after 1504. Two medals of Venetians seem to date from this last period.

He was naturally enough, but not happily, influenced by Pisanello, if influence can be said to be seen in the fact that he quite shamelessly caricatured his exemplar, adapting to his own purposes some of Pisanello's most beautiful reverse compositions. Thus the reverse of the medal of Carlo Grati is a preposterous parody of Pisanello's Novello Malatesta. Some of his portraits, such as those of Giovanni II Bentivoglio, do, however, possess a certain dignity. One, that of the poet Carbone, even verges on the pathetic. In the Salting collection at South Kensington is a pretty plaquette-portrait of Eleonora of Aragon, made out of one-half of the joint medal of Ercole d'Este and his consort. It has been carefully finished, probably, however, not by Sperandio himself, who seems to have been too lazy or too much pressed to chase his productions. Charming though it is, a good deal of the character which seems to be present in the rougher original has apparently evaporated. Sperandio—characteristically enough, for he did not lack audacity—made one or two attempts at three-quarter face portraits. The medal of Francesco Sforza shows how hopelessly such a treatment exposes his native lack of fine feeling. The old condottiere was doubtless a 'rough specimen', but he did not lack dignity, as Sperandio would have us suppose. How dull and uninspired is the building on the reverse! Other works of his, such as the portraits of Bartolommeo and Giuliano della Rovere (Plate 8), may pass muster as vigorous if plebeian portraits. But the less said about his reverse designs the better; I will only quote Fabriczy's criticism of the medal of Jacopo Trotti as an 'appalling example of Sperandio's tasteless allegories'.[111] The muddled composition on the reverse of the medal of Tartagni is little better. One of his best known medals represents the good Duke Federigo of Urbino; but the portrait has not much dignity, and the draughtsmanship of the reverse is wretched. Yet it was this medal that Goethe most admired.

To sum up: in Sperandio what is admirable to us is his vigorous characterization, which is, however, apt to degenerate into mere vulgarity or brutality. These defects are especially visible in the medal, which by its nature, like the sonnet, its analogue in the art of poetry, seems to call for careful and refined workmanship. One does not notice it so obviously, for instance, in a terracotta bust, such as that in the Berlin Museum, where the material responds naturally to a rough handling. (It is true that the antiquity of this particular bust has been doubted.) But even in a stone relief like the striking portrait of Ercole d'Este in the Louvre[112] one sees that a dashing style does not altogether serve to cover up shallowness of conception and carelessness of execution; note how inadequate and at the same time violent are the incisions marking the wrinkles about the nose and mouth.

Without congratulating ourselves on having better taste than the Germans of a century or so ago,[113] it is strange to reflect that by Goethe and his circle Sperandio was put at the head of the Italian medallists, and Pisanello in the second place. Possibly in time to come opinion will veer, as it so frequently does in matters of artistic taste, but it is hard to believe that Sperandio will ever again be set above the great Veronese master.

Parma produced but one medallist of note, Gianfrancesco di Luca Enzola, whose working period, so far as we know, covered about a quarter of a century, from 1456 to 1478. Goldsmith, medallist, maker of plaquettes, and engraver of seals and coins, he is interesting for two reasons. One is that from 1456 to 1471 he seems to have experimented with a view to making dies for striking medals, instead of casting them. Nearly all his medals of this period were small struck pieces (Plate 11.5), which are extremely rare in their original struck form, being represented in most collections by after-casts. But after a time he seems to have tired of these experiments, possibly because he found it difficult to get sufficient power for his purposes; for he probably used a hammer and not any kind of mechanism. There is little doubt that Enzola engraved his design straight into the metal of the die. Naïve as his technique may appear, his design would surely have been worse had he used punches for its separate elements.

His cast medals are much finer than his struck ones, so far as the handling of the portraits is concerned. Two very fine portraits—and this is Enzola's second claim on our interest—of Alessandro and Costanzo Sforza of Pesaro were cast between 1473 and 1475. The portrait of the handsome young Costanzo (Plate 6.8) is surely one of the most noble things in Italian art; this profile is worthy to rank beside some of Pisanello's. But in his treatment of details Enzola fails badly. Notice first of all how mean is the inscription—which, by the way, looks as if it has been engraved on a separate metal band and impressed in the mould. On the reverses elaborate, nay fantastic, detail often quite obscures the meaning of the type, as in the extraordinary treatment of the horseman's crest on one of the reverses of the medal of Costanzo. Enzola's last and largest medal was made in 1478, when he portrayed Duke Federigo of Urbino. This piece is known to us only from an impression in leather in the Vatican Library;[114] evidently it pleased Federigo well enough for him to have impressions of it put on the bindings of some of his books, from one of which these scraps of leather have been cut. This medal also suffers greatly from over-elaboration of detail. The fact is that the Italian custom of beginning by training most artists as goldsmiths had its bad as well as its good side; any artist without a strong sense of proportion was lost.

The mention of Federigo of Urbino makes it opportune to allude here to other medallic portraits of this remarkable and attractive personality. The medal made in 1468 by an obscure and mediocre artist, Clement of Urbino, need not detain us. Paolo of Ragusa's[115] little portrait made nearly twenty years earlier, that is not later than 1450, is chiefly interesting because it represents the young man before his beauty had been irretrievably ruined by an accident in a tournament in 1450, when his nose was broken. Nothing more is known of the artist except that he made two other medals of Alfonso V of Naples, about the same time (Plate 5.2). The style of all these medals is unassuming but good.

But by far the finest medallic portrait of the Duke of Urbino (Plate 6.7) was made, if I am right in my attribution, by the versatile Sienese artist—painter, sculptor, engineer, in fact, as he has been called, a Leonardo da Vinci *au petit pied*—Francesco di Giorgio.[116] This is a unique medal in Mr. Rosenheim's collection which appears to present close analogies with certain other works attributed to Francesco.[117] Among these are the relief in the Carmine at Venice, with incidental portraits of Federigo and his son; and the famous *Discordia* relief at South Kensington, which has been the subject of so much dispute among critics that is certainly deserves its name.[118] Verrocchio, Leonardo,

Antonio Pollaiuolo and Bertoldo have also been advanced in the most reckless fashion as its author; but in the course of the struggle Francesco's voice has gradually made itself heard with ever-increasing distinctness. Now Vasari says that Francesco made a medal or medals of Federigo; and I believe we have it here. Unfortunately it is a 'waster'; i.e. it was never finished, and indeed part of the design—the head of the monster whom the horseman is attacking—has been deliberately jabbed out. The same design recurs as a plaquette, where the detail is more visible; but the medal, wreck though it be, is a fine and spirited thing. It was probably made at Urbino about the time when Francesco first visited the court of Federigo in 1478.

Sperandio's medal of Federigo has already been mentioned; and of a restoration by Torrigiano I shall speak later.

From Urbino we may retrace our steps to the north, to Venice by Padua; and Padua need detain us but a little time, since cradle though it was of the Italian medal, and inspiring to all artists as must have been the presence of Donatello there from 1443 to 1453, it produced, so far as we know, but one medallist in the fifteenth century, and he indeed only regarded medal-making as a minor and ancillary art.

This was Bartolommeo Bellano or Vellano,[119] a pupil of Donatello with that tendency to the ungainly and grotesque, which is certainly visible in his master, developed to a curious degree. It would seem that the impulse, which elsewhere showed itself in the making of medals, was in Padua directed to the purely decorative minor art; thus was produced Riccio, the greatest master of decorative and fanciful bronzes, a consummate craftsman without any care for the intellectual content of his productions. Medals have been attributed to him on, I believe, quite inadequate grounds; certainly that which shows his portrait seems to me to be posthumous, and at any rate belongs to the sixteenth century. But this is anticipating. Bellano, whose life covers the years from 1430 to 1498, is said by Vasari to have made medals of the celebrated philosophical professor Antonio Royzelli, the Monarch of Wisdom as he was called; of Platina, the acrid biographer of the Popes; and of Pope Paul II. None of the extant medals of Paul II can be associated with Bellano; nor is any medal of Platina known to exist; but the medal of Royzelli with its gaunt uncouth portrait and contorted figure on the reverse is essentially Bellanesque in style. It enables us to attribute to Bellano the still uglier portrait of another Paduan legal professor, a churlish controversialist named Bartolommeo Cepola, whose character has certainly been well caught by the artist.[120]

The Venetian school of medallists begins in the reign of that unfortunate doge Francesco Foscaro, who died of grief on being deposed in 1457; for we have a medal representing the doge, with Venetia on the reverse—a fine sturdy portrait and a dignified reverse design, probably adapted from the relief on the façade of the ducal palace. The signature AN may just possibly indicate Antonio da San Zaccaria, the father of the more famous medallist Gambello.[121] At any rate the medal is not by the same hand as one signed ANT, representing the doge Cristoforo Moro (1462–71), and probably the work of Antonello della Moneta, who was active at the Venetian mint from 1454 to 1484.[122]

Between the two doges just mentioned comes Pasquale Malipieri (1457–62). Portraits of him and of his wife Giovanna were made by a native of Fano who called himself Petrus de domo Fani;[123] but this artist's best medal is one of Lodovico Gonzaga, Marquis of Mantua, made between 1452 and 1457, and thus earlier than the Venetian pieces. The portrait, although perhaps lacking in significance, shows a fine broad style. On the reverse is a curious allegory: a little genius seated on a rock, with a hedgehog beside him. The hedgehog is hardly studied from the life; but the genius or wingless Cupid, holding bow and arrow, is quite admirable. We shall see that it gave an idea to a Venetian medallist a few years later.

Nothing further is known of Pietro da Fano save that he was later (in February 1464) in the service of Lodovico Gonzaga, whose medal he had made some years before.

In the use of a curious jargon which he supposed to be Latin, Pietro has a companion in his contemporary Marco Guidizani.[124] This artist's best piece represents Bartolommeo Colleoni, the fine soldier immortalized by Verrocchio's statue at Venice. But in the very rare medal of Pasquale Malipieri (Plate 6.9) there is a homely dignity in the portrait of the doge, and the lettering and composition are distinctly good; the monumental touch is there. The squat figures on the reverse, in a design supposed to be modelled on the antique, are childishly artless.

The imitation of the antique advances a considerable stage further in Giovanni Boldù,[125] who is known to have worked in Venice, both as painter and as medallist, from 1454 to about 1477. He lacks the monumental quality of his predecessors, but makes up for it not only by finish, but also by an elaborate parade of scholarship. Thus on a portrait medal of himself he gives his name in Greek and Hebrew (making the words alternate in the two languages), and also in Latin. He is full of classical reminiscences, affects the nude, and copies the types of ancient coins; in fact his study of gems and coins is probably responsible for the wiry character which we observe in the technique of some of his medals. The charming Caracalla (Plate 9.*1*) is, however, free from this; and the *memento mori* device (of the artist seated with his head in his hands, and a little genius resting on a skull), which occurs as the reverse both of this and of one of his own portraits, is extremely attractive.[126] In this composition Pietro da Fano's earlier design has been drawn upon for the figure of the genius.

With Boldù we pass from what may be called the primitives of the Venetian medal to the fully developed style. The author's reputation as a painter perhaps makes it necessary to mention the medal of the Sultan Mohammad II which was cast by Gentile Bellini.[127] But the achievement, which dates from 1479, when Bellini went to Constantinople, or soon afterwards, does him no credit, especially if compared with Costanzo's splendid piece, or even with Bertoldo's.

The portraits of Gentile Bellini himself (Plate 11.*3*) and of his brother Giovanni are known to us from two admirable medals, the work of Vettor Gambello or Camelio.[128] Gambello worked as engraver to the Venetian mint from 1484 to 1523, and was probably making medals before then, as there is one by him of Sixtus IV (1471–84) which does not seem to be posthumous. Like Enzola of Parma, Gambello experimented with struck medals; perhaps it would be truer to say that he got beyond the stage of experiment, for there is no hesitancy in such a piece as the little portrait of himself, dated 1508 (Plate 9.*2*). But, as it was with Enzola, so it is with Gambello; the cast medals are incomparably the finer. Even in the latter, practised as he evidently was in the engraving of dies, one sees the cramping influence of the engraving process, and the inability to attain to largeness of style except when modelling freely in wax. Some of the Milanese engravers surmounted the difficulty; but with that exception it is no exaggeration to say that the Greeks stand alone and above all comparison, as modern photographic enlargement demonstrates.

Almost contemporary with Gambello is another most pleasing artist, generally known as Fra Antonio da Brescia.[129] To this artist M. de Foville, one of the few serious students of the Italian medal, has devoted a study which I am bound to confess seems to me to be radically misleading.[130] He proposes to interpret the artist's signature—which is sometimes F.A.B., but in its fullest form FRA. AN. BRIX—not as Frater Antonius Brixiensis, but as Franciscus Antonii, Francesco son of Antonio; or else to take AN. as a surname. He does not, however, adduce any parallel instance from this period of the father's name being thus given, without the addition of F. for filius. It is true that the abbreviation FRA. might be meant for Franciscus; true also that Frater would more naturally be shortened into FR. But the rules that govern abbreviations in manuscripts cannot be rigidly applied to medallic inscriptions, so that the current interpretation of the three letters may be allowed to stand. It is a point worth mentioning that a later medallist of Brescia, evidently by his style a follower of the man we are concerned with, was also a friar, and signs himself beyond all possibility of error, 'Frater Iulius Brixiensis'.[131] Finally, I may add a proof conclusive that the second element in the signature is the artist's name and not his father's, and probably his Christian name; and that is, that on one of his finest medals he signs himself simply 'A'.

But the man's name is less important than his work. Now there are portraits of half a dozen people, some of them signed by our artist, others undoubtedly by the same hand as the signed ones. One of these represents a man who died in 1487; another commemorates the defence of Osopo against the imperial troops by Girolamo Saorniano in 1513. We may, therefore, date the activity of this artist from shortly before 1487 to shortly after 1513. On the other hand there is another group of medals, so many of them dated 1523 that their maker is generally known as the 'Medallist of 1523'. Not one of these bears a signature; and, to my mind, not one of them has the peculiar intimate treatment that is characteristic of the man whom we may continue to call Fra Antonio. But M. de Foville boldly proposes to give to the earlier artist all these works of the 'Medallist of 1523'.

It will suffice to ask one question, which seems to go to the root of the matter. Why, if M. de Foville's theory is sound, did the medallist, having signed a good proportion of his medals during his first period, entirely drop the practice of signing them during his alleged second period?

If we have spent more time than might seem necessary on what may appear a minute point of criticism, it is because the works of the two men, the Brescian friar and the Venetian of the next generation, are both in their way very remarkable. In a piece like Fra Antonio's portrait of Nicolò Michiel and his wife Dea Contarini (Plate 10.1), which must have been made about 1500, we reach the high-water mark of a certain form of realism, the analogue of which in painting we find, as Fabriczy has remarked,[132] in the portraits by Giambattista Moroni of Bergamo. Unflinching fidelidy, not without dignity, but inspired by no high intellectual ideal—this is the characteristic of the good friar's work. The transparent honesty of the artist never fails to reconcile us to the lack of imagination which he shows in his compositions.

The other master, the so-called 'Medallist of 1523',[133] is totally different in feeling and conception from his predecessor. The superficial resemblances are in the way of cutting off the bust and in certain tricks of lettering; the O which leans backwards, for instance. He may have learned this from his predecessor; but it occurs on other contemporary works, such as certain medals of Antonio and Pietro Grimani which have no claim to be by either artist, so that it was doubtless merely the fashion of the time. And, indeed, a reference to early printed books shows that the form occurs in Venetian printing as early as 1477 in the founts used by Bernard Maler and Erhart Ratdolt.

Apart from such superficial resemblances to the work of Antonio of Brescia, the later medallist shows little affinity with him. In contrast to the earlier man's unassuming sincerity, there is a distinct tendency to pose; there is a 'swagger' about the portraits; the men he represented have the air of grandees of State or Church rather than of plain citizens or clerics. The portrait of Sebastiano Renier (Plate 10.2) is typical; but perhaps the finest of the medals attributed to him is one of Altobello Averoldo, a Brescian who was Bishop of Pola and Papal legate at Venice. The splendid group of figures unveiling Truth on the reverse is perhaps the finest composition in the Venetian series. Now in 1527 a bronze-worker named Maffeo Olivieri completed for the same Averoldo a pair of candlesticks which are now in St. Mark's;[134] and the design on the reverse of this medal, as Mr. Max Rosenheim first noticed,[135] has certain affinities to the workmanship of those candlesticks. There is also a curious correspondence between the inscriptions on the two works of art. It is thus a plausible conjecture that the artist of this whole group of medals may be no other than the bronze-worker Maffeo Olivieri.

Another Venetian artist who has recently been identified is Giovanni Falier,[136] who signs his name 'Ioannes Faletro' on a medal of an unknown priest Marco; and he is probably to be identified with the author of a medal of the future doge Andrea Gritti, while still procurator of San Marco. On this the signature resembles a Greek Φ followed by F, but the first sign is really a monogram of IO. We shall see later that another medallist, Giovanni Zacchi, adopted the same way of signing his name. But Giovanni Falier is not a medallist of much importance. Chronologically he should perhaps precede Maffeo Olivieri, since the medal of Gritti was made before he became doge in 1523, and commemorates one of his feats in the wars against Brescia in 1512 and 1516.

We shall return to Venice later to deal with her medals of full sixteenth-century style; for the present we may take leave of her. But Verona, Bologna and Milan demand our attention before we can follow the stream of artists which set steadily from all quarters towards Rome. Verona in the fifteenth century seems to have exhausted herself in producing Pisanello and Pasti. The crushing domination of Venice, as I have said before, was probably also un-favourable to the development of the intensely personal art of the medal. Thus it is not until 1518 that we find a Veronese of any note making a medal; and that was made far from Verona, at Casale, for the young Marquis of Monferrat, Bonifazio VI, by the painter Gianfrancesco Caroto.[137] But it is Caroto's only medal. Of considerably more importance are Giulio della Torre and Gianmaria Pomedelli. Giulio della Torre[138] is the type of the good amateur. He was by profession a lawyer. I do not know exactly what it is that makes his medals, in spite of their amateurishness and manifold faults, so very attractive; it is, however, partly their simplicity of treatment, their unconventionality, and their genuine intimate feeling. He was born perhaps about 1480 and lived until 1540, but his only dated work is of 1529. Quite a number of his medals portray members of his family, two himself. One of the latter, where he represents himself led by his guardian angel, might easily be criticized; but the composi-tion is so natural and unaffected, and expresses the idea with so touching a sincerity, that one prefers not to dwell on the roughness of the technique and the poorness of the modelling. Again, the unsigned medal of an unknown teacher of the law, Angelus Marinus Regulus (Plate 11.*1*),[139] delights us by its playful reverse of the master discoursing gravely to a young bear which responds by raising a paw.

Gianmaria Pomedelli[140] belonged to a noble family of Villafranca near Verona. He was born in 1478 or 1479, and lived until 1537 at least; he is thus exactly contemporary with Giulio della Torre. He too has left us a graceful little portrait of himself (Plate 11.*4*), with a reverse imitating an ancient coin of Thasos. He worked not only as medallist, but also as painter and engraver, and frequently signs his medals with an apple (for the first part of his name) com-bined with a monogram of his baptismal name, and flanked by a graver and a punch. A full signature, however, appears on the charming medal of an anony-mous lady (Plate 10.*3*), with an inscription which in its clumsiness looks like an anagram, and a richly composed reverse of Cupid and a nude kneeling figure carrying a basket of fruits. Though he is not known to have travelled from Verona he made—doubtless from materials supplied to him—fine portraits of Charles V and François I. His style, if more accomplished than that of Giulio della Torre, is distinctly less virile.

At Bologna, as we have seen, the influence of Sperandio was profound towards the end of the fifteenth century. But in its last years a new power, a gentler star, arose in the able, if over-smooth and dulcet, painter Francia—a singular contrast to the coarse strength of his predecessor. In 1494 the Emperor Maximilian granted the Lord of Bologna, Giovanni II Bentivoglio, the right of coinage; and he employed Francia to engrave the dies for his portrait coins or testoons (Plate 11.6).[141] An extraordinarily able and expressive portrait it is, though far from pleasant. It is probable that Francia worked from a relief or large-size model; for there remains, in the church of San Giacomo Maggiore at Bologna, a marble relief reproducing the type of the coins, but with the head turned the other way.[142] The relief is signed by one Antonio Bal . . . in his eighteenth year in 1497, therefore subsequently to the issue of the coins. Now it is not copied from the coins, because the head is reversed. But it may have been copied from a similar relief, perhaps by Francia; and that relief may have been Francia's model for the coins, because, if he engraved the die with the profile directed the same way as the model, it would come out reversed on the coins struck with that die.

Among the medals which can with some probability be assigned to Francia is a fine one of Tommaso Ruggieri. We may notice, as a small detail, that the ear breaks through the hair in just the same way as on the testoon of Giovanni Bentivoglio. And with this portrait of Ruggieri we may associate a medal of Ulisse Musotti. There is also an extraordinarily accomplished medal of Cardinal Francesco Alidosi, Julius II's legate at Bologna (Plate 11.7).[143] The Pope's own nephew, Francesco della Rovere, afterwards Duke of Urbino, killed this man at Ravenna in 1511. No portrait could better express the sneering insolence which gained for the prelate so bitter an enemy, and hastened for him that ascent to the stars to which the type of the reverse alludes. Obviously inspired by this medal, but as some think from another and a heavier hand, is one representing Bernardo Rossi,[144] Bishop of Treviso, who came in 1519 to Bologna as vice-legate, an office which is mentioned on the medal. This evidently cannot be by Francia, who died in 1517. The question is: does it carry with it the medal of Alidosi, or can we leave that to Francia with the medals of Ruggieri and Musotti, in spite of its close resemblance to the medal of Rossi? It is a nice question; but I am inclined to agree with those who, like M. de Foville,[145] remove both medals from the painter and ascribe them to some pupil. The Louvre possesses a bronze relief portrait of Francesco Alidosi, which would seem to be by the same hand as the medal.

We are not here concerned with the coins which came from Francia's hand, although the Bentivoglio testoon is of so medallic a character that we could hardly pass it by. But Francia engraved dies for the mints of Ferrara, Pesaro, and Rome, as well as of Bologna. Of course, therefore, Papal medals have been attributed to him, but all such attributions are disputable.

Francia had an enormous number of pupils; but in the medallic art the only one whose name is known to us is Giovanni Zacchi.[146] From his hand come a few signed medals, the best known of which is one representing the Venetian doge Andrea Gritti, cast in 1536. This medal is signed IO. ZACCHVS. F. on the reverse, which has a well-modelled though somewhat conventional figure of Fortune standing on a globe entwined by a sea-monster. But he sometimes signs merely IO. F. And I think that we may also attribute to him, on the ground of the signature Φ, which as in Giovanni Falier's signature is a monogram of IO, a fine medal of Girolamo Veralli, a Papal official of high rank in the Veneto (Plate 16.9). But this carries with it a medal of Julius III before he became Pope, while he was governor of Bologna; the portrait on the obverse of the latter is so like the portrait of Veralli as to be almost indistinguishable from it. To the same group, again, certainly belongs a medal of Fabio Mignanelli, who like Veralli held some high ecclesiastical post in Bologna or the neighbourhood. Zacchi was in high favour in Church circles, and worked for Paul III in Rome, though none of his Papal medals is signed, and it is difficult to identify them. He was active as late as 1555.

One could mention other medals showing the distinctive character of the Bolognese school of the period, but these will suffice. In their general handling they illustrate the fact that the leading art of the time in Bologna was not sculpture but painting. The busts, as compared with the sculpturesque work of the late fifteenth-century medallists, makes one think of painted portraits, seated half-figures like those which dominated the Venetian school of the time.

More or less contemporary with Zacchi and the other nameless Bolognese of the period 1525 to 1550 was a Modenese artist, Nicolò Cavallerino of Mirandola.[147] There is a mystery about him, which is perhaps more interesting than anything in his actual work. We know that he was mint-master at Modena in 1539. One Girolamo Muzio, more or less his contemporary, says in an undated letter that he made numerous medals *di conio* (i.e. struck from dies) of Guido Rangoni. Now there are four different medals of that man, some struck and some cast. The cast ones, at any rate, are of a very distinctive, though far from fine, style. On the basis of these cast medals, some half dozen other cast medals can be attributed to the same hand, including a unique one of Giambattista Casali in the Fitzwilliam Museum at Cambridge. None of these bears any signature. But now comes the difficulty. Indisputably belonging to the same group is a cast medal of Ascanio Gabuccini of Fano, which on its reverse bears the signature Ant(oniu)s Vicen(tinus) F(ecit). Thus the only signed medal of a group traditionally attributed to Nicolò Cavallerino turns out to be by some one else. Was Antonio of Vicenza a pupil of Cavallerino? Or is the attribution to Cavallerino unfounded? What was Muzio's authority for his statement? These are questions which for the present must remain unanswered. As matters stand the solution of the difficulty which appears most probable is that only the struck medals of Guido Rangoni are by Cavallerino; the cast medals (which indeed do not resemble the others very closely, except in subject), and all the group to which they seem to belong, must be given to Antonio Vicentino.

Through the Bolognese artists Francia and Zacchi we have naturally been brought into contact with the Papal court, since after the overthrow of the Bentivoglio dynasty Bologna was in the hands of the Popes. The remaining northern school of medallists which we have to mention, the Milanese, also sent its chief master to Rome. This was Caradosso Foppa,[148] one of the most famous goldsmiths of his time, of whom Cellini has given us a most enthusiastic appreciation. We hear of him from 1475 to 1527. In the former year he entered his mark, as required by the statutes of the goldsmiths of Milan; and if he was then recognized, it is not unreasonable to suppose that he may five years earlier have made the very attractive medal of Galeazzo Maria Sforza which is dated 1470, and shows certain indications of being the work of an inexperienced artist.[149] More than this in favour of the attribution we cannot say. As an expert in gems and jewellery employed by the Sforza, he travelled much; but apart from such incidental journeys he worked chiefly in Milan until the fall of Lodovico il Moro. In the end of 1505 he settled in Rome for the remainder of his days. It is possible that he had occasional commissions from the Popes before then; and two medals of Alexander VI, one representing his coronation, the other apparently alluding to the triumphal return to Rome in the summer of 1495 after the French expedition ('ob sapientiam cum fortuna coniunctam'), suggest themselves as having some claim to be from his hand. But the truth is that Caradosso's work is involved in considerable obscurity; a careful examination of the documentary evidence reveals the disconcerting fact that almost all the traditional statements about him, even as regards his name, which is generally but wrongly given as Ambrogio, are without foundation or definitely wrong, and that any account of him can be little more than a tissue of more or less plausible conjectures. I have already mentioned the medal of 1470 which may perhaps be his, although it has with no less probability been attributed to one Lodovico of Foligno, who is known to have been working for the Milanese court about that time. There is some plausibility in the traditional attribution to Caradosso, not merely of a number of testoons or portrait coins of the Sforzas, Giangaleazzo Maria, Lodovico il Moro, and Beatrice d'Este, but also of a remarkable series of eleven coin-like medals or medal-like coins, probably all made during the reign of Louis XII as Duke of Milan, and representing him and his predecessors, from Giangaleazzo Visconti onwards—a sort of medallic manifesto of Louis's claim to rule over Milan. The testoons above-mentioned are the finest of all Italian portrait-coins, perhaps, so far as portraiture is concerned, the finest coins produced since antiquity.[150]

Besides striking coins for his Milanese patrons, Caradosso also, if we accept the current opinion, made cast medals of Lodovico il Moro and of the founder of the Sforza dynasty, Francesco; these were cast about 1488.[151] To him, moreover, is generally assigned a characteristic portrait of the old warrior Giangiacomo Trivulzio.[152] When he settled in Rome—we have already seen that he may have previously had commissions from Alexander VI—it appears that he cast some famous pieces for Julius II (Plate 12.6), as well as an excellent portrait of Bramante (Plate 12.7). The architect of St. Peter's is shown in a heroic guise; the treatment of the bust as if it were of marble is a piece of pseudo-classicism which one can understand in Rome at the time. Later in the century it became an affectation much favoured by a certain school of Italian medallists. One of the medals of Julius II is also associated with Bramante, since it shows his design for St. Peter's.[153]

Finally, we must not forget to mention—especially as it appears to be the one piece of which Caradosso's authorship seems to be documentarily attested—a struck medal of Federigo II Gonzaga, fifth Marquis of Mantua. The portrait is dull, but the reverse, executed in low relief, with the design of David playing his lyre, while a Victory places a wreath on his head, is a fine piece of technique. Federigo's agent in Rome mentions this work in a letter dated September 26, 1522.[154]

In spirit, these medals have practically nothing of the quattrocento left in them. They belong to the sixteenth century, not merely in date, but in style; whereas the cast medals produced in the north, some as late as 1540, which we were considering just now, still retained a good share of the fifteenth-century spirit. It is a difference difficult to define, but easy to appreciate if one is familiar with the work of both the centuries. Caradosso—if he made all the pieces we have described—was the great transformer of the medal. Benvenuto Cellini learned much from him, as he himself admitted; we do not need to read between the lines of the famous *Autobiography* in order to see how much the arch-braggart was indebted to his elder contemporary; and who influenced Cellini influenced the whole subsequent course of medallic art.

III

Rome and Florence
in the Fifteenth Century

But before dealing with these new development we must consider the earlier progress of the art in Rome.[155] The Papal series of medals, taking it as a whole, is artistically most disappointing; a proper appreciation of it is also made exceedingly difficult owing to the reprehensible custom, which from quite early times prevailed in the Papel mint, of reissuing medals at a later date by re-striking them with the old dies which had been preserved, and, what is even worse, of issuing hybrids, combining a reverse of one Pope with a portrait of another, and touching up old dies with a shameless disregard of the responsibilities of a mint official.[156]

There are no contemporary medals of Popes earlier than Nicholas V (1447–55); and for portraits of him, and of his successors Calixtus III (1455–8) and Pius II (1458–64) we depend on a Florentine medallist, Andrea Guaccialotti or Guazzalotti of Prato (1435–95).[157] He generally counts as a member of the Florentine school, but as almost all his medals are directly or indirectly connected with Rome, we may fitly place him here. He was a clerk in the Papal Curia until he retired to a canonry at Prato in 1467. There he combined with his clerical duties, which were doubtless light, a foundry where he cast his own and other artists' works, whether in medallic or in other forms. His medal of Nicholas V, though I have called it contemporary, was really cast just after the Pope's death, which it records. It is clumsy, coarse and heavy in treatment, but genuine enough in feeling; evidently the work of a beginner—the worthy clerk was only twenty then—groping his way. The medals of Calixtus III and Pius II[158] are technically far more successful. The Pelican of the latter is copied from Pisanello's medal of Vittorino da Feltre. Guaccialotti at first inscribed this reverse 'Ales ut haec cordis pavit de sanguine natos'; then, finding out his error (for the verb should refer to the Pope) he took the T of PAVIT out of the mould and replaced it by a small ornament. Under Paul II (1464–71) Guaccialotti ceased to work for the Papal court; but in the reign of Sixtus IV (1471–84) he was again employed, and produced an interesting medal of the Pope.[159] On the reverse is a figure of Constancy, and at her feet are represented, partly by engraving, the Turkish captives who had been taken at the liberation of Otranto. The capture of Otranto in 1480 had horrified the Christian world; its recovery by Alfonso Duke of Calabria in 1481 was a fit subject for commemoration, and accordingly Guaccialotti was commissioned to portray the young duke (Plate 12.*1*). Though, as a rule, hardly an enterprising artist, he ventured, not without success, on a three-quarter face rendering of the portrait. The reverse represents the triumphal entry of Alfonso into Otranto, driving his Turkish prisoners before him. There is another medal of the same duke with a reverse practically the same as on the medals of Sixtus.

These are Guaccialotti's latest medals. His only other signed piece represents one Nicolò Palmieri, Bishop of Orte, apparently a patron of the artist; it exists in two forms, one of them made before his death and inscribed with no name, but merely with the motto *Nudus egres(s)us sic redibo*;[160] while on the other his name and the date of his death, 1467, have been engraved. Of unsigned medals attributed to Guaccialotti, the only one with a good claim is an early portrait of the famous Archbishop of Rouen, Cardinal Guillaume d'Estouteville, made before 1461; it is very close to the medal of Calixtus III. A characteristic of the artist, not very praiseworthy in modern eyes, is the freedom with which he borrowed ideas from other medallists, especially Cristoforo di Geremia, to whom we now come. Cristoforo seems to have succeeded Guaccialotti as Papal medallist during the reign of Paul II; but to plagiarize his rival's works was an odd way of showing dissatisfaction, if the good canon felt it. Yet it is true that he lifted a group of figures on the medal of Alfonso of Calabria from Cristoforo's medal of Lodovico Scarampi;[161] that his favourite reverse composition of Constancy is derived from that on a medal of Dotto of Padua, plausibly attributed to Cristoforo; and that he seems to have adapted the reverse of Cristoforo's medal of Constantine the Great to make a reverse for a new medal of Sixtus IV.[162] We have already noted his debt to Pisanello for the Pelican on his medal of Pius II.

Cristoforo di Geremia of Mantua,[163] a sculptor, gem-engraver and medallist, was at work in Rome as early as 1456, though not in the service of the Pope. By 1461 Cardinal Lodovico Scarampi had secured his services; and to him we owe the finely characterized portrait of his patron (Plate 12.*2*). Scarampi died in 1465, and Cristoforo then worked for Paul II; there can be little doubt that some of the unsigned medals of the Pope are from his hand, although it is equally clear that the neat little medals, made when Paul was still Cardinal Barbò in 1455, have nothing to do with him. Paul had a passion for burying medals, specially made for the purpose, in the foundations of his buildings, and many have been recovered thence, especially from the Palazzo di Venezia; further, there is documentary evidence that Cristoforo was paid for making medals to this end.[164] It has been suggested, not without some reason, that a famous medal of Cosimo de' Medici, made after his death (since it gives him the title Pater Patriae which he received posthumously), may be by Cristoforo; and if this is so, there is something to be said for the suggestion that the beautiful portrait by Botticelli in the Uffizi of a young man holding that medal may represent Cristoforo himself.[165]

However this may be, we have two medals signed by the artist. One represents not Augustus, as it is generally supposed, but Constantine the Great, with a pseudo-classical group on the reverse; it seems probable that this group represents the Constantinian Peace of the Church, though the precise relevance of the allusion remains obscure.[166] The other signed medal is of Alfonso V of Aragon; it may, however, have been made after the king's death. Fabriczy, indeed, points out[167] that the treatment of the king's bust is exactly similar to that of the bust of Federigo of Urbino on a medal by Clement of Urbino, dated 1468, when Alfonso had already been dead ten years. It is possible, however, that Clement copied these details from Cristoforo. The medal has been highly praised; and, indeed, with the medals of Paul II and Scarampi, it marks out Cristoforo as one of the most powerful portraitists of his time. He must also be regarded as the founder of the Roman school, with its characteristic dependence on antique models. And his influence on the Mantuan school, as seen in Melioli and Ruberto, was very marked.

The medals of Paul II[168] throw an interesting light on the Pope's keen classical sympathies (his medals are for all the world like Roman imperial sestertii) and also on the methods of the Papal mint of the time. Having once obtained a model of the bust or of the reverse design, the mint used it for all it was worth, combining the obverse with different reverses, altering the legend, remodelling the decoration on the orphrey of the cope, and so on. The medallic series of this Pope numbers about thirty-five varieties, but of essentially different portraits there are barely half a dozen. The most considerable artist employed by him was the man whom we have already mentioned, Cristoforo di Geremia. Aristotile Fioravanti[169] of Bologna, a celebrated engineer who anticipated the modern achievement of moving buildings bodily—he moved, for instance, the Torre della Magione at Bologna—seems also to have been employed; and so was the Pope's favourite jeweller, Andrea di Nicolò of Viterbo.[170] It was possibly this last man who engraved the dies of a large struck medal commemorating the Consistory of December 23, 1466, which condemned George Podiebrad, the heretic King of Bohemia.[171] So large a piece, struck with dies, was a remarkable achievement for its time. It is, however, coin-like and not medallic in style, the relief appearing to be nearly flat. There is no real evidence, we may say before leaving Paul II, to confirm Vasari's statement that Bartolommeo Bellano made a medal of this Pope.

Cristoforo di Geremia was followed by his nephew, whose real name is unknown. Under the pseudonym of 'Lysippus the Younger', the artist[172] is mentioned by Rafael Maffei of Volterra as being the nephew of Cristoforo di Geremia, and as the author of a medal of Sixtus IV. Two medals bear his signature: one (known only from an engraving of the seventeenth century) represents Giulio Marascha, an unknown youth; another has the portrait of Martino Philethico, who was Professor of Greek at Rome about 1473. The former has on its reverse the words 'Lysippus amico optimo' in a wreath; the latter, a copy of Pisanello's group of the Pelican in her piety and the words ΕΡΓΟΝ ΛΥΣΙΠΠΟΥ ΝΕΟΤΕΡΟΥ, 'the work of Lysippus the Younger'. On the basis of these two medals, which have a very distinctive style, it has been possible to attribute to the artist, with as much certainty as is ever possible in the case of unsigned works of art, a score or so of pieces. The only dated medals among these belong to the year 1478. By far the most interesting of Lysippus's medals is the perfectly fresh and delightful portrait of a young Roman clerk (Plate 12.4), with a metrical inscription which may be rendered:

> This side the likeness of your servant shows;
> Turn me, and 'twill your own fair face disclose.

There can be no doubt that the reverse of the piece—which in all known specimens is smooth—was meant to be polished and serve as a mirror, while the head that we see is the portrait of the person who presents the medal, and therefore most probably of the artist. The simple unaffected charm of the portrait makes it one of the most pleasing of all medals. It does not, perhaps, go very deep, but it is unpretentious. Another good medal[173] represents a brilliant young Milanese jurist, orator, and poet, Giovanni Alvise Toscani, who was in the service of Sixtus IV and died in 1475. All these pieces show the characteristics of Lysippus: his sincerity; his pleasant relations with his sitters, who seem to have been nearly all connected with the Papal court from about 1470 to 1485; his fondness for Greek; his lack of power to design a reverse; and his quite admirable lettering and sense of proportion. Of course several attempts have been made to pick out the medal of Sixtus IV which, as Maffei tells us, he made; I have little doubt that it is one which represents the Ponte Sisto, with the inscription CVRA RERVM PVBLICARVM, rather than any of the others which have been suggested.[174]

Among the medals which have been attributed to Lypsippus are two beautiful pieces (the smaller is shown in Plate 12.3), which seem to me to be by different hands, and possibly neither by the master, representing Giovanni Candida.[175] This was a man of Neapolitan origin who came young to Rome and grew to distinction in the diplomatic service. Of late years he has emerged from the obscurity, into which most fifteenth-century diplomatic agents have sunk, as a medallist of very considerable interest. Of the two portraits, that in the Dreyfus Collection is nearest to Lysippus's manner;[176] but it is not quite near enough, and as Candida was evidently influenced if not actually taught by Lysippus, it may well be the work of his own hand. However that may be, while still young, probably not more than twenty-five years old, he went to Flanders, where he became secretary of the Duke of Burgundy in 1472. Documents have recently been discovered which have been held to suggest that he was also responsible for the medals of Charles the Bold and Anthony, Bastard of Burgundy,[177] as well as the equally admirable little portraits of Jehan Le Tourneur and of the Neapolitan Jacopo Galeota. But there seems to me to be a radical difference in style between these pieces and those which can certainly be given to Candida. In 1479 the artist was imprisoned at Lille for some offence, when he made a medal of his gaoler Jean Miette. But by 1483 he was settled at the French court, and from now until 1504 we hear of him from time to time as royal councillor, ambassador, secretary to Charles VIII, protonotary apostolic, and once indeed as 'sculptoriae artis atque plastices hac aetate omnium consummatissimus'. But his marvellous works as sculptor have not been identified, if by that phrase his panegyrist means anything more than medals; and even as a medallist he cannot by any means rank above all his contemporaries.

Some authorities[178] have denied to Candida any claim to a number of medals of Frenchmen made at the end of the fifteenth century and during the first three or four years of the sixteenth. But these medals are so closely connected in style with the earlier pieces which are generally admitted to be his, and so different from anything produced just afterwards, that, failing documentary evidence to the contrary, we must allow his claim. Apart from these portraits of Frenchmen, among the earlier pieces is a beautiful medal representing Maxilimian I of Burgundy and his first wife Mary (Plate 12.5); this was doubtless cast on the occasion of their marriage in 1477, and at any rate not after Mary's death in 1482. It is much broader in style than the medals of Charles the Bold and the Great Bastard. A fine portrait of the brothers Clemente and Giuliano della Rovere (the latter afterwards Julius II) doubtless belongs to one of the artist's visits to Rome; no one, I imagine, credits this to a French hand. Typical of the broad but refined treatment, the almost Holbeinesque dignity, which this artist could attain, is the medal of Louise of Savoy, Duchess of Orléans and Countess of Angoulême, the mother of François I.

After 1504 we hear no more of Candida. He marks the first penetration of the Italian influence, so far as the medallic art is concerned, into Flanders and Northern France. How that influence worked we shall see later.

We have now traced the history of the Roman school of medallists down to the end of the fifteenth century. It may seem strange that we should have left to the last the works of the Florentine medallists. Surely the city which during the quattrocento ranked so easily first, both in sculpture and in painting, should have been more in the foreground of our sketch. There are, however, good reasons for the disposition we have adopted. The Florentines paid comparatively little attention to the medal until the last third or quarter of the century. Again, the Florentine school of medallists has an unusually independent character; the remaining schools are connected with each other, they influence and are influenced by each other.

To deal with the Florentines in any place except the first (which would be chronologically absurd) or last would spoil the unity, slight as it may be, which it has been possible to preserve.

The Florentine series begins with a small struck piece, done by some coin-engraver, commemorating the Council of Florence in 1439. This hardly counts as a medal. Quite insignificant artistically, and a mere curiosity, is the portrait medal of the sculptor and architect Antonio Averulino, called Filarete, the maker of the famous bronze doors of St. Peter's. It is evidently by himself, and was probably made while he was in the service of the Duke of Milan, between 1451 and 1465. Only two specimens of this rare medal are known, one in the Victoria and Albert Museum, the other at Milan.[179]

Of Andrea Guaccialotti we have already spoken, so we may pass at once to Bertoldo di Giovanni[180] (c. 1420–91), Donatello's pupil and Michelangelo's master. He was not—in spite of the works due to him—strictly a bronze-worker; for, having made his models, he left the casting to be done by others, especially by Adriano Fiorentino. Whatever may be thought of his large bronze reliefs, his one signed medal and those others which may be safely attributed to him show a dryness of technique and carlessness in design which quite belie his reputation as an artist. The signed medal represents the Sultan Mohammad II of Turkey—not from the life, but perhaps after Gentile Bellini's rather mediocre medal. On the reverse is a triumph-scene—three chained female figures, representing Greece, Trebizond and Asia, carried in a car. The design, though less confused than on some of the medals attributed to him, is ill-balanced and restless. Two somewhat similar reverses, representing the Triumph of Chastity, one attached to a portrait of the Venetian lady Letitia Sanuto, the latter divorced from its obverse, if it ever had one, are, I think, imitations by a coarser hand. But von Bode's attribution to Bertoldo of the medal (Plate 13.*1*) commemorating the Pazzi Conspiracy of 1478, when Giuliano de' Medici was killed, and Lorenzo escaped, is quite convincingly right. We observe exactly the same crowding of the space with small figures, and, if possible, a still greater failure to see that the composition should be suited to the circular field. The two portrait heads are absurdly placed. One of them, that of Giuliano, is copied from the painting by Botticelli;[181] possibly there was a similar original for the portrait of Lorenzo also. It is noticeable that, as in the painting, the heads are not in pure profile, but slightly turned to the front—a representation unique, I believe, in medals of the period. This must have been the medal referred to by Guaccialotti in a letter to Lorenzo de' Medici, in which he says that he has made four casts from a model by Bertoldo (September 11, 1478).

The medals of Filippo de' Medici and of the Emperor Frederick III are also plausibly assigned to the same artist; the latter is as early as 1469, while the others we have mentioned seem to be ten or twelve years later. Fabriczy has also suggested[182] that Bertoldo is the author of a medal of Alfonso of Calabria, whose portrait by Guaccialotti we have already described. This commemorates Alfonso's victory over the Florentines at Poggio Imperiale in 1479. The delicately vague modelling and picturesque treatment of the portrait, the comparatively simple composition of the reverse seem to me to be as foreign to Bertoldo as they are to Guaccialotti, to whom the medal used to be ascribed.

A priori, also, although Italian artists were not over-scrupulous in their patriotism, the event was not of the sort that we should suppose a Florentine would be chosen to commemorate. It is probably by some unknown Neapolitan; such a man, for instance, as made the beautiful medal of the young prince Federigo of Aragon with the unicorn reverse.[183]

Bertoldo's style is very distinctive, and there is no sort of danger of confusing his work with that of the greatest representative of the medallic art in Florence during the last quarter of the fifteenth century and the early years of the sixteenth—Nicolò di Forzore Spinelli. It is a misfortune that, under the stimulus of the mania for attributing works of art to a definite name, Nicolò has been made responsible for nearly all the Florentine medals of his period. So long as we regard a name like his as a sort of symbol merely, no harm is done,—so long, that is, as we realize that when we say 'this is a medal by Nicolò Fiorentino' we only mean 'this is a medal of the school of which Nicolò is the most distinguished representative'. But how few critics use the words in this significance, and how fewer far are those who understand them when the writer means them so!

There are, indeed, a few anonymous Florentine medals which have escaped the net which has been flung so wide on Nicolò's behoof. Most striking among these are the remarkable portraits of Piero and Giovanni de' Medici, both sons of Cosimo il Vecchio.[184] Each is described as 'Cosmi P.P.F.', 'son of Cosimo Father of his Country'. This title was not awarded to Cosimo until after his death, therefore the medals were cast in 1465 at the earliest. But they are reproduced in a manuscript of Aristotle in the Laurentian Library which is not later than 1469; so that we can date them between 1465 and 1469. They are fine, bold portraits, absolutely unlike anything else in Italian medals; so much so that they may be regarded as the creations of some sculptor not accustomed to medallic work. Who he was, however, must be a mere matter of conjecture; they are simply two busts, such as are so common in Florentine work of the period, translated into relief on a small scale. In feeling, in pose, however, they come extraordinarily near to such a bust as Benedetto da Maiano's Filippo Strozzi in the Louvre. If one is seeking for an attribution, Benedetto's name suggests itself.

There are other medals of the period which at once suggest that a sculptor has been experimenting with relief portraiture on a small scale, under the common but mistaken impression that to make a medal one has only to reduce a large relief composed in a circle. A medal is at once something more and something less. You cannot make a sonnet by boiling down an epic. An instance of a medal that is no medal, however greatly we may admire its verve, its power of characterization, but merely a relief on a small scale, is provided by the remarkable portrait of the condottiere Jacopo Sassetta in the British Museum (Plate 13.2).[185] The relief is extraordinarily high—12–13 mm. above the background, with only 92·5 mm. diameter. The artist has been content to incise his inscription instead of building up the lettering on the medal. There is no reverse, but merely a rude design of a castle, perfunctorily engraved, whether by the artist or by some one else we cannot say. All the principles which the experience of the medallists showed to be sound are neglected. The relief bears no relation to the background; if we look at the piece sideways, we see that the relief proper only begins at some distance from the background, the head being, so to speak, modelled on a platform which is raised above the actual background. That is a mere trick to give an appearance of vigorous relief; and tricks in art are annoying when they are discovered.

In Florence, where sculptors were so numerous and so flourishing, it is but natural to find that they were disinclined to be hampered by any rules that the professional medallists were accustomed to observe elsewhere. Why not, indeed? It is no crime for a sculptor to make a small relief in bronze, on the same principles as might serve him for a large relief, without troubling about lettering or the recognized convention that a portrait should have a reverse design attached to it. Nevertheless in medal after medal in the Florentine series we are saddened by the thought that what might have been made into a beautiful and finished whole has been treated with so much carelessness and neglect that it makes the same impression as a noble painting in a mean and makeshift frame.

However this may be, there is no doubt about the skill in portraiture of the Florentine medallists of the last third of the quattrocento. But only one name stands out with any significance among all those who must have made the many medals which have come down to us. That is the already mentioned Nicolò di Forzore Spinelli,[186] called Nicolò Fiorentino, a grand-nephew of the painter Spinello Aretino. He was born in 1430 and died in 1514. We have only five medals signed by him, the earliest being of the year 1485. We are fortunate in that one of these signed medals represents Lorenzo de' Medici. It is a most uncompromising likeness, sombre, not to say sinister, in expression. The reverse—which is generally so badly cast that the artist's signature is barely visible—is almost childish in execution: the figure of Florence, holding lilies and seated under a tree, presumably an olive, is clumsy, ill-proportioned and badly drawn. There is the same contrast between the portrait of the young Alfonso d'Este and the reverse of his medal (Plate 14.*1*). It is signed and dated in 1492, and a document of that year records the payment of 18 lire to 'Maestro Nicolò Forzore di Spinelli' for having composed a silver medal of the most illustrious Don Alfonso. The portrait is fine, sympathetic, well composed. On the reverse we have a feeble design of an armed figure—presumably Alfonso—seated on a triumphal car drawn by four prancing horses; and so sensible was the artist of his weakness, that he simply lifted this group of horses bodily from the ancient cameo, now in the Naples cabinet, on which the engraver Athenion had represented Jupiter in his chariot thundering against the giants.

The five signed pieces are nearly all that we have to go upon if we wish to distribute the Florentine medals of this period among their artists. They have been considered by Dr. von Bode sufficient to justify the attribution to this one artist of over 130 pieces. That is by no means too large a number for any one medallist to have produced; but this wholesale attribution of good, bad, and indifferent work to Nicolò Fiorentino has never been taken seriously by any one but its inventor. On the other hand, the old division of the medals between the Hope Medallist, the Eagle Medallist, and the Fortune Medallist, because a number of portraits share these subjects as reverse types, is also impossible. As well might we invent a Medallist of the Graces, because the famous antique group of the Three Graces is found reproduced as a reverse type on a number of medals. One thing is clear, and that is that the reverses have so little significance in the Florentine series, that two portraits which share the same reverse must not be regarded as necessarily from the same hand. It was quite customary for an artist, having made the model, to entrust the casting to another hand; and the reason why we find two portraits very dissimilar in style sharing the same reverse is doubtless that these reverses were attached to them in the foundries. The ruthless way in which this was done is well illustrated by the medal of Rafael Martin,[187] of which the reverse is patched up out of that which served for the medal of Giovanna Albizzi, the inscription being altered from the names of the Graces to IN EO GRATIAE MVSAS PROVOCARVNT.

No attempt will be made here to classify all the material, a task to make the stoutest attribution-monger quail. I propose merely to deal with certain outstanding medals, or groups of medals.

First comes a remarkable piece, a unique medal in the Berlin Cabinet, representing Anthony of Burgundy,[188] the natural brother of Charles the Bold; a powerful portrait, with the man's motto ('Nul ne si frota' for 'Nul ne s'y frotte'), so apt to the haughty Bastard's expression. On the reverse is a device for casting fire from battlements, with flames issuing from it, and the same motto repeated. There can be no doubt that a Florentine hand modelled this forceful bust. It might have been made in 1475, when the Grand Bastard visited Italy. But, as a matter of fact, we know that a man described as Nicolas de Spinel was in 1468 employed as seal-engraver at the court of Charles the Bold, where he cut, among others, the splendid great seal of the duke;[189] did not Memlinc also paint him, in a beautiful panel in the Antwerp Gallery, holding a coin of Nero in his hand?[190] Even so, a sceptic might hesitate to identify this Nicolas de Spinel with the Florentine medallist, did not Leonardo da Vinci himself come to our aid. In the Leicester MS.[191] Leonardo speaks (about 1505) of a method of diverting the course of a stream which was employed in Flanders, as was told him by Nicolò di Forzore. There can be no doubt then that the Florentine medallist did go to Flanders, and the attribution of this medal to him may be taken as fairly established, seeing that it bears a considerable resemblance in style to the signed medals. It carries with it other pieces, such as that of one Pietro Maria (Plate 13.3), of whom nothing more is known. With the medal of Alfonso d'Este we must also associate that of Pierfrancesco de'Medici, one of a set of family medals made about 1490, doubtless at Lorenzo's orders. This Pierfrancesco, a cousin of Lorenzo's, had died in 1477.

In fact, whenever one takes up a medal of this period, with a few exceptions, such as the portraits of della Sassetta and of Pietro and Giovanni de' Medici already mentioned, one finds that it has points of contact with others, which gradually lead one away from the starting-point. This only means that we are dealing with a strongly characterized school, rather than with the works of a single man.

A very distinctly marked group is provided by a series of portraits of Frenchmen. These were all evidently made in 1494–5, at the time of King Charles VIII's expedition into Italy. They include the king himself:[192] a portrait characterized by a vacillating and melancholy expression. The reverse design is almost identical with that on a medal of the famous virago, the heroine of the defence of Forlì, Caterina Sforza-Riario. Here, on the medal of Charles, we have a figure of Peace preceding the chariot of Victory, although the legend says, 'Peace shall follow Victory'. Victory holds a sword and palm-branch. On Caterina's medal, the horses that draw the chariot are winged; no figure precedes them, and Victory holds only a palm-branch; the legend is, 'Fame shall follow Victory'. Which is the earlier? The medal of Caterina exists in two forms;[193] on one she wears the widow's veil, on the other her head is bare; both heads are, however, from the same original model, which was modified to make the later of the two versions. This of course is easily done; you cast a wax reproduction of the piece and work on that as much as you please. Caterina married in 1477 Girolamo Riario, Lord of Imola and Forlì; he was murdered in 1488, and his widow's defence of Forlì against Innocent VIII is famous. The reverse type seems meaningless in reference to her before the siege, yet it occurs attached to the portrait without the widow's veil, as well as to the other. Perhaps it was really made only for the widow's portrait, and recklessly attached to both. However that may be, as we may date it certainly before 1497, when she re-married, and probably very soon after 1488, it would appear to be earlier than the medal of Charles VIII, which cannot be earlier than the autumn of 1494. These medals of Caterina have been attributed to the Florentine gold-smith Domenico Cennini, who was in her service. We know nothing about his work, so we cannot deny his authorship. But it seems clear that he did not also make the medals of Charles VIII and of his suite; among whom, by the way, was a Frenchman of Scottish descent, Béraud Stuart d'Aubigny, represented by a unique portrait-medal in Mr. Whitcombe Greene's collection.[194]

These French medals are, however, by no means the masterpieces of the school. Few, on the other hand, will dispute the claim to this title of the portrait of Giovanni Tornabuoni,[195] with the figure of Hope on the reverse, although this figure must not be included in the praise. We have here a specimen of what could be done in the way of rendering a vigorous but perhaps not too refined or intellectual personality. Turn next to the exquisitely beautiful portrait of Giovanna Albizzi (Plate 14.3), the wife of Lorenzo Tournabuoni, and therefore daughter-in-law of Giovanni. This and the portrait of Nonnina Strozzi,[196] by the same hand, have a pure beauty, at once romantic and serene, that places them on the level where criticism can find no foothold. Intellectual refinement, again, is the keynote of the wonderful portrait of the philosopher, Giovanni Pico della Mirandola (Plate 14.2), who died so young in 1494, leaving a name—though not many read his *Discourse on the Dignity of Mankind* now—as distinguished as any other in Italian philosophy, not excepting Marsilio Ficino. Filippo Strozzi, the great financier who lived so long in exile in Naples (we may still read the touching letters of his mother to her exiled sons) and who began in 1489 the noblest monument of Florentine domestic architecture, the Strozzi Palace—him too we find portrayed, in a very different manner from any of the medals we have mentioned.[197] The reverse is one of those which account for but do not excuse the invention of the Eagle Medallist; it is a mere piece of shop-work. So is the Fortune reverse which comes, for instance, on the medal of Alessandro Vecchietti. A quaint, and also far from masterly, design occurs on the reverse of a medal of Carlo Federighi, made in 1498—three figures, like the three Graces, labelled Fortitude, Beauty, and Love. This medal, again, seems to stand almost by itself. So do the powerful portraits of Gioacchino della Torre (Plate 15.2), the Venetian General of Dominicans who played so important a part in the tragedy of Savonarola; and of Benedetto Tiezzi, the friar of Foiano.[198] So does the large medal of Savonarola himself, holding a crucifix[199] (Plate 15.1). How far any of the Savonarola medals—and there are many—go back to Fra Luca and Frate Ambrogio della Robbia, it is almost impossible to decide.[200] Vasari says that these two friars were much attached to Savonarola and portrayed him 'in that manner which we see to-day in the medals'—an odd way of saying, if he meant to say, that they made medals of him. The largest medal of Savonarola is by no means artistically the best, but its devotional expression has earned it popularity.

A fine little work of the school we are dealing with is the small portrait of Ercole I d'Este, which has been left, in the unique specimen in the British Museum, with a curious rough margin.[201] And of special interest to Britons is the splendid portrait of John Kendal (Plate 13.4) of the Westmorland Kendals, who was prior of the English Knights of Rhodes and commander of the cavalry who protected the pilgrims against the Turks (Turcopolier). He is described as Turcopolier at the time of the siege by the Turks in 1480, though as a matter of fact he was just then not in Rhodes but in the West, raising funds for his Order; and it was probably about this time that he visited Florence and had his portrait made. Or it is possible that it may have been made in Rome, for there is no doubt that, even if Nicolò Fiorentino did not himself work at Rome, the Florentine school at this time was exerting an influence there. There are certain medals which approximate to the style of Cristoforo di Geremia and Lysippus, and yet show such strong Florentine characteristics that one hesitates whether to call them Florentine or Roman. There can be little doubt, however, that the large medal of Innocent VIII with three figures on the reverse (Iustitia, Pax, Copia) is Florentine;[202] although there is nothing in the traditional attribution thereof to Antonio Pollaiuolo.

A work which by its size claims to be one of the most important productions of the school, although it lacks some of the finest qualities, is the portrait, without reverse, of the philosopher Sebastiano Salvini—a unique piece in the possession of the Società Colombaria at Florence. The incised inscription contains a reminiscence of a phrase in Ecclesiasticus; Salvini is described as the follower of wisdom who 'alone compasseth the circle of the heavens'.[203]

There exists, besides the medals of comparatively well-known persons, a certain number of anonymous portraits which belong to this school. Typically Florentine in its unaffected simplicity is the portrait of the nameless youth, the reverse of which shows a leopard seated before a laurel tree. This medal is at Vienna.[204]

It was natural that at the time when all Florence was having itself portrayed in medals, some artists should have thought of making in this medium portraits of some of the earlier heroes of Florentine history. Thus it was that medals of Dante, Boccaccio, Petrarch, Coluccio Salutati came into existence. Of these only the first has much claim to consideration as a work of art; it is a dignified portrait, based doubtless on the Giottesque type, and in some ways no finer head of Dante exists. On the reverse is a compressed rendering of the painting in the Duomo at Florence, by Domenico di Michelino, of Dante standing before the Mountain of Purgatory.[205]

A peculiar interest attaches to the last group of Florentine medals of this period on which we shall touch.[206] It will be remembered that Matteo de' Pasti did a medal with a head of Christ. The medallic type which he originated did not have much vogue, although it is copied in a painting by Montagna in the Brera. But shortly after 1491 a new medallic type was introduced, which was to enjoy an extraordinary popularity. There is in the Berlin Museum a profile bust of Christ on a panel formerly attributed to Jan van Eyck; it is at any rate of the Flemish school, but not earlier than the end of the fifteenth century. The panel is probably half of a larger picture, the other half of which doubtless contained a bust of the Virgin. This picture, or more probably an earlier one with the same type—and it doubtless existed in a good many replicas—must have found its way into Italy. At any rate, it appears, copied most faithfully, on certain medals of Florentine work (though they may have been made at Rome) about the end of the fifteenth century. But the curious thing is that the earliest of these medals bear on the reverse an inscription referring to two portraits of Christ and St. Paul, supposed to be carved on an emerald which had been preserved by the predecessors of the Grand Turk with great care, and sent by the Sultan, Bajazet II, to Pope Innocent VIII, as an especial treasure, to the end that the Pope might retain the Sultan's brother in captivity. Bajazet's brother had been taken prisoner by the Rhodian Knights and was considerably exploited by the princes of the West, until he died in 1495. Now, though we need not doubt that Bajazet sent an emerald, it is fairly clear that this medal reproduces no Byzantine type, but merely a Flemish type which had become popular in Italy, and which the medallist made use of, because it was ready to his hand, to be the vehicle of his pious fraud.[207] There is a companion medal of St. Paul, and in fact a whole series descended from this pair; but to discuss them would lead us too far afield. I only mention here that the medal became so popular that we find it copied in German woodcuts, in stone reliefs, on bells, in paintings, in tapestries. It appears, for instance, on a wretched little devotional panel painted in England in the sixteenth century, with an inscription which is a broken-down descendant of that on the reverse of the original medal. As to the medal itself, a specimen is described in an inventory of 1590 as 'a special picture of Christ cast in mould by Raphael de Urbino brought into England by Cardynall Poole'. Thus Raphael's great name was dragged in to help in the imposition. Recently, Verrocchio's name has been mentioned in connexion with the medals, presumably on the ground of a superficial resemblance of the type of Christ to that which is seen in his group of the Incredulity of St. Thomas.

Fairly early in the sixteenth century another type, more or less inspired by the type of Christ created by Leonardo, found its way on to the devotional medals. This, in a somewhat degraded form, with a blundered Hebrew inscription on the reverse, became immensely popular. Miserable casts of the medal are still made and sold to the credulous as reproductions of a first-century portrait of Christ.

Let us return from this side-issue to the main line of development of the Italian medal. One puzzling group of transitional medals remains to be mentioned before we proceed to deal with the full sixteenth century. They are associated with the name of Adriano de' Maestri, called Adriano Fiorentino,[208] who died in 1499. He was a bronze-worker who was employed by Bertoldo to cast some of his models. Fabriczy has, however, constructed for him, on a rather slender basis, a whole œuvre of medals. If Fabriczy is right, he worked for Frederick the Wise, Elector of Saxony, whose bust he made in bronze, or rather gun-metal; and, while in his service, he made a medal of Degenhart Pfeffinger, Provincial Marshal in Lower Bavaria (Plate 6.5). The portrait is magnificent, the heraldic reverse childish. Towards the end of his life he was at Naples, in 1493; and several Neapolitan medals can be assigned to him with some show of proba-ability.[209] There is documentary evidence that he made medals at Urbino in 1495, of Elisabetta, Duchess of Urbino (the chief character in that famous dialogue, the *Courtier* of Baldassare Castiglione), and of her sister-in-law, Emilia Pia. These two pieces have many features in common with others attributed to him: such are the curiously ugly way of rounding off the back of the bust and the wide spacing of the legend. But, strange to say, the designs on the reverses of both seem to refer to events, unfortunate for the sitters, which happened after the death of Adriano. It is possible, indeed, that he only designed the obverse portraits, which are clearly companions, and that some pupil added the reverses later.[210]

There is a little medal of the poet laureate Agosto da Udine, with a graceful portrait on the obverse. On the reverse is a nude, but not graceful, figure of Urania—Agosto was astrologer as well as poet. On grounds of style alone I have suggested that this might be by Adriano. The suggestion seems to me to be strongly confirmed by the general resemblance in proportions between the Urania figure and a bronze statuette of Venus in the Foulc Collection which is from Adriano's hand.[211]

Whatever we may think of this group of medals, it reveals a very distinct, not wholly attractive, artistic personality, standing quite aloof from the Florentine development as shown in the other Florentines of the time.

IV

The Italian Medal
in the Sixteenth Century

Arrived at the sixteenth century, we must perforce pick and choose, from amongst the great crowd of medallists, good, bad and indifferent, those who seem most worthy of mention. The general improvement in the mechanical side of medal-making, the increasing perfection of the process of striking, may not have been the real cause of the decay in the art; but it was a contributory factor, for it enabled technical excellence to disguise emptiness of conception and design. Again, the court medallist now becomes an important personage; various series of portraits of the Medici are turned out by efficient but un-inspired craftsmen; and nothing can exceed in dreariness the Papal medals of the sixteenth century except those of the times that succeed.

In this century the old smaller centres of the art, Verona, Ferrara, Mantua, have lost their importance. We have to deal with Florence and Rome and Milan, and to a less degree with Venice. It is to be noted that these are at the same time the centres of political importance. Of Padua and the Emilia we shall also have something to say; but Naples still stands aside from the current of our art.

A Florentine sculptor—for we shall begin with Florence—must first be mentioned here, although but one medal can be attributed to him. This is Pietro Torrigiano, of special interest to us, perhaps, because thanks to the quarrel with Michelangelo which ended in the breaking of the master's nose, Torrigiano had to flee his native city, and found his way to England, where he worked from about 1509 to 1519. Among the works attributed to him during his stay in England is a bronze medallion supposed to represent Sir Thomas Lovel, and it is the resemblance, thereto of a large medal of Federigo of Montefeltro, Duke of Urbino, that suggested to the late Max Rosenheim that this medal is by Torrigiano. It is clearly not contemporary with the duke, who died in 1482. But, as it represents him as Knight of the Garter, it is quite probable that Torrigiano made it for Henry VIII in connexion with some Garter celebration.[212]

Notes to this chapter begin on p. 177

Another Florentine sculptor also appears as a medallist: Francesco di Giuliano da Sangallo (1494–1576).[213] His violent, so to speak 'slogging,' methods seem painfully out of place in a quiet gallery of medals. High relief and coarse execution combine with a bourgeois conception which would be less surprising on the other side of the Alps than in Florence. His portrait of himself is an exact replica of the relief in Sa. Maria Primerana at Fiesole; his wife, Elena Marsuppini, large nosed and high cheek-boned, is a vivid Latin type of an unprepossessing kind. The unsigned medal of Lelio Torelli (Plate 16.2) perhaps shows the artist in his least offensive form.

Here we may mention two or three medals, one of which has been given to Francesco, though it has nothing in common with him but its high relief. This is the large medal of Leo X. Like the portrait of Fernando of Aragon, mentioned before, this seems to be cast from a wooden model. It is a good portrait, but a clumsy piece of work. By the same hand are large medals of Giuliano II de' Medici, Duc de Nemours, and of Antonio Ciocchi del Monte.[214]

Another Medici, who is represented by at least five medals, is the famous condottiere Giovanni de' Medici of the Black Bands, son of that famous virago Catarina Sforza whose medals we have already discussed, and father of the Grand Duke Cosimo I. He died young in 1526, fighting against Frundsberg near Mantua. One of his medals is signed by Sangallo; of the four others, the largest, with a poor portrait, shows a cavalry fight (evidently his last battle) on the reverse; another shows him riding out to battle with another horseman; but in some ways the most interesting are the remaining two. Their reverse is very simple: merely a thunderbolt issuing from a cloud. But in its very simplicity there is something impressive; something that stirs the blood, like the trumpet sound of the words that accompany it: FOLGORE DI GVERRA, the Thunderbolt of War. Probably all the medals of this warrior were produced after, some perhaps many years after, his death.[215]

These medals and the works to which we now come are poles apart. Sooner or later one must mention Benvenuto Cellini[216] if one is to consider the minor arts in Italy in the sixteenth century. So consummate a craftsman—for it is impossible to deny him this title—could not be without influence on the art of the medal. It is true that his reputation as an artist has been magnified tenfold by his literary talent as an autobiographer. But, even when we have made allowance for that fact, and when we have discounted the poverty of his ideas, and his entire lack of power to compose, his mere technique as a metal-worker remains matter for admiration.

Born in 1500, Cellini came as a young man, about 1524, to the notice of Pope Clement VII. He struck two medals of the Pope, which he himself describes; one (Plate 17.*1*) refers to the Peace of 1530 to 1534; the other, with Moses striking the rock, to the well which Clement built at Orvieto. The modern official medal, with frigid classical allegory, is the lineal descendant of this Peace medal of Clement.

Cellini was proud of these medals, and of others which he struck (such as the medals of François I[217] and that of Alessandro de' Medici which was actually being prepared when the duke was murdered). But he also produced a certain number by the casting process. The best is that of Cardinal Bembo (Plate 16.*1*).[218] As early as 1537 he was preparing dies for a medal of Bembo, who was then wearing his beard short. These dies were never finished; about 1539–40, however, Bembo, now a cardinal, was portrayed by Cellini with a long beard, on a cast medal. This cast piece is not mentioned by Cellini, but those who have denied his authorship have produced no more satisfactory attribution. It is quite his best achievement as a medallist; the portrait is sympathetic, refined and scholarly, and the objections which have been brought against the Pegasus on the reverse seem to be hypercritical.

It is difficult, however, to find any words of praise for the large medal of Ercole II of Ferrara which Cellini describes himself as modelling in 1540. It is pretentious and vulgar. Only the obverse has been preserved; an early cast from the model, before it was quite completed or lettered, is at Weimar; and a lead cast of the completed obverse is in Mr. Maurice Rosenheim's collection.[219] The reverse, which has not come down to us, represented Peace, doubtless as on the medal of Clement VII. We need not regret its loss.

There are certain other cast medals—one of Cardinal Jean de Lorraine; one of the Milanese Pietro Piantanida; others of the Cardinal Scaramuccia Trivulzio, sometimes attributed to Caradosso—which seem to form a group round Cellini, even if they are not from his own hand. Through them we see his influence radiating out to other schools, such as that of Milan.[220]

Other Florentine medallists of the first half of the sixteenth century are Domenico di Polo de' Vetri (after 1480 to about 1547), who worked for Alessandro I and Cosimo I, and Francesco dal Prato, a capable maker of cast medals, some of which have long been attributed to Domenico.[221]

By the side of the Florentine medallists we may without impropriety place a son of Siena, Pastorino de' Pastorini,[222] who was born in 1508 and died in 1592. In his youth he was a glass-painter, achieving some distinction in the art;

but from about 1540 to 1578 he seems to have devoted himself with extra-ordinary energy to modelling portraits in wax and casting them, usually in lead, and usually without reverse designs. Over 200 portraits, the majority of them signed with his initial P, can be attributed to him. He was a very fashionable artist. In a letter of 1551 one Trappolino says:

> I went to see Pastorino's things, and quite fell in love with a portrait in lead of a Tullia Tolomei; on my word as a gentleman, 'tis too great! Now think what will happen to me when I see the ladies alive, if these, which are without breath, do thus affect me! I tell you truly that I have seen no more lovely profile, nor any other portrait of a Sienese lady, not that of della Valle, nor of a lady of Perugia, the flame of . . . , which indeed is most lovely, &c.—but this leaves all the others behind. See now, if I be not a soft-hearted fellow.

This somewhat incoherent enthusiasm was probably shared by all Sienese society. Pastorino's fame spread rapidly, and from 1552 onwards he was called away to make medals and engrave coins at various mints, such as Ferrara (where he worked from 1554 to 1559 and also later); in 1576 he settled finally at Florence in the service of the Grand Duke Francesco. But no medals later than 1579 can be attributed to him, though he lived until 1592.

His medals may be divided broadly into two classes, distinguished by the absence or presence of a border of rather large pearls, ranged on a kind of raised band. The class without the border consists of small, unpretending pieces, often of considerable if rather superficial charm. They are the earlier; they are comparatively seldom signed and still more seldom dated; but, roughly speaking, they range from about 1540 to 1554. The others, with the border, are usually signed and dated; the border probably occurs first in 1551, on that very medal of Tullia Tolomei that Trappolino raves about, and after 1554 it is found exclusively (Plate 31.3). These later pieces are extraordinarily skilful, evidently the work of an artist of great facility; but after seeing a few of his medals one begins to realize that his portraits are only skin-deep. Charming and accomplished as they are, they have no real intimacy. Some pieces, usually included among his work, which appear to possess this quality, seem rather, on closer examination, to be the work of another artist.[223] But the medal of Giulio Cesare del Grosso (Plate 17.3) is a characteristic and also, being signed, an indubitable specimen of his earlier style. Equally typical is the unsigned Isabella Spagiari (Plate 17.2). Quite delightful also in their way are the companion medals of the two pretty daughters, aged 17 and 15, of the Duke of Ferrara, two of the first medals made by Pastorino when he entered the duke's service in 1552. The portrait of Ariosto which, though the poet had long been dead, Pastorino was moved or commissioned to make, doubtless about the same time, is, as one might expect, uninspired. It is one of the few of the artist's medals that has a reverse. His reverses are banal, and he was wise not to trouble himself to make many. Very characteristic of him, more so doubtless than of the lady, is the portrait (Plate 16.6) of Isabella Rammi, the wife of Francesco d'Este, dated 1555, which was probably the year of her marriage. To the next year belongs a curious portrait (Plate 16.4) of a Turk, Cassan Ciaussi, i.e. Hassan the Envoy; he may have come to Italy in connexion with an alliance which was concluded with the Sultan in that year.

These medals suffice to indicate Pastorino's style. Two of his latest pieces are those of Francesco de' Medici and the notorious Bianca Cappello, dated 1579. They do not do him credit; but it must have been difficult to make a work of art out of the grand duke's mean features, or the opulent charms of his duchess.[224]

Two brothers of the family of Poggini[225] worked as medallists; they were sons of a gem-engraver. Giampaolo (1518–82), as a medallist, is known only by a series of pieces of Philip II and his family, made in Spain. His workmanship is very good and delicate, but his scope limited. His younger brother Domenico (1520–90) won repute as an accomplished sculptor as well as medallist. His sculpture, and the statuettes which can be attributed to him, show the high-water mark of sixteenth-century academicism. We turn from them with some relief; but his struck medals are often even less inspired. In his cast medals, however, he seems to be more at ease, at any rate in the portraits. Thus the portrait on the large cast medal of Cosimo I, known by a unique example in the British Museum (Plate 16.3), is something more than merely accomplished, academic though the reverse with Victory crowning Cosimo may be. Domenico's portrait of Benedetto Varchi (Plate 16.7) has also been justly praised. And if the struck medals, such as that of Francesco de' Medici, appear poor and dry beside these, they are greatly superior to those of some contemporary die-engravers, like Michele Mazzafirri.

Another medallist of the Medici was Pier Paolo Galeotti;[226] born at Rome, he was known as il Romano, and signed his medals PPR. He ranks next to Pastorino, though he makes a bad second, in the number of his works, over seventy are signed by him. The medals of Francesco Taverna (Plate 16.5) and Jacopo de' Medici, Marquis of Marignano, are characteristic of his extremely efficient workmanship; the reverse of the former also shows his tendency to a pictorial style. He worked a good deal in the north of Italy, and one sees in these medals the affinity to the school of which Jacopo da Trezzo is the most famous example. But from 1550 to 1584 Galeotti was settled in Florence, and produced a large number of portraits of the Medici family.

It is impossible even to mention all the minor Florentine medallists of this period. The original wax model for the reverse of a medal of Fernando I by Michele Mazzafirri[227] (1530–97), in Mr. T. W. Greene's collection, shows the extreme delicacy of workmanship which often, as Fabriczy has remarked, demoralizes the eye of the beholder whose taste is not quite assured. Fabriczy makes this remark à propos not of Mazzafirri but of Gaspare Mola[228] or Molo, a famous armourer and goldsmith as well as medallist, who takes us well into the seventeenth century; for he worked at Florence from 1598 to 1627, and did not die until about 1640. He made medals for Fernando I, Cosimo II, and Fernando II; and the struck medal of Vincenzo Gonzaga is a good specimen of his style: very suave, very accomplished, and withal very uninteresting.

Turning now to the sixteenth-century medals made in Rome, we may notice first a curious piece, which for over 200 years has exercised the ingenuity of Hebrew scholars. It was found in 1656 at Fourvières near Lyon, and is therefore sometimes included among French medals.[229] It is, however, purely Italian in style. The fine head is probably a fancy portrait of a Roman emperor, but its significance remains obscure in spite of all attempts at explanation. The long Hebrew inscription is an acrostic, giving the name of a Jewish physician known at Rome in the fifteenth century, Benjamin son of Elihu Beër. Of all the attempts—and there are many—which have been made to explain the enigmatic legends, the last, by S. Ferarès, seems to come nearest the mark. With extraordinary ingenuity he has explained some of the words and sentences as chronograms, giving the dates 1497 and 1503; and the date D·III·M on the reverse was, as he shows, probably so expressed that it might be read as either 1497 or 1503. These are the dates of the oppression of the Jews by the Inquisition; and he supposes the medal to have been cast after the election of Julius II, to celebrate a new era of liberty for the Jews. There are some things that remain doubtful in his argument; one at least of his chronogrammatic interpretations is certainly wrong, and his attempt to connect the medal with Giancristoforo Romano will not be regarded seriously by many critics. But a very great advance has been made in the interpretation of a piece which is something more than a mere riddle; for the head has distinct artistic quality.

Rome is not the most important centre of the medallic art after Florence in the sixteenth century, any more than it was in the fifteenth. We find there the usual influx of artists from all quarters, from Milan, from Parma; nay, even from Cyprus there comes a *Graeculus*. The Papal mint gave employment to a considerable number of workmen whose productions, in their efficient mediocrity, are even more distressing than those of contemporary Florence. But there are a few outstanding artists whose works are certainly worth a moment's consideration. The merit, for instance, of the medal of Gianpietro Crivelli (Plate 16.8) is unquestionable, so far as the portrait is concerned. At once delicate and sure in modelling, broad in conception and full of character, it ranks very high indeed. The ornamental border, very unusual in medals, but just the kind that a jeweller might use, suggests that it may well be, as is generally supposed, the work of Crivelli himself.[230] This Milanese goldsmith, who was born in 1463, came to Rome before 1508, and is probably identical with Cellini's friend Gianpietro della Tacca. His house, decorated outside with reliefs depicting scenes from the life of Paul III, still stands in the Via dei Banchi Vecchi. None of the jewellery for which he was famous seems to have been preserved; if it showed anything like the fine quality of this medal, we could have spared some of Cellini's work for it. The medal of one Benedetto Crivelli[231] which has been attributed to Gianpietro seems to me to be by quite another hand. He died in 1552.

Giovanni Bernardi[232] of Castelbolognese (1496–1553) is best known as an engraver of crystal and other precious stones; his chief work in this line being the Farnese Casket in the Naples Museum. From his engraved crystal plaques casts in metal were often taken, and probably this is the origin of most of the plaquettes which bear his signature, or are attributed to him. His actual medals are of comparatively small importance. One or two, mentioned by Vasari, representing Alfonso I of Ferrara and the Cardinal Ippolito de' Medici, have not been identified if they have survived at all. The medal of Clement VII with Joseph and his brethren on the reverse is said by Vasari to be his, and the ascription is certainly borne out by the style (Plate 17.4). Vasari also says that he made a die for a medal of Charles V at the coronation at Bologna in 1530, which so pleased the emperor that he invited the artist to Spain. Bernardi, however, preferred to return to Rome. Now there is a large cast medal of Charles, mentioning his coronation, which is generally placed among Bernardi's works.[233] But in style it bears no resemblance to his accredited work, and Vasari's story applies to a struck medal; so that Bernardi's piece must be sought elsewhere; nor can it be found in the little piece commemorating the expedition to Tunis, since that only took place in 1535. Bernardi accordingly remains an almost unknown quantity as a medallist; but the work which can be identified as his shows a minuteness of execution and hardness of detail which are not surprising in a man accustomed to engrave in crystal.

Tommaso d'Antonio Perugino, called il Fagiuolo, succeeded Cellini as engraver to the Papal mint in June or July 1533, and held the post until 1541. To him possibly, or at any rate to some skilful artist with the initials T.P., working in Rome about this time, we may attribute a charming group of eight or nine medals, of which six or seven are signed with the monogram P̄. Frequently mistaken for P, this signature has led to the inclusion of these pieces among the work of Pastorino of Siena, to which they are much superior in conception, and quite equal in technique, as the portrait of Cardinal Bembo, illustrated beside some portraits by Pastorino (Plate 17.5) will show.[234]

Alessandro Cesati,[235] called il Greco or Grechetto, was the son of an Italian father and a Cypriote mother. Born in Cyprus about 1500, he came to Rome before 1538, and took service under Cardinal Alessandro Farnese. From October 1, 1540, for about twenty years he was master of the Papal mint, and he worked also for the local mints of Parma, Camerino, and Castro, belonging to members of the Farnese family. In 1561 he went to Piedmont as engraver to the Duke of Savoy; in 1564 he is last heard of as being on his way to Cyprus. Cesati's chief fame, in his time, rested on his gems. Unfortunately the whole subject of the stones attributed to him is in great confusion. A head of Phocion mentioned by Annibal Caro and Vasari used to be identified, one knows not why, with a fine onyx cameo now in the British Museum.[236] But the cameo bears not the slightest resemblance to his work in medals or to any of his signed gems now traceable. As to his medals, if Vasari has reported correctly, Michelangelo bestowed the most overwhelming praise on Cesati's medal of Paul III, the reverse of which represents Alexander the Great kneeling before the High Priest of Jerusalem, in accordance with Jewish legend. Let us hope that Michelangelo has been misreported; but great artists often seem to commit remarkable solecisms when they play the critic. Probably the best, or most characteristic, example of Cesati's style is the medal of the same Pope with Ganymede on the reverse (Plate 17.6). In smoothness and dexterity of execution it is certainly without a rival; but it leaves us cold. Besides Paul III, Alessandro Farnese,[237] Julius III, Emanuel Philibert of Savoy and his duchess, Margaret of France, were all portrayed by Cesati, not to mention other persons of whom medals are mentioned but cannot be identified. The artist had a great reputation also a counterfeiter of ancient coins—which was in those days a respectable profession. A group of medals representing Priam, Dido, Homer, Artemisia (with the earliest attempt at a restoration of the Mausoleum at Halicarnassus) may, on grounds of style, be with some reason assigned to him.[238]

I have dwelt at some length on Cesati because he represents the classicizing, academic Roman school of medallists at the acme of its accomplishment; although the freshness which marked the work of Cristoforo di Geremia is gone, although Cesati's ideas are frigid, it is still possible to look at his medals with interest, even though it be to lament that such marvellous skill should be employed on such conceits. There is a stage in the history of art when even the utmost skill on the artist's part is unable to defeat the boredom which his ideas produce; that stage had not quite been reached in Cesati's time.

Cesati evidently made some important technical improvements in die-engraving. The extreme finish of his work seems to indicate some new process of finishing the detail of his dies. He is also said to have struck medals in two metals, with the bust in gold on a silver ground.

Giannantonio Rossi[239] of Milan (1517 to about 1575), Cesati's successor at the Papal mint, was a very different kind of artist. Although he too was a gem-engraver, he has, in his cast medals, nothing like his predecessor's finish; the handling is, if anything, rather rough. But his struck pieces are quite in accordance with what had now become the tradition at the Papal mint. The same applies to artists like the Bonzagnas, Giangiacomo (1508–65), and Gianfederigo (died after 1586). Fabriczy[240] describes the latter's medals, with some truth, as 'works of desperate dryness of technique and of commonplace conception, inspired solely by the dictates of routine'. These medallists are followed by others whom it would be tedious to enumerate; for there is nothing to relieve the monotony of their achievements. The palm for dullness may perhaps be assigned to Giovanni Paladino, who struck a series of medals representing Popes from Martin V in the early fifteenth century to Pius V (1566–72), in whose reign presumably he worked. These 'restitutions' are a constant stumbling-block to the amateur; but when once warned against them no one ought to be deceived. Yet the chances are ten to one that any illustration of a Papal medal in a popular book will turn out on examination to be the work of this mischievous, though doubtless well-meaning, medallist. A series of cast medals representing St. Peter and all his successors down to John XXII, thus supplementing Paladino, is said to have been made by the Milanese Giovanni Battista Pozzi, Paladino's contemporary. They are so childish that they may be regarded as the worst example of that human failing which is responsible for series such as the Holyrood portraits.

It is a relief to leave Rome for the north of Italy. There the old tradition of the superiority of the cast over the struck medal is maintained throughout the century. Some artists, it is true, engraved dies; but the only man who obtained any great reputation by struck medals alone was Giovanni dal Cavino; and his success, as we shall see, was essentially a *succès de scandale*.

Padua enjoyed a great reputation, from the time of Donatello's visit onwards, as a centre of the bronze-worker's art. Towards the end of the century, Andrea Briosco, better known from his curly hair as il Riccio, was the head of the school; but although he was distinguished as a maker of figures on a large scale, it was essentially as a master of the minor works of decorative art that he won his wide reputation. In these, indeed, he is acknowledged to be without a rival; the wonderful candelabrum in Sant' Antonio at Padua is perhaps the most remarkable achievement in the art of decorative bronze-work in the whole world. Numerous figure-plaques were turned out by Riccio and his school, and it is natural that medals should have been attributed to him. I confess that I can see no reason for accepting any of these attributions; in particular the portrait medal of Riccio himself (Plate 17.7) is in all probability posthumous, as seems to be half-suggested by the wording of the inscription: 'Andrea the curly-haired of Padua made the bronze candlestick for Sant' Antonio', and by the reverse type—a dead laurel-tree with a fresh shoot, a star above, and the motto OBSTANTE GENIO.[241] It was probably the work of some younger contemporary, such as that one in whose house in Padua the Anonimo Morelliano saw many medals partly by his own, partly by other hands.[242]

Riccio finished his candlestick in 1516, and died in 1532. A younger contemporary of his was Valerio Belli (about 1468–1546);[243] though a native of Vicenza, he ranks as a Paduan artist. Like Giov. Bernardi, he won his fame chiefly as an engraver of crystal, the Medici Casket at Florence being his masterpiece. He also made a very large number of pieces—at least fifty— which were dignified with the name of reproductions of coins. They are, as a fact, fancy portraits of distinguished persons of antiquity, showing little or no imagination, and a peculiar shagginess in the treatment of the hair which makes them easy to recognize. It has already been remarked that Rouille of Lyon used them as models for his engravings. These pieces were all originally struck, although numerous casts were made afterwards. There are two, if not three, medals representing Valerio himself.[244] I do not feel at all sure that the two variations known to me are by the same hand; the treatment of the hair, for instance, and the lettering are wholly different. The larger medal is decidedly the better work of art; and in its lettering it shows more resemblance than the other to the medal of Bembo (Plate 17.8), which is with some show of reason accepted as Valerio's, and which is certainly the work of a gem-engraver.[245] All the specimens of the larger portrait that I have seen are cast, but possibly the original was struck. It is a curious fact that the medallic work of the great plaquette artists, l'Antico, Giovanni Bernardi, Riccio, Valerio Belli, always seems to be involved in a certain amount of mystery.

The Paduan Giovanni dal Cavino[246] (1500–70) is the most famous, not to say the most notorious, of all imitators of ancient Roman coins. The designation 'Paduan' indeed is commonly applied to all sixteenth-century imitations of Roman sestertii and the like. Cavino's are often dangerous counterfeits, and the attempts which have been made to whitewash their maker may be summarily dismissed. A large number of his dies have been preserved and are in the Paris Cabinet; but a few which cannot be his have been mixed with them. In addition to his false coins, he struck a certain number of portrait medals of his contemporaries (Plate 17.11); also a medal of Julius III referring to the re-establishment of Roman Catholicism in England, and two medals of Christ. His style is arid beyond all possibility of description, and as an artist he merits but little consideration.

A medallist of a very different type is Lodovico Leoni[247] (1531–1612). His work at the Papal mint under Gregory XIII need not detain us; but the cast medals which he produced in his native Padua are of no small merit. In fact, in these he shows himself to belong less to the tradition of Padua or the Venetian district than to the school of the great wax-modellers of Milan; it seems clear, in fact, that he had learned much from Leone Leoni, of whom we have yet to speak. Of some interest to us is his portrait of the Englishman Richard White of Basingstoke,[248] a scholar of no little distinction in his time, whose medal he cast at Padua in 1568. White was a Fellow of New College, Oxford, who in 1564 forfeited his fellowship by absence; at Padua he became Doctor of Laws, and published in 1568 a treatise on the famous riddling inscription of Aelia Laelia Crispis. Lodovico's portrait of the aged Jacopo Tatti (Plate 18.3) is full of character and pathos, far superior to Vittoria's bust, and fit to be mentioned beside Tintoretto's portrait in the Uffizi.

Although it is not by Lodovico Leoni (to whom it has been attributed) I may mention here another interesting medal of an Englishman which was made at Padua; this is of Sir John Cheke,[249] the well-known humanist who was tutor to Edward VI. In 1554 Cheke went abroad, and spent the year 1555 in Italy (his biographer mentions that he lectured at Padua on Demosthenes), returning to England in 1556. The medal is a good specimen of the academic Paduan style of the time. It has also been attributed to an obscure medallist named Martino of Bergamo; but this attribution, though better than the one mentioned above, still leaves much to be desired.

The fame of the Italian medallists penetrated early in the sixteenth century to Poland. Thus it was that Giovanni Maria Mosca, a Paduan sculptor, migrated to that country, where in 1532 he cast some medals, more curious than beautiful, of Sigismund I, his wife, and his son.[250] In 1539, or more probably 1538, Sigismund summoned thither the well-known engraver Gian Jacopo Caraglio of Parma.[251] A medal of the musician Alessandro Pesenti, one of Sigismund dated 1538, and (more doubtfully) one of Bona Sforza, have been identified as his work. Finally among the products of these emigrants we must not omit to mention a really fine medal of Sigismund II, dated 1548 and signed by Dominicus Venetus.[252] Whoever he was, this Domenico Veneziano understood both vigorous characterization and—what so few Italians of his time had any inkling of—heraldic composition.

The Venetian medals after the first quarter of the sixteenth century are to a certain degree disappointing. The meagre, dry compositions of Andrea Spinelli,[253] who struck medals between 1534 and 1542, although he was actually employed at the Venetian mint for another thirty years, are among the few that bear signatures; unfortunately they are also among the least interesting. He distinguished himself, it is true, by the enormous cast medal of Bernardo Soranzo, which has been mentioned earlier (p. 14) as one of the things that a medal should not be.

The chief forces in Venetian sculpture in the sixteenth century are the Florentine Jacopo Tatti (1486–1570), called Jacopo Sansovino[254] after his master Andrea Sansovino, and Alessandro Vittoria (1525–1608). No medals can be attributed to the former, although it seems possible to discern the influence of his stately and dignified style in such a figure as the Fame on the reverse of the medal of Antonio Bosso.[255] From Vittoria's hand[256] we have two or three medals, notably the famous one of the 'Scourge of Princes', Pietro Aretino (Plate 18.*1*). There is also the very rare medal which, giving the portraits of Vittoria himself and the painter Bernardino India, and being entirely in Vittoria's style, may without hesitation be assigned to him.[257] These portraits

have a dull and heavy effect—'stodgy' perhaps is the just if slangy term—
which is not out of keeping with Vittoria's work as a portrait sculptor, as
exemplified, for instance, in his bust of Jacopo Tatti in the Seminario at Venice.
His portraits of plump women (Plate 18.2) have a certain attraction, though it
is not intellectual.

Far more interesting than Vittoria's medals is a group of portraits all made
about the middle of the century by an unknown artist.[258] Nearly all the persons
represented seem to belong to Venice or the neighbourhood. Many of the
medals portray a pair of brothers, a mother and daughter, a mother and son,
or a man and his wife. There is a charming intimacy about the portraits; the
women are buxom and pleasant, if not always pretty. Occasionally, as in the
case of Titian's friend, Elisabetta Quirini (Plate 17.9), they even achieve beauty.
The artist stands in some sort of relation to Vittoria, although he has much more
liveliness and geniality. M. de Foville has called him the Venetian pupil of
Riccio, on the supposition that he made the portrait medal of Riccio which
we have already discussed. But this hypothesis seems to me insecure, and it is
safer to call him merely the Venetian medallist of 1550. His strength lies certainly
in portraiture; but occasionally he produces a charmingly graceful reverse, as in
the figure of Friendship on the medal of Francesco Comendone (Plate 17.10).

We now come to the Milanese school, in some respects the most important
school in Italy in the sixteenth century, not excepting the Florentine. For it
includes Leone Leoni, or, rather, he is its foundation; and he is an artist of more
intellect than Cellini or Pastorino and of nearly, if not quite, as fine execution.
The best Milanese medallists retain a good deal of the sculpturesque quality
of their predecessors in the fifteenth century. Skilful though they were as
wax-modellers, one feels that they did not abuse the facilities which their
medium gave them. Their attitude towards the wax model is different from
that of a Pastorino or, to mention artists who will occupy us later, Ruspagiari
or Antonio Abondio. These seem to look upon the wax model as the end and aim
of their labours; if it is reproduced in metal, then that metallic reproduction is,
so to speak, only a means of preserving a record of work done in a more perish-
able medium. Very different is this feeling from that of the earlier masters, to
whom, even if they did not use the waste-wax method, destroying the model
entirely, the model was nevertheless only a stage in the production of the medal.

It is true that we have no definite statement by any artist which justifies the
distinction which we have drawn. But we can, I think, safely conjecture it from
the varying styles, and support our conjecture by the patent fact that now in the

sixteenth century not only were wax models, from which medals had been cast, preserved, repaired, coloured, and otherwise ornamented, but actually the making of wax portraits, without any view to the casting of medals, was developed as an independent art.

Leone Leoni[259] was born about 1509, probably at Arezzo; he calls himself Aretinus, indeed, which should suffice for us, but Menaggio has also been claimed as his birthplace. His life was a changeful one. From November 1537 to 1540 he was employed as die engraver to the Papal mint. It was he who succeeded in causing the imprisonment of his rival Benvenuto Cellini in 1538. Two years later he committed a violent assault on a German jeweller (Pellegrino de' Leuti) in the Pope's employment, and was himself in consequence committed to the galleys. But Andrea Doria, the great admiral of Genoa, procured his release.[260] From 1542 to 1545, and from 1550 until his death in 1590, he worked for the Milanese mint; but he also executed commissions elsewhere, as at Venice, Parma, and Rome. In 1549, the Emperor Charles V invited him to Brussels, and ennobled him. On a medal, once if not now in the Ambrosian Library at Milan, he calls himself 'Leo Aretinus Sculptor Caesareus'. On this appointment followed a busy period, during which he made statues and busts of Charles and members of the Imperial family. He finally, after visiting Spain, returned to Milan in 1558, and did not, so far as we know, leave it again. One observes that even at this mature age he retained his old habits, for on one occasion he nearly murdered the son of Titian with the object of robbery. It is interesting also to note that neither this, nor any of the other crimes of which he was guilty, is mentioned by his fellow-townsman, Vasari, in his biography, judging from which Leone might have been a most respectable member of society, instead of belonging, as he did, to the same category as Cellini.

But he was a most admirable artist. The medals which he made to commemorate his release from the galleys are not among his finest works, but his own portrait on them is clever, and the admiral's head is full of dignity (Plate 18.4).[261] He is at his best in his medals of Charles V; the great medal with Jupiter thundering on the Giants, or the smaller, less ambitious work with the Salus Publica reverse, are equally fine from a technical point of view. His portrait of Michelangelo is without doubt in the first rank as a record of the master's appearance; in fact it may, with some reason, be described as the best portrait of Michelangelo in existence (Plate 18.6). We are fortunate in possessing also, in the British Museum, a portrait of Michelangelo modelled in wax, evidently from Leone's hand.[262] It differs in certain details from the medal.

Leone portrayed a number of celebrities besides those whom I have mentioned, and he was specially successful with certain members of the Hanna family. Martin de Hanna was a wealthy Flemish merchant who settled at Venice. We have medals of him (Plate 18.5), of his sons Daniel and John, and of Paul the son of John, all probably from Leone's hand, and all singularly attractive.[263] A medal of Titian is also, without much reason, attributed to Leone, and he signed one of Vasari.

Contemporary with Leone Leoni is another famous Milanese medallist, Jacopo Nizolla of Trezzo.[264] He was born about 1515 or 1520, and worked first in Milan. All Milanese artists of any note in this period naturally came into the employment of the emperor. Thus it was that in 1555 Jacopo went to the Netherlands, and in 1559 to Spain, where he remained until his death in 1587. The Spanish monarchs employed him as sculptor, architect, gem-engraver, and metal-worker, as well as medallist. When Philip II married Mary Tudor, Trezzo came to England, and produced a well-known medal of the pair. The two portraits are also found singly (Plate 18.9) with allegorical reverse designs, much in the same manner as the allegorical designs of Leone Leoni, but rather more academic in spirit.[265] There are also some exceedingly skilful versions of the same type, consisting of the two heads with less bust. Some specimens are masterpieces of chasing. We have, further, a remarkable unsigned medal, representing the Cremonese engineer Gianello della Torre, which has been assigned both to Leone Leoni and to Trezzo. It is one of which neither might be ashamed. The portrait, it is true, is not attractive; but the subject is to blame, and there is no lack of character in the features. But the reverse (Plate 18.8), the 'Fountain of the Sciences', with a stately figure supporting an urn from which flow the streams of knowledge, to be eagerly caught by figures bending at her feet—this is a nobly monumental design, than which the academic art of the sixteenth century has produced nothing better. I confess that I find it difficult to decide whether it is the work of Leone or of Trezzo. It is true that Leone quarrelled violently with Gianello, and called him an ox in human shape: his portrait betrays a certain stolidity which may have prompted the phrase. But such a quarrel is insufficient proof that Leone could not have made a medal of Gianello before the quarrel or after a reconciliation. Pending the discovery of a document the medal may instructively remain as an indication of the way in which the styles of the two masters approach each other.

Passing over Annibale Fontana, a younger contemporary of Trezzo, and the author of one or two medals, unsigned but well authenticated, we may briefly mention Pompeo the son of Leone Leoni (born about 1535, died 1610). He had great vogue as a sculptor and medallist at the Spanish court. But he lacked his father's strength and power of composition.[266]

Before dealing with the last important representative of the Milanese school, Antonio Abondio, who will take us to the north of the Alps, it is desirable to round off our outline of the history of the Italian medal by a few words about one or two minor medallists who cannot rank as great artists, but are consummate masters of the technique of modelling in wax in low relief. Alfonso Ruspagiari[267] was born at Reggio d'Emilia in 1521. He was made superintendent of the mint of his native town in 1571, and died in 1576. He works in extremely low relief; he delights in representing thin drapery with numerous fine folds, and elaborately ornamental headdresses. The bust is usually shown to front or from the back, with the head turned in profile. Another mannerism consists in truncating the arms so that the medal looks like the reproduction of a sculptured bust, an effect which is sometimes enhanced by placing the bust on an ornamental bracket. These tricks are less pleasing when he is representing a man, such as Ercole II d'Este; but it is impossible not to take pleasure in so exquisite a piece of modelling as the portrait of a nameless woman (Plate 18.*11*) who is represented in profile to right with the face of another person looking at her as it were from the edge of the frame of the medal. The artist's understanding of flesh and texture is quite masterly.

Allied to Ruspagiari is a medallist who signs his medals with the letter S. He has been identified with Nicolò Signoretti,[268] who was engraver to the mint at Reggio from 1556 to 1612; he carries some of Ruspagiari's mannerisms to even greater excess.

The third medallist of this group is Andrea Cambi,[269] called il Bombarda. He was a goldsmith of Cremona, whose chief activity dates from about 1560 to 1575. As a specimen of his pictorial style one may instance the pretty reverse of his medal of Giambattista Pigna: the nymph Pitys, beloved of Pan and Boreas, is being changed into a tree, while Pan looks on.[270] In his portraits of ladies he shows as great virtuosity as Ruspagiari; witness his pretty medal of Lodovica Poggi (Plate 18.7).

These medallists may not be great artists, but there is one fact which makes it possible to enjoy their work, that for the most part they do not fly at very high game. The pretentious works of the court medallists of Florence and Rome too often irritate us by the emptiness of their performance compared with their claims. These portraits by Ruspagiari and his like do not make so loud a challenge; the persons represented are as a rule comparatively obscure, and we take them simply for what they are worth.

An inferior member of this school, Agostino Ardenti, who signed himself A·A·, produced a certain number of rather rough portraits evidently inspired by Ruspagiari.[271] A mechanical interpretation of the signature led older writers to incorporate all his medals in the work of a much greater medallist, Antonio Abondio, who sometimes signs in the same way. They are, however, easily distinguishable by their style.

Antonio Abondio[272] was of Lombard, perhaps Milanese origin; at any rate he may rank as a pupil, direct or indirect, of Leone Leoni. He was born in 1538 and died about 1596. In 1566 he was, like all the other leading artists of the time, called to the Imperial service, and went to Prague. He exercised an over-whelming influence on the Austrian medallists of his day. From June 1571 to March 1572 he was in Spain, and while there met Jacopo da Trezzo, of whom he cast a fine medal. But with the exception of occasional visits to the Netherlands, Bavaria, and North Italy, nearly all his life was spent in Prague or in Vienna.

We have little from his hand that we can assign to his pre-Austrian period; but the stately medal of Nicolò Madruzzo, which has only recently been recovered in its entirety, is probably one of these comparatively early works. Until Mr. T. W. Greene's specimen (Plate 18.*10*) was published,[273] the portrait was known only with Leone Leoni's reverse of a Gigantomachy, belonging to his medal of Charles V, attached to it. This hybrid already existed as early as 1610, when it was engraved in the work of Luckius. But we now have the true reverse, on which Madruzzo rides after Fortune, accompanied by or dragging after him seven women, *per tot discrimina rerum*. Madruzzo, originally an ecclesiastic, became a soldier in 1547, and held important commands in the Imperial army. The medal dates from about 1560 to 1565, possibly from the time when his life was already overshadowed by a quarrel with the Archduke Ferdinand.

The medal is a good specimen of Abondio's technique; but perhaps a more advanced stage of his art is seen in the medals of Rudolph II and the Austrian archdukes, or still more in the remarkable large medal of Maximilian II,[274] of which the original wax model, coloured and repaired, is still preserved at Vienna. The reverse attached to this wax model I cannot believe to be by the same hand; indeed, were its existence at the beginning of the seventeenth century not attested, one would suspect its authenticity, if one judged merely by the motives and types. The obverse is, however, characteristic of the artist.

The British Museum possesses what is apparently the best of the existing lead castings from this model. The little medal of the Empress Maria (Plate 17.*12*) is typical of the artist's work on a small scale.

Antonio Abondio had a son Alessandro[275] (1580–1653), well known first as a wax-modeller, and later, when he left the Austrian service for that of the Elector of Bavaria, as a medallist. His medals have been highly praised; they are, it has been said, equally free from all courtly stiffness or insipid idealization. When German art came under the domination of Italy, it was natural that the new Italianate style should lack vigour. The praise given to Alessandro Abondio shows, by contrast, the tendency of the time towards an academic Italianism. The great period of the German medal was over. It had had a short life and a vigorous one, much more independent of Italian influence than was the case with its fellows in France and the Low Countries. It is for that very reason fitting that we should briefly survey the history of the German medal before dealing with the less original schools of the other northern countries.

V

German Medals

Mr. C. J. Holmes has remarked that the intense imaginative insight which accompanies D rer's amazing manipulative power may be due to his Hungarian ancestry, since no parallel to it appears in other Teutonic work. He adds that 'of genuinely German art Holbein is perhaps the greatest manifestation, and the gap which separates Holbein from Rethel and Menzel, the most considerable figures in German art of modern times, is filled with names that survive only as synonyms for misdirected effort'.[276] Sweeping as this criticism may seem, it is well to bear it in mind as a corrective to the enthusiasm which many students and collectors of German medals feel and express. The German medal seems to hold more or less the same relation to the Italian, as Roman sculpture does to Greek. The analogy is doubtless far from perfect, but it is sufficiently close to be instructive.

It is only within the last seven or eight years that the study of German medals has been placed on a really critical footing. Erman, in 1884, made an admirable beginning, by giving a careful classification of the material known to him. He was followed by various writers of monographs; certain artists, such as Peter Flötner, were exalted to great heights, and then subjected to a course of destructive criticism. In 1909 Georg Habich began the publication in the *Jahrbuch* of Berlin of his articles on the German Renaissance Medal. He deals with an enormously comprehensive collection of material, both in actual medals and models, and in documents. The material foundations of the study are soundly and truly laid.[277] What follows in this chapter is little more than a summary of Habich's researches on the historical side. It is hardly necessay to say that for the estimate which is here given of the artistic value of the German medal small support will be found in his pages.

The wax model, the basis of the Italian medal, did not play nearly so great a part in the German school. The two schools, however, were alike in this respect,

Notes to this chapter begin on p. 181

that neither seems to have had any direct connexion with the craft of engraving dies for coins. The Carrara medals, as we saw, coin-like productions as they were, remained isolated, without influence on the subsequent development of the art. Similarly, the earliest examples met with in Germany stand quite out of relation to what follows. The Berlin Museum possesses a remarkable piece cast in silver and gilt, representing Duke John of Cleves, which was produced as early as 1449. On the obverse is the duke on horseback in full armour, wielding his sword; on the reverse are the arms of Cleves and Mark. The style of the whole is so extraordinarily seal-like that it is impossible to resist the conclusion that the duke's seal-engraver made it. Another work of the fifteenth century, produced on the lower Rhine, is a thin, coin-like, struck medal of Arnold of Egmont, Duke of Gelderland (1423–65). But this belongs rather to Holland than to Germany; whereas the medal of the Duke of Cleves is thoroughly German in style.[278] Yet it is in no artistic sense an ancestor of the later German medal, and need be mentioned here only as a curiosity.

More distinctly related to the later medals are the *Schauthaler*, or 'show dollars', struck from engraved dies, which make their appearance in the last quarter of the century. Yet even these and the medals proper remained for a long period without influence on each other, except for an occasional instance of one being copied, so far as design was concerned, from the other. Not until the decline, says Habich, does one find modellers like Tobias Wolff trying to render the technique of struck medals by means of stone models, and engravers like Valentin Maler obtaining a wax-model effect with their dies.[279]

The German medal had two sources, one in ordinary metal-casting, the other in goldsmithery. Nuremberg was the centre of the latter, Augsburg of the former technique. The models for both forms of work were carved in wood or stone, indifferently.

The German medal remained, until the end of the period with which we are concerned, a straightforward application of the artists' stock-in-trade to the new demand for portrait-medals. On the obverse was a portrait; on the reverse, if there was a reverse, a coat of arms. The goldsmith had been accustomed to engrave seals; accordingly craftmanship acquired in seal engraving was applied direct. In this sense the medal in Germany is not a new discovery as it was in Italy. Its sole merits lie in the vividness of the portraiture, in the skill with which the heraldic reverse is designed, and in the craftsmanship with which the whole is executed. Personal ugliness, which the Italian artist understands how to dignify and inspire with pathos or interest, is allowed by the German to work with unmitigated force; grossness and stupidity are revealed with a directness which shows that the medallists regarded them without aversion. The element of imagination does not enter into the construction of the medal in Germany. What had the plain, matter-of-fact German burgher of Nuremberg or Augsburg to do with such frivolities as *imprese*? If, therefore, the Italian portrait-medals are sometimes monotonous, the German are ten times more so.

These generalities do not become applicable until after the first stages, which are the most interesting stages, in the history of the art. Habich has pointed out that the three primitive medals of Peter Vischer the Younger and his brother Hermann,[280] of the years 1507, 1509, and 1511, are quite different in feeling and technique from any other German medal. He thinks the design was cut negatively (i.e. sealwise) into a piece of stucco (i.e. hardened wax) or plaster. He regards this as an Italian method, although he does not adduce any evidence for the use of such a process in Italy. As to Italian influence on the types, there can be no doubt.

What was the part played by Albrecht Dürer[281] in the history of the German medal? The Vischer medals had no effect on the development of the art; and the same is almost as true of the medals connected with Dürer. There is some controversy about the question whether Dürer actually made any medals himself, or merely provided the designs. In the case of struck medals, for which dies would have to be made, naturally the work of professional die-engravers, there can be no doubt that he did no more than supply the designs. A most interesting example is to be found in the splendid piece presented by the city of Nuremberg to Charles V as an act of homage, in 1521.[282] There is documentary evidence that Dürer, advised by Willibald Pirckheimer, provided designs for the dies. These were reproduced by woodcutting, and a copy submitted to Charles's court historiographer, who was requested to say whether the titles and arms and the device of the columns of Hercules and the Imperial eagle were correctly set forth. The finished medal was in some respects not unworthy of the great artist who designed it, or of the occasion. The depth of the relief is remarkable. The richness of the effect would be oppressive were it not carried off by the freshness and verve of the cutting. So far as this factor is concerned, one feels that the art of the die-cutter is still a living art, in which everything is due to skill of hand, and nothing to machinery; every stroke of his graver has its meaning, and there is no mere exhibition of the craftsman's skill for its own sake, nor has the life been taken out of the details, as it has in so many equally rich baroque designs, which are consequently only tedious. But if the ornamental and heraldic part of the design is still alive, that is not so true of the portrait, which has wholly lost the Düreresque penetration of character, and become merely the craftsman's work, a purely ornamental element in the general design. This fact may make us hesitate to accept Habich's view that the engraver was Ludwig Krug, since the portraits which it seems possible to attribute to that artist are distinguished by their power of sympathetic characterization.

Very different, because not struck but cast, and also because it is nearer the master's own hand, is such a masterpiece as the supposed portrait of Michael Wolgemuth, dated 1508, and marked with Dürer's monogram (Plate 20.*1*). There is no reason to deny that Dürer may himself have made the model for this. Certainly neither Hans Daucher, nor any other contemporary who has been suggested, has a style of carving or modelling which approaches the medals of 'Wolgemuth', of Willibald Pirckheimer (1517), of the 'Dürer's Father' of 1514, of the nameless bust (Plate 19.*1*; also of 1514) of which the stone model is in the Vogel Collection at Chemnitz, or of the ideal head which has already been mentioned (p. 19) in another connexion, the so-called Eve or Agnes Dürer or Lucretia, of 1508. This last belongs, as Habich says, to the series of female heads drawn by Dürer from 1506 to 1509 under the influence of his Italian studies. As regards the technique of these pieces, it is to be remarked that, rather than medals properly speaking, they are thin, hollow-cast pieces of metal, real goldsmith's work, and have almost the appearance of being repoussé. We remember the Duke of Berry's medallions and note that here again the goldsmith provides us with the incunabula of the medal. Equally we find that this form of hollow-cast shell is rejected by the professional medallist when he comes into existence. Italy had found a great artist ready to take up and develop the medal. But in Germany, Dürer, the only artist of absolutely the first rank who ever troubled himself about anything approaching medals, did not care to take up the task, so to speak, professionally. Dürer's medals are the work of an amateur from the medallic point of view. German system does not tolerate the amateur. Therefore these works had no influence on the subsequent development of the art.

Hans Daucher,[283] the Augsburg sculptor, has already been mentioned in connexion with the theory, suggested but not to be accepted, that he may have executed medals from Dürer's designs. He became a citizen of Augsburg in 1514, obtaining the right to exercise his craft at the same time, and died in 1537. His style is very marked; clearly his *métier* was the carving of low relief in stone, and indeed it is signed reliefs of this kind that have made it possible to locate his medals. He is one of the few Germans who understand the value of lettering as an element in decoration. Characteristic of his style are the facing portraits, with a great bust, filling nearly half the available space, and a broad hat in the Henry VIII style. Indeed, there is little doubt that we have a medal of Henry VIII (1526) from his hand, though it can hardly have been done from the life; probably it was inspired by a Holbein portrait.[284] This is closely akin to the medal of Otto Heinrich, Count Palatine, dated 1527 (Plate 19.2).

Daucher's work as a medallist seems to be confined to the period from 1515 to 1529, although he lived for another eight years, occupied doubtless with work on a larger scale.

Daucher was indeed more a sculptor than a medallist. The first professional medallist, properly speaking, in Germany was Hans the son of Ulrich Schwarz of Augsburg,[285] born about 1492 or 1493. He is mentioned as an apprentice in 1506 in the register of the painters, goldsmiths, sculptors, &c. His earliest known work is dated 1516. As early as 1519 he was working, full of commissions, at Nuremberg, though in 1520 he was expelled thence for political reasons. Thereafter he seems to have wandered about until 1527, the year to which belongs the latest dated medal that can be assigned to him, and after which he disappears, except that his presence is recorded in Paris in the beginning of the thirties. There is no good reason to suppose that he is identical with a painter of the same name who is mentioned in 1540, though he did use the same monogram.

To his short career of about ten years can be attributed over 130 medals. The great majority of them are simple portraits, without reverses. His occasional attempts at reverse designs have met with praise from amateurs of the German medal; it is, however, to be feared that in the dearth of good German reverses, other than purely heraldic, these have acquired an exaggerated importance. The figure of Hope, on the reverse of the medal of George, Bishop of Speyer, is a ludicrous example of the fussy and vulgar treatment of drapery which is so appallingly common in German art of the time. There is much more to be said for his portraits. Schwarz is indeed the only German medallist—always excepting Dürer—who succeeds in attaining really powerful expression without inevitably falling into vulgarity. Nor does even he always escape; after all, some of his subjects must have been such that escape was impossible for the most noble-minded of artists. But, although a highly refined type may have caused him embarrassment, he does not give one the impression that he coarsens everything he touches. The portrait of Lucia Doerrer (1522), the tenth Muse and the glory of Germany—a glory, alas! somewhat faded now, for how many have heard of her?—shows his power of composition and characterization (Plate 19.5). The coarseness of feature and expression that is undoubtedly discernible is not, one feels, due entirely to the roughness of his handling. Equally characteristic, though much uglier, is the Conrad Peutinger (1516–17). This medal (Plate 19.3), strong as the portrait may be, shows how inadequate an idea of the subordination of inscription and minor decoration to the main subject the best German artists sometimes had. The restless decoration of the borders detracts enormously from the effect of the whole. The medal of Matthäus Lang, Cardinal Archbishop of Salzburg, is much more satisfactory, and that of Charles V (c. 1520), uncompromising as it appears in the rendering of the Hapsburg lip, is doubtless more true to life than many portraits of the emperor. One of the most attractive medals of this group represents 'Urban Labenwolf ain Augsburger' (1518); the face is thoughtful and refined (Plate 19.6). But it is to be noticed that Habich labels it 'manner of Hans Schwarz' only. It does perhaps lack strength. A certain number of Schwarz's medals are of foreigners, some (like the Count Jan of Egmont, Plate 20.3) perhaps done on journeys, others (like the Henry VIII of England, Plate 19.4) more probably at second-hand.[286] It cannot be denied that in his rough, bold way, Schwarz was the greatest portraitist among the professional German medallists, perhaps the only one who had real genius as distinct from talent. He has great simplicity and directness, great power of blocking out a relief, so as to give the most effective play of light and shade. Habich describes him, rightly, as the only German medallist who in simplicity of pose and energy of characterization can be compared with the Italian masters of the quattrocento.

Christoph Weiditz[287] was the author of a large series of Augsburg medals which have long been grouped together, although it is only within the last few years that Habich has succeeded in discovering the name of their maker. He is first met with at Strassburg in 1523. In 1525 he moved about, eventually settling in 1526 at Augsburg. In 1529 he visited Spain; returned to Augsburg in the next year; and left almost immediately to visit the Rhineland and Netherlands, perhaps in the train of Charles V. In 1532 he was back in Augsburg, where he worked certainly until 1536, perhaps even to the forties.

None of his medals bears a signature; but documentary evidence proves his authorship of one or two, those of Christoph Mülich and of Johann Dantiscus, the former a man of business and public affairs with a tinge of Italian culture, the latter a man of letters, diplomat and church dignitary. Like other medallists, Weiditz had trouble with the Augsburg gild of goldsmiths; in fact, he seems to have owed his right to be a master of this craft to a special privilege conferred on him by the emperor in the teeth of the opposition of the Augsburg gild. He died in 1560, but seems to have given up making medals during the last twenty years of his life.

Weiditz differs from Schwarz and most other German medallists in taking considerable care of his lettering, which was actually carved on the models and not punched into the moulds with type. His style is broad and sculpturesque, though not so virile as Schwarz's. One of his best works is the medal of the celebrated Fernando Cortes,[288] which was made in Spain in 1529. It is a masterly study, expressing indomitable will and keenness, though hardly nobility of character. A gentler type is the medal of Lienhard (Lux) Meringer, made at Augsburg in 1526 (Plate 20.2). This is surely the German medal at its best: a proud and dignified profile, beautifully composed and quite free from constraint.

Weiditz invented more reverse designs than his immediate contemporaries, but none of them can be called successful. The subjects are usually treated on too small a scale for the field of the medal, and remind one in their scratchy composition of some of the less successful medals of Neapolitans by Adriano Fiorentino, though they are better modelled. As Adriano worked in Germany, it is possible that some of his designs may have been known to Weiditz. Italian influence of other kinds is discernible in many of his medals, but he cannot be taken seriously as a designer of anything but portraits.

One of the most prolific among the German medallists was Friedrich Hagenauer,[289] a younger rival of Schwarz and Weiditz. He was a Strassburger, and probably left his native town owing to the iconoclastic mania which raged there from 1520 to 1530, making it an unprofitable home for a sculptor.

The medals which can be attributed to Hagenauer, either because they bear his signature or on the ground of style, show that he was in Munich in 1525, 1526, and 1527. From 1527 to 1532 he lived in Augsburg. It is significant that Hans Schwarz's activity as a medallist came to an end—not, as we know, because of death—in this year 1526. In the same year also, if we except a single piece dated 1529, ends the medallic work of Hans Daucher. It would appear that Hagenauer either ousted the two or acquired the goodwill of their businesses. His great success as a 'Konterfetter' aroused the jealousy of the gild of painters and sculptors of Augsburg, who, after he had been working there five years, i.e. about 1531, sought to restrict his activity, since he was not a member of the gild. He contended that the art of the medal was a free art, not subject to gild law. In Speyer, Worms, Mainz, Frankfurt, Heidelberg, Nuremberg, Regensburg, Passau, Salzburg, Munich, and Landshut he had never been interfered with. But here in Augsburg, where the medal had evidently been born from sculpture, we can understand the protest of the gild. The quarrel is significant of the status and character of the art. For one thing, a portrait-medallist was bound to travel about, to get commissions; and that was difficult to reconcile with gild conditions. The German tendency to bring this, which should have been as in Italy a free art, into the cast-iron system of the artistic gilds accounts in some degree for the limitations of the German medal.

The opposition of the gild, mentioned above, seems to have been successful; for in 1532 we find Hagenauer back at Strassburg, making, among others, the neat medal of Paul Lauchberger and his wife Agnes Wicker (Plate 20.5). The years from 1533–6 he spent chiefly in Baden and Swabia, with occasional visits to Strassburg, and perhaps to Basel. The portrait of the corpulent Count of Nellenburg and Thengen—'der dicke Thengen', as he was called—belongs to that period (1534). From 1536 to 1546 is his Cologne period, and to this belongs the fine, thoughtful, medal of Philip Melanchthon, made in 1543 (Plate 20.6). In all, Habich has classified under Hagenauer's name some 230 pieces, either actual medals or wood models.

One of the most remarkable of these models is in the Munich Cabinet; it was cut in 1534 out of maple-wood, not out of the usual box-wood, and represents the already mentioned Christopher, Count of Nellenburg. Berlin possesses the fine model for the medal of Melanchthon.

These 230 pieces show that Hagenauer was in no sense a genius like Hans Schwarz, but a craftsman of great efficiency, with remarkable finish and skill in the handling of low relief. He avoids the strong shadows and contrasts that please Schwarz. With more refinement, he is proportionately weaker. He is not at his best with a subject like 'Fat Thengen'; he has not caught the jovial good humour which history tells us characterized the count. Indeed, the expression is that of a man overburdened with the weight of his cares, doubtless mainly corporeal. But the gentle scholar Melanchthon, or the alert diplomat Michael Mercator of Venloo (Plate 20.4) and a dozen other gentlemen appealed to him. Of course he could also do justice to a vulgar subject, such as were too plentiful to his hand: witness the large wood model of Sebastian and Ursula Ligsalz (1527).

Habich has justly observed that whereas Schwarz is essentially sculpturesque, Hagenauer's affinity is with painting, and with the Augsburg painting of the time; it is this that has inspired his principles of pose and composition.

A stately medal of Wilibald von Redwitz, Canon of Bamberg, cast in 1536 on the large scale of 113·5 mm. diameter, stands apart from most other German medals in its sculpturesque quality. It has recently been attributed[290] to the Würzburg wood-carver and portrait-sculptor Peter Dell the Elder, who is known to have been working from 1501 to 1549.

Another sculptor, Conrad Meit,[291] signs his name in full on a medal of the Nuremberger Peter Harsdörffer (Plate 20.8): *Peter Harstorffer, alt 20 Iar, kontrfet von Conrad Mit*. The influence of sculpture is manifest, but as a medal it does the artist little credit.

An able craftsman, with a great capacity for detailed ornamentation, but little more than respectable power as a portraitist, is Hans Kels of Kaufbeuren.[292] He is best known for his elaborate draughtboard and set of draughtsmen in the Vienna Museum, signed and dated 1537. He is first heard of in Augsburg in 1529, and died between October 1, 1565, and April 1, 1566. A wood medallion representing Charles V and Ferdinand I with their wives, signed fully and dated 1537, is in the Hamburg Museum. There are also a wood model with the portrait of Adam Oeffner of 1540, signed ᴴᴋ, and medals of Ferdinand I and Matthäus Schwarz of 1550, similarly signed. Such is the foundation for the attribution to him of a goodly number of medals and wood models. A fair specimen of his work on a small scale is the little medal of Sebastian Gienger, made in 1532, with the reverse design of a boy asleep with his head on a skull. (Plate 20.7).[293] One of the best of his wood models, at Vienna, represents the three emperors, Maximilian I, Charles V and Ferdinand I (1540).[294] Although these carvings of Kels could serve as models, it must not be forgotten that they were complete in themselves, and that casts from them are always too reminiscent of the wood model to make satisfactory medals. At the same time, it must be admitted that the relation which artists like Kels continued to maintain with sculpture on a large scale was beneficial, in that it kept their style broader and more free than it might otherwise have become. We feel this at once when we come to the other artists, chiefly of the Nuremberg school, whose affinity is distinctly rather with goldsmithery than with sculpture. In Schwarz, Hagenauer and Weiditz we have seen at least the elements of that greatness which breaks out through the restrictions of a minor art, just as the finest Greek coins and Italian medals show a largeness of style which places them on a level with sculpture.

The attribution of the medals of the early Nuremberg school, from 1525 onwards (Plate 20.*9* and *10*; 21.*1–6*), is still in a state of great uncertainty. The admirable portrait of Marquart Rosenberger, and the two pieces, dated 1525, representing Wilhelm of Brandenburg and Hans Schenck, which are associated with it in style, have lately been attributed to Ludwig Krug.[295] Krug paid the tax which gave him the right to call himself Master in 1522. He had the reputation of being a particularly skilful engraver of portrait dies; and the refinement of his style may be due to the fact, recorded of him, that he worked from wax models. The medals just mentioned are cast, but, as Krug was a friend of Hans Schwarz and worked with him, it is possible that some struck thalers after the manner of the Augsburg medallist, such as those of Matthäus Lang of Salzburg, are from dies by Krug.

Many other medals have been attributed to him, especially among the Nuremberg portraits of 1525 to 1527. But the truth is that with extraordinary technical ability the artists of this school frequently combined so little individuality of style, that nothing short of authentic signatures or documentary evidence can suffice to distinguish the members of a group of artists. Erman gave to Krug a whole group of Nuremberg medals of 1526 and 1527, among them a medal of Dürer which is now shown, by the statement of a contemporary, to be by Mathes Gebel. Hampe, who has done more than any other writer to reconstruct the work of Gebel, leaves to Krug certain excellent medals, such as the Albrecht Scheuerl of 1527; but Habich, having provided Krug with the three pieces above-mentioned, is inclined to sweep into the net of Mathes Gebel the whole group of medals of 1525–7 which had hitherto been assigned to Krug. It seems clear that any one who chooses to go into the question is likely to make a different partition, and that for the purposes of the study of the artistic development of the medal these attributions are of small significance, since they are based on infinitesimal differentiae where they are not due to purely subjective reasons.

Round Mathes Gebel[296] is gathered an ever increasing number of medals dating from about 1526 to 1544. Some of these, whether by him or by another, are among the most finished productions of German art. There is, for instance, a medal of Christoph Kres of Kressenstein (Plate 20.*9*) which is probably surpassed by few existing medals in delicate truth of modelling. In this respect it stands comparison admirably with the best Italian work of the sixteenth century; nor (and this is remarkable in a German work) does it come far behind it in delicacy of feeling. It is noticeable, however, that in the treatment of the heraldic reverse there is not the same distinction. Neither Italian nor German heraldic design can for a moment bear comparison with the best French or English, even although in the sixteenth century neither of the latter schools was in its prime.

Mathes Gebel, who signs, when he signs at all, with his initials M·G·, became a citizen of Nuremberg in 1523 and worked steadily until 1554; he did not die, it seems, until 1574. He has but recently come into notice. This is due to the fact that documentary evidence has been published, proving that he made an unsigned medal of Christoph and Katharina Scheuerl in 1533. We also know that the medals of Albrecht Dürer of 1527–8, and of Johann Stöffler of 1530 (1531), are by his hand. His signed medals belong to the years 1539, 1542 (Jörg von Embs, Plate 21.1), and 1543. Now the medal of Scheuerl used to be attributed to Peter Flötner, and the result of the new evidence has been to suggest that the whole mass of medals attributed to Flötner (except two which are signed P·F·) should be transferred to Mathes Gebel. Thus Hampe, who discovered the new fact about the Scheuerl medal, transfers to his hero some sixty-five unsigned medals of Nurembergers from 1526 to 1553 or 1554, and Habich is equally of opinion that the mass of the Nuremberg medals of this stretch of years are the work of one hand, or at least one shop, and that is Mathes Gebel's. Domanig, one of the most uncritical of the adherents of Flötner, to whom he, on his side, had assigned an extraordinarily miscellaneous assemblage of medals,[297] retorts that the majority of these are of much finer workmanship than the pieces signed by Mathes Gebel, which are comparatively coarse in execution. The two medals of Raimund Fugger (Plate 21.4) and one of Philip Count Palatine are typical of the best work attributed to Flötner by Domanig. The judicious critic will probably say that though some of the signed medals by Gebel do show such inferiority, there is little to choose, for instance, between the medal of Jörg von Embs, which is signed by Gebel (Plate 21.1), and such a brilliant piece of technique as the medal with the three portraits of Heinrich Ribisch, Georg Hermann, and Konrad Mair (Plate 21.3). Whoever made the latter was a consummate master of the sympathetic delineation of bourgeois types.[298]

But the two signed medals by Flötner really decide the question. One represents the head of Christ, with a satirical reverse caricaturing the Pope. The other commemorates the restoration of the walls of Nuremberg in 1538.[299] Domanig argues that if Flötner was commissioned to make a medal of such importance, he must have already gained a reputation as a medallist. Experience of the motives which govern the distribution of commissions by public authorities lends little support to this argument. Flötner was doubtless well known not merely as a wood-cutter but as a maker of plaquettes and a worker in metal; that would be enough, as it is enough for a committee of the present day, in search of an artist to make a medal, to know that the person to whom they give the commission is a sculptor. Flötner's two signed medals are in any case, unlike his plaquettes, of not the slightest artistic importance. But their subjects were not inspiring; and it may be that he was more successful with portrait-medals. Nevertheless the fact remains that if he made any of the portrait-medals which used to be ascribed to him, they are indistinguishable among the mass of medals which, as we have seen, are now grouped round the name of Mathes Gebel; further, that none of these medals bears any sort of affinity in style and workmanship to the two medals which bear Flötner's signature. In view of the peculiar character of German craftsmanship, which we have seen may make it so difficult to distinguish different hands in a group of men who work together, it is not altogether impossible that Flötner may have made some of the medals which were formerly attributed to him. But, without documentary evidence, it cannot be made to seem even probable.

The reconstruction of Flötner's work as a medallist must accordingly be based on the two signed medals; and on this basis Habich is able to place to his credit some half dozen more pieces (e.g. that of Charles V, Ferdinand I and Maria of Hungary, Plate 19.7).[300] The famous modeller of plaquettes can no longer count as one of the leading German medallists. The clearing up of the confusion which reigned in this corner of the history of German art is one of the most satisfactory pieces of work of the kind that has been done of late years.

The medallists with whom we have just dealt, although their ideal may not be very high, are sincere and often pleasing. In contrast to them, another medallist, Hans Reinhart the elder,[301] who became a citizen of Leipzig in 1539, and died in 1581, must be mentioned here as an awful example of the deplorably bad taste of which the shool was capable. Reinhart's 'masterpiece' is the Trinity medal,[302] a monstrosity which won so great approval that it was issued in no less than four different versions, in 1544, 1561, 1569, and 1574. It was originally cast to the order of Duke Moritz of Saxony, at a time when great efforts were being made to reconcile Protestants and Catholics. A representation of the Trinity is combined with extracts from the Athanasian Creed and a hymn in honour of the Trinity.[303] Technically regarded, the medal is a *tour de force*. Various portions of it such as the head of God the Father, the hands with sceptre and orb, the Crucifix, etc., are made separately and soldered on. The curls of God the Father's beard appear to have been cast separately and fastened in. The result is, of course, a merely vulgar display of wealth of decoration, with as little claim to artistic merit as the Crucifixion scenes, carved in nutshells, which were a favourite with certain German craftsmen and still excite the admiration of the crowd.

Reinhart's ordinary portrait-medals are less offensive than this because they are less pretentious. But his Charles V of the year 1537, one of the best of them (Plate 19.*8*), has not the distinction of the portraits of the emperor that we have mentioned before. In fact, Reinhart must be regarded as a signal example of that misdirection of effort to which reference is made in the passage with which this chapter opens.

Ludwig Neufarer,[304] who was perhaps of Tyrolese origin, worked from about 1530 to 1562, chiefly in Nuremberg and Austria, being eventually (in 1545) taken definitely into the service of Ferdinand I and in 1547 made a warden of the Vienna mint and court goldsmith. In 1558 he became mint master at Prague; in 1562 he was pensioned off. His larger medals, from wood models, differ considerably in style from the smaller, which are mostly from stone, being, as Habich remarks, chiefly portraits of Nurembergers and therefore produced by the process usual at Nuremberg; and his struck pieces, again, naturally differ from those which are cast. His style inclines to be dry and mechanical, but he is usually quite unpretending. Thus his portrait of Charles V gives the features doubtless truly enough, but without dignity; and the composition of the reverse, with the Imperial eagle manipulating the columns of Hercules as if they were clubs, is ridiculous (Plate 21.*11*).

Hans Bolsterer,[305] who signs with the initials H B and a house-mark, was a competent medallist who worked at Nuremberg from 1540 to 1567, with intervals of absence. During one of these he was at Frankfurt, where in 1547 he made at least seven medals. He died in 1573. Technically he excelled in very fine hollow casts, often casting the two sides separately and joining them together, so as to make what are called shells. This technique is a jeweller's rather than a medallist's, as we have already seen. It was occasionally adopted also by Hans Reinhart. In the seventeenth century the medallists of the Dutch school often joined two repoussé designs together in this way to make a medal. Erman (whose opinion on the point is quoted with reverence by most subsequent writers) praised this artist as one of the best German medallists, on the ground that his work is distinguished in equal measure by technical perfection and by agreeable conception (*gemütvolle Auffassung*). In this limited sense of 'best' we may agree. He does not, however, approach the Augsburgers of whom we have already spoken in any of the greater qualities. The medals of Sigmund von Nanckenreut, dated 1551 (Plate 21.8), and of Wilibald Gebhart, dated 1555 (Plate 21.7), give a good idea of his style; other of his medals show perhaps a more 'agreeable conception', and it would be easy to find even among the works of his contemporaries medals in which the composition is more dignified, less 'all-over-ish'; but the Nanckenreut is undoubtedly a strong portrait.

Joachim Deschler[306] was one of the most productive of German medallists. Born about 1500, he became a citizen of Nuremberg in 1537. At some time between 1530 and 1547 he spent two years in Italy—with singularly small benefit, be it said, to his conception of what a medal should be. As early as 1543 he was in relation with Maximilian, the future emperor, and he worked from 1548 for the courts of Austria, Saxony, and the Palatinate, living at Nuremberg or in Austria. Maximilian II made him Imperial sculptor and 'Konterfeiter in Stain'. He died after October 1, 1571, perhaps not before 1572.

He is seen at his strongest in the extraordinary facing portrait (1553) of Hieronymus Paumgartner, a Nuremberg churchwarden (Plate 19.9).[307] It is impossible to deny the cleverness of this brutal exposure of his sitter's pompous vulgarity. But a doubt arises, whether the exposure is conscious. Too large a proportion of the works, not merely of Deschler, but of most German medallists, stand on the verge of caricature for us to believe that a sarcastic or humorous intention lay behind them. It is easier to suppose that they were executed in deadly seriousness, and, as the artists were nothing if not conscientious, none of those superficial vulgarities, which may cover the most estimable of characters, was allowed to escape. We have seen that there were Italian artists like Sperandio and Francesco da Sangallo whose touch seemed to have the faculty of coarsening nearly all that came under it. But they never produced anything that was ridiculous, however much it may have lacked refinement. Therein lies the difference between the artist with an artistic ideal, and the craftsman without imagination.

The medal of Georg Olinger, another Nuremberger (1556),[308] shows Deschler in a much less offensive form. The technical excellence of the casting of his medals, as clean as if they were struck from dies, is worthy of notice.

Tobias Wolff was a very popular medallist of the second half of the century.[309] He was established in Breslau by 1561; his medallic activity, however, probably did not begin until about 1564 at the earliest; in 1574 he received an appointment at the court of Augustus of Saxony. He lived into the seventeenth century, his latest signed piece being dated 1604. His works are very numerous, very neat and elegant; his mannerism of presenting the eyes small and narrow, almost as if they were blinking, has been remarked. His workmanship is so fine, his technique so subtle, that his medals, though cast from stone models, give the impression of being struck. It is only as examples of extraordinary technical ability that they are of interest (Plate 21.*10*).

I do not propose to carry the history of the German medal beyond the time when it fell so completely under foreign influence as to lose its character. But a few other prolific German medallists, who, like Wolff, mark the transition to the seventeenth century, must be mentioned.

Valentin Maler of Iglau[310] belongs to the school of Nuremberg, but was considerably influenced by foreign examples. His fondness for medals without reverses recalls the example of some Italian artists, such as Pastorino; and his predilection for the oval shape may be due to Netherlandish influence. Maler worked for a time in Prague, where he came into touch with Antonio Abondio, who influenced him strongly. The fact that Habich is inclined, though doubtfully, to accept as Maler's work, and perhaps as evidence of a visit to Italy, the medal of Guido Panziruolo (1563) of Reggio d'Emilia, shows how near his style must come to some of the Italians of his time. This piece, which is signed ·A·A·, is by an Emilian artist, whose work has been uncritically classed with that of the much more accomplished Antonio Abondio.[311] Maler was active from about 1563 to 1593, very busy with portraits of Nuremberg dignitaries, clerics, and members of the court of Saxony (Plate 21.*9*). A few of his portraits, brilliant examples of wax-modeller's technique, have also great liveliness and character.

Baldwin Drentwett,[312] a Frisian born in 1545, lived and worked as a goldsmith in Augsburg from the early seventies until 1627. On the basis of a single piece signed B·D· and representing Joachim Rieter von Korenburg (1614), Habich has grouped under Drentwett's name nearly a hundred medals, many of which have been attributed to Antonio Abondio, Valentin Maler, or Matthäus Carl. The series begins in 1572 and goes down to 1619 or 1620. If Habich's classification is correct, Drentwett's work is a good example of the eclectic character of German medallic art at the time. Matthäus Carl,[313] the last German medallist with whom we shall concern ourselves, may have been a pupil of Drentwett in Augsburg. His career as a medallist extends from 1584 (when he appears in Nuremberg, where he became a citizen and master in 1585) until a year or two before his death in 1608 or 1609. In Carl again we see the influence of Antonio Abondio, as also of the Netherlandish school, and he has little power of expressing character.

The series of German medals of the sixteenth century is a long one, and contains no small proportion of works which are characterized by fine technical execution; nor in any series shall we come across a larger number of lifelike portraits. Yet it is impossible to deny that their general effect is monotonous, not to say tedious. The reason appears to lie in the lack of that artistic imagination which alone can redeem a long series of technically admirable works from monotony, and which alone can raise an ordinary 'speaking likeness' above the level of the skilful photograph. Mere technical perfection soon cloys the palate; nay, it makes it more difficult to be fair to the artists, since it leads one to expect more from them, and to ask for an intellectual content on a par with their manual dexterity. This lack of imagination, coupled with a high ideal of craftsmanship, corresponds in art to that characteristic of the German mind which has been expressed so incisively in the statement of a German that the Germans possess knowledge but not culture: 'Kenntnis ohne Kultur'. The epigram of course employs the word 'Kultur' in its old sense, which has been distorted by recent usage. There can be no doubt that the medals reflect with great exactitude the general spirit of German art at the time. They will always remain deeply interesting to those who look at medals as personal portraits rather than as works of art. It is true, as I have urged at the outset, that personal interest was the cause that brought the medal into existence. Only in Italy the medallist could not help producing a work of art at the same time; in Germany he seldom produced more than a good likeness.

VI

Medals of the Netherlands

After Germany it seems natural to pass to the Netherlands in our consideration of the history of the medal. We observe there a much less homogeneous material than in either of the two countries that we have yet dealt with. Throughout our period we find a friendly struggle proceeding between the native school and foreign influence. Not until the second half of the sixteenth century can we speak of a definite Netherlandish style.

The connexion of Flanders and Brabant with the Empire meant that foreign artists flocked thither whenever the presence of emperors or archdukes attracted them. Italians came on visits and influenced the local artists; or they settled and became thoroughly Flemish in their style. A medallist like the Netherlander Stephen H. developed an Italianate style which in some cases makes it difficult at first to distinguish his work from Italian. As in politics, so in this minor art, the country was a kind of playground where all sorts of opposing forces met. One or two fine medals are the result; but there is no tradition, no long succession of masterpieces.

The invasion of Flanders by Italian medallists began late in the fifteenth century. We have already seen (p. 77) that Nicolò Spinelli was employed at the court of Charles the Bold in 1468, and that he probably executed then the wonderful medal of Charles's natural brother, Anthony. Further we have seen (p. 71) that for at least seven years, from 1472 to 1479, Giovanni Candida occupied an important position at the Burgundian court, and made medals of Maximilian and Mary as well as of less exalted personage in their entourage.

Despite these powerful examples, the Flemings remained blind to the possibilities of the medal, until, just as in Germany, the impetus was furnished by a great native artist. Exactly as in Germany, again, although the impetus to the art was given, the great artist exercised no influence on the subsequent development of the medal so far as style and manner are concerned. It is a strange fact, for which the explanation is yet to seek, that Quintin Metsys, though his example it doubtless was that incited other Belgians to make medals, had no more influence on their style than Dürer had on that of the German medallists.

The history of the medal in Belgium is still involved in a great deal of obscurity. A somewhat ambitious attempt to deal with it has been made by Dr. Julien Simonis,[314] but a mistaken form of local patriotism combines with a not too profound scholarship to lessen the value of his contribution to the study. It is to him, however, working chiefly over ground prepared by Pinchart,[315] that we are indebted for nearly all the available material.

There are three or four medals that have been ascribed to Quintin Metsys.[316] None of them is signed, nor is there any documentary evidence of his having made them. But one of them is a portrait of Quintin himself, and the other represents his sister-in-law Christine. Allowing for a certain coarseness in the lettering of the portrait of the brother, due perhaps to the only known specimen of the medal not being an original casting, we can have no doubt that these two are by the same hand. It is of course absurd to assume that every unsigned medal of an artist, even if he be a medallist, is necessarily by himself. When, however, we find portraits of a brother and sister-in-law by the same hand, and when the brother-in-law is known to be a worker in metal, the presumption that he made both grows in force, though, as we shall see, it is still no more than a presumption. The portrait of Quintin is said to be dated 1495 (though this is not visible in Simonis's reproduction); that of his sister-in-law has the date 1491 incised on it. Quintin, who was born about 1460 at Louvain, was received into the painter's gild in that same year 1491. He worked at Louvain and Antwerp, dying at the latter place in 1530.

The medal of Christine is charming in its *naïveté* and freshness. There is no outside influence visible here; it is just an unassuming, direct portrait in relief of a modest young woman of Brabant. It looks as if the model had been carved in wood rather than in stone or wax; that is the impression given, especially by the lettering. The cutting off of the right elbow is a little unfortunate, but otherwise the work is very skilful.

By the same hand as these two pieces is undoubtedly a third, a most interesting medal of William Schevez, Archbishop of St. Andrews (Plate 22.*1*). As Dr. R. F. Burckhardt[317] has shown, the modelling, the lettering of the inscription, the moulded border, and the diameter (77 mm.) are all exactly similar to those of the Metsys medals. Now we happen to know that Schevez was summoned to

Rome by the Pope on January 2, 1491, and that he stopped at Louvain on his way; for the archives show that he was presented with a quantity of Rhine wine and Beaune at the expense of the municipality on February 3/4 and about June 2, 1491. The medal is actually dated 1491. The conclusion that it is by the same artist as the Metsys medals is irresistible.

But now we are brought up against a difficult problem. We know that Quintin Metsys cast in bronze a portrait of Erasmus.[318] (Erasmus, by the way, owned one of the three or four known specimens of the Schevez medal, and, if Metsys made it, Metsys may have given it to him.) In 1528 Erasmus wrote to a friend: 'I wonder where that sculptor of yours got my portrait; unless perhaps he has the one which Quintin at Antwerp cast in bronze. Dürer has painted me, but nothing like.' Now there exists a magnificent medal of Erasmus, bearing the date 1519 (Plate 22.2), and it is very generally assumed that this is the piece to which Erasmus refers as having been cast by Quintin Metsys at Antwerp. The Basel Museum possesses Erasmus's own collection of medals, and among these are two specimens of this large medal, and one of the reduction thereof, which cannot be the piece referred to in his letter of 1528, since it is of later date. We are almost driven to the conclusion that the medal of 1519 is the one which was cast by Quintin Metsys. It is indeed worthy of a great painter, and must rank as one of the greatest portrait-medals in the world. Not even Holbein could surpass the purity of this scholarly profile, IMAGO AD VIVA(M) EFFIGIE(M) EXPRESSA, to which is added the remark, in Greek, that 'his writings will exhibit it better'. On the reverse is Erasmus's own device, a terminal figure, inscribed 'Terminus', with the three mottoes, 'I yield to none', 'Death is the final goal of all things', and 'Keep in sight the end of a long life'.[319]

Now the problem is this: between this medal and the three of the Metsys and Schevez, there is not one jot or one tittle of resemblance in style, fabric, conception, or execution. Either, therefore, we must suppose that Quintin completely changed his style between 1495 and 1519, and changed it not in the way of a natural development but, so far as we can see, so radically that all connexion between the two styles seems to be lacking; or else we must suppose that the Erasmus is not by the same hand as the others. The latter is the view taken by most critics; and, indeed, I do not see how we are to escape from it. And as we know that Quintin did cast a portrait of Erasmus, whereas there is no definite statement that he made medals of himself, his sister-in-law or Schevez, it is only reasonable to assign the medal of Erasmus to Quintin, and the others to some unknown artist. Christine's own husband, Josse Metsys, was a locksmith and clockmaker; and there was a younger brother, Jan, who was a painter. I make no definite suggestion; but there must have been plenty of artists, if not in, then among the friends of, the family.[320]

Simonis, bent on attributing the Metsys medals to Quintin, has hit upon a fantastic theory which enables him to give the Erasmus to a later artist, Jean Second, who was just eight years old in 1519, the date on the medal. He supposes that it was copied by Jean Second at a later date from some portrait which bore the date 1519. He lays stress on the phrase 'ad vivam effigiem', which he says cannot mean *ad vivum*, 'to the life', but only 'from a lively portrait'. Exactly the same phrase occurs on Dürer's engraving of Erasmus: 'Imago Erasmi Roterodami ab Alberto Durero ad vivam effigiem deliniata', with the same allusion to his writings as able to supply a better portrait. But of course the whole point of the phrase lies in the contrast between the modelled or engraved portrait and the literary one. This, it says, is the image of Erasmus according to his living form or likeness: if you want the spiritual essence of the man, look in his literary works. The idea, in fact, is in part that of Shakespeare's seventy-fourth sonnet, where he is speaking of his own verses:

> But be contented: when that fell arrest
> Without all bail shall carry me away,
> My life hath in this line some interest
> Which for memorial with thee shall stay.
> When thou reviewest this, thou dost review
> The very part was consecrate to thee:
> The earth can have but earth, which is his due;
> My spirit is thine, the better part of me.

If further evidence is required that 'ad vivam effigiem' means nothing more than 'ad vivum', it may be found in the title of one of the epigrams of Jean Second himself (Lib. i. 16): 'Inscriptio imaginis formosae virginis ad vivam effigiem a semet ipso caelatae'. It would be absurd to take this to mean that the artist copied some other portrait of the girl.

There exists yet another medal of Erasmus dated 1526, with the same Greek inscription on the reverse.[321] I have not seen it, but it is described as having the bust of Erasmus three-quarters facing, and as evidently inspired by the piece of 1519. As M. Victor Tourneur suggests, this is probably the portrait referred to by Erasmus in his letter of 1528. M. Tourneur is said to have discovered documentary proof in the correspondence of Erasmus that the medal if 1519 is by Quintin Metsys; but whether this amounts to more than the letter of 1528 is not stated.[322]

Jean Second,[323] the brilliant if lascivious scholar, of whom Burmann said that, Dutchman though he was by birth, he might rightly be counted among the classical poets, and whose 'Elegies' and 'Kisses' are as famous as anything of the kind outside of the classical period—this poet was also a medallist of merit. He was born at the Hague, November 14, 1511, his father Nicolas Everaers being President of the Council of Holland. In 1527 Nicolas settled at Malines as President of the Emperor's Grand Council, so that his son came into touch with the most important circle of society at the time. In 1532 he was sent to Bourges to finish his education; returning next year to Malines, he found his father dead, and accepted a secretarial post which took him to Spain. In 1535 Charles, attracted by his talent as a poet, seeing perhaps in him a *vates sacer*, made him his secretary, and took him on the expedition to Tunis. His health, sapped it would seem by excesses, both of work and of other less honourable kinds, broke down, and he returned to his country only to die on September 27, 1536.

His earliest medal represents one Philibertus Panicerius, and is dated 1527.[324] Next comes, in the following year, a portrait of his father. Others succeed; and among them is a portrait (Plate 23.*1*) of his mistress Julia: 'Vatis amatoris Iulia sculpta manu.'[325] Though undated, it must be of 1528 or early in 1529, for he made the acquaintance of this voluptuous lady when he first came to Malines, and she deserted him in 1529. The modelling of the bust is distinctly amateurish, but the genuineness of the feeling that inspires it makes it very attractive.

Simonis has attributed to this medallist, in addition to some pieces which may be his, a rather miscellaneous assortment of medals by other hands, such as one of Erasmus already mentioned, and two of Dantiscus which are probably by Christoph Weiditz. One of the most interesting of Jean's medals has recently been discovered, in the shape of the original box-wood of Nicolas Busleyden.[326] Were it not for the signature 'Per Ianum Secundum', one would say that it was the work of Hagenauer, though the lack of accomplishment in details is not quite characteristic of the careful German. Jean Second's work would perhaps have lost some of its spirit had he taken the trouble to finish it. A sort of impressionistic dash is characteristic of him. He was evidently, as we should expect from his life-story, a passionate artist, without much capacity for taking pains.

But in a medal like this he succeeds in expressing the character of a poet and musician, such as Busleyden is known to have been; and throughout his work he shows that sincerity of feeling which one often notices more distinctly in the not wholly professional artist of the type of Giulio della Torre; presumably because it comes out in contrast with a certain amateurishness of execution. And Jean Second, in spite of the fact that he was so strongly influenced by Hagenauer, always retains his own fresh individuality.

It is characteristic, perhaps, of Jean Second's impulsive nature that most of his medals are known only in rather badly executed casts. He probably never had the patience to master this portion of his work. Even the medal of Julia exists, so far as we know, only in two poor lead castings, one at Brussels, the other in the British Museum. The artist modelled sometimes in stone (as in the case of the portrait of Frans Craneveld), sometimes, as we have seen in the medal of Nicolas Busleyden, in box-wood, and sometimes in wax.

It will be remembered that in dealing with the work of Hagenauer we mentioned certain medals of Michael Mercator of Venloo (Plate 20.4). This man, who was born in 1490 or 1491, was in the service of Floris of Egmont, Count of Buren, in 1527; and in this year he came to England, where he gained the good graces of Henry VIII. The king knighted him in 1539. He finally returned to Venloo about 1540, and died in 1544.

Now a seventeenth-century authority, Erycius Puteanus, in a rare book published in 1630, says that Michael was an admirable maker of portraits on metal and that he alone was allowed the privilege of making a medal of Henry VIII. But there are numerous medals of Henry by different hands; and this last statement belongs to a very common class, being doubtless an exaggeration of some such fact as the grant of permission to execute an official portrait of the king. However this may be, since we have no less than three medals of Mercator himself and one of his wife Elizabeth, it has very naturally been suggested that, being a metal-worker, he made them himself; and among the medals of Henry VIII one, or rather an old reproduction of one in glass paste, has been thought to be his work.[327] This last is doubtless—like, indeed, nearly all so-called English medals of the time—of foreign origin; but I confess that I cannot see the slightest resemblance between it and the medals of Mercator. On the other hand it does show signs of German style, and may be best described as belonging to the school of Hans Schwarz. There are also other medals which have been brought into connexion with those representing Mercator. One depicts Jan of Egmont, the uncle of that Floris who was Mercator's employer. And there are two medals of Charles V, which have been classed with it. All three are as a matter of fact to be connected with Hans Schwarz (see p. 106).

The attribution to Mercator of the medals of himself was summarily rejected in 1904 by Julius Cahn,[328] who has been followed by Habich[329] in attributing them to Hagenauer. One does not like to throw aside an old authority like Puteanus, but he is, after all, a century later than the medals concerned; nor does he say anything about Mercator having made medals of himself, but only of King Henry. Now if Mercator had made three medals of himself, and one of his wife, it would be unlikely that he should have made them all in the same year. All four bear date 1539; and even if one of them has been re-engraved, so far as the incised inscription is concerned, it cannot be earlier than that year, because it mentions that Mercator was knighted by Henry. Now it is significant that it was in the same year 1539 or in 1540 that Sir Michael returned to Venloo, and that Hagenauer at that very time was on a visit to the Low Countries. The presence of the famous German medallist for a short time may well have induced Mercator, proud of his newly-acquired knighthood, to have himself portrayed three times over in the same year.

Though we need not deny that Mercator made medals—he may indeed have made one of the extant medals of Henry VIII—we shall be safest in saying that there is no good proof that any of the medals of Henry VIII are by the same hand as the medals of Mercator, which themselves bear a strong resemblance to the work of Hagenauer and may well be credited to that artist. On the other hand, the resemblance of one of the medals of Henry VIII to one of Jan of Egmont, with whom Mercator may have come into contact, raises a slight presumption that these two may be from his hand. But we shall be wiser, pending the discovery of documentary evidence, if we leave these medals to Schwarz, in whose manner they are.

Among minor medallists, passing mention may be made of a young scholar and archaeologist, Antoine Morillon,[330] who was born at Louvain about 1522 and died prematurely in 1556. He attempted the art of the medal, but his works, which include a fancy portrait of Seneca, are not of any artistic importance. A better artist was Jacob Zagar,[331] a man of letters and a lawyer, and like Jean Second an *alumnus* of the Bourges school of law. In 1557 and 1567 he occupied high positions in the municipality of Middelburg. Here then is another amateur medallist. But his medals show a finish and—particularly that of Frederic Perrenot[332]—an academic spirit which is quite lacking in the medals which we have previously met with. It is true that we are now far on in the century; the medal of Perrenot is dated 1574. Zagar's best work, the portrait of Levinus Bloccenus de Burgh (Plate 23.3), is earlier, being dated 1566, and shows considerable skill in the handling of low relief.

The most prolific of Flemish medallists, though by no means the best artist among them, was Jacob Jonghelinck.[333] He was born in Antwerp in 1531 and died there in 1606, and was working from about 1555 until his death. He thus comes upon the scene shortly after Leone Leoni's visit to Brussels in 1548, in which the influence of Italian on Flemish art, so far as the medal is concerned, may be regarded as culminating. He was of considerable repute as a sculptor, and was employed by Philip II in 1558 to make the sumptuous tomb of Charles the Bold in Notre-Dame at Bruges. His bronze statue of Alva, erected in the citadel of Antwerp in 1571, was destroyed by the people six years later; and he made in 1570 eight bronze statues, representing Bacchus and the seven planets, which were offered to Alessandro Farnese on his triumphal entry into Antwerp in 1585. From 1556 he was seal-engraver to the king, to the Order of the Fleece, and to various other important institutions; from 1572 he was Master of the Mint; and in addition to all this he was evidently exceedingly active as goldsmith and medallist. Of his early life we know almost nothing; the suggestion that he was trained by the painter Frans Floris is a conjecture merely; but Simonis's supposition that he made a journey to Italy has recently been confirmed by the discovery of documentary proof that he went thither in 1552, and in fact worked especially under Leone Leoni in Milan. We know also that, when Leone was in Bruges, he employed Jonghelinck to cast his models in bronze. This sufficiently explains the traces of Italian influence in his style.

We may, with good reason, question the attribution to Jonghelinck of a group of medals, closely allied to each other in style, and all but two of them dated 1552. These represent Antonis de Taxis (Plate 22.3), Frans Floris the painter, Reinart van Busdal, Jan Lotin of Bruges (undated), Adrienne de Mol, and Ursula Lopez (1555). They have also been attributed to Frans Floris's brother, Cornelis, apparently only because he was the brother of Frans. Simonis claims them for Jonghelinck, on quite insufficient grounds. On the other hand, a medal of Christoph Volkmar[334] dated 1553 might very well be the work of the young Jonghelinck while under the influence of the unidentified artist of these other medals.

The signature IVNGELI F occurs on certain small medals of Charles V and Philip II (Plate 23.2), which appear to have been made about the time of the abdication of Charles in 1555 and the victory over the French at St. Quentin in

1556. And a letter from Francesco Marchi to the Cardinal Alessandro Farnese at Parma, written in 1567, tells us that Jonghelinck made a medal of Margaret of Austria, Duchess of Parma and Governess of the Netherlands (Plate 22.4). This medal, dated 1567, is more ambitious than the little pieces of twelve years earlier. The portrait is treated with considerable skill, but without sympathy; the workmanship shows no sense of texture; and the reverse, with Margaret in armour, palm and sword in hand, enforcing the Catholic religion throughout the land, FAVENTE DEO, is restlessly composed. Reverse-compositions, indeed, are not Jonghelinck's strong point. But the medals of Charles V and Philip and of the Governess of the Netherlands between them make it fairly certain that he is responsible for quite a number of other pieces, of which one of the best known represents Philippe de Montmorency, Count Horn, and his wife Walbourg de Nuenar. Simonis has run riot with his attributions in this case, as in others; but, after discounting improbabilities, a large number of medals of a very distinct homogeneity remain to Jonghelinck as their most likely author. Viglius of Zwichem, president of Philip's Privy Council, who appears on four medals from 1556 to 1571; Eric, Duke of Brunswick and Luneburg; Charles de Berlaymont, Governor of Namur; William, Duke of Cleves; Antoine Perrenot, Cardinal Granvelle;[335] and Antonis van Stralen (Plate 23.5) are among the distinguished persons who sat to him. It is instructive to compare one of the Flemish medals of Granvelle with that which was made by Leone Leoni. With all his skill the northerner retires hopelessly into the background; in dignity, in sympathetic understanding, in composition, the Italian easily surpasses him, and that although the personality of the sitter does not give the impression of being inspiring or easily seized.

Among the most curious medals of the period are the little badges worn by the confederates, when they assumed the title of Gueux, used of them in contempt by Berlaymont. They—the Prince of Orange, the Counts of Egmont and Horn and their followers—wore round their necks small medals, with a portrait of the king and the legend EN TOVT FIDELLES AV ROY; on the reverse of the best-known variety are clasped hands and two beggars' wallets, with the motto IVSQVE A PORTER LA BESACE 1566. A letter of the same year from Antoine Morillon to Cardinal Granvelle proves that Jonghelinck had something to do with these badges, or at any rate with some of them[336] Originals are not very common; as happened with some of the English Royalist badges of Charles I and Henrietta Maria, innumerable after-casts were made from a comparatively small number of originals.

Though unsigned, it seems fairly clear that certain medals of Alessandro Farnese, third Duke of Parma, are by Jonghelinck; one, in particular, with Alessandro in a car crowned by Venus, and dated 1565, is mentioned in a letter from the Low Countries by Francesco Marchi, who employed Jonghelinck; he says a clever artist is engaged on it, though he does not name him. Others dated twenty years later, and referring to the siege of Antwerp, do not seem to be by the same hand. Then there are various portraits of archducal personages, Mathias, Albert and Isabella. A gold specimen in the Vienna Cabinet with the portraits of Albert and Isabella cannot be one of the four gold medals which the artist delivered in 1598 on the commission of Albert, since it is dated 1601; but it is doubtless a reproduction with the date altered. It is a highly accomplished work, with the smooth and cold perfection of a portrait by Pourbus. We must not forget also the medal of Alva, dated 1571, when Jonghelinck was working for the duke, and made his colossal statue which was soon afterwards destroyed. A bust, which he offered to the duke when he left Flanders in 1574, has survived; it is signed and dated 1571. Jonghelinck evidently had no more objection to working for the oppressor of his people than an artist like Nicolò Fiorentino had to being employed by members of bitterly opposed factions in Florence. The workmanship of the Alva medal is very close to that of the Governess of the Netherlands.

Jonghelinck sometimes worked from other people's designs. Thus in 1568 Cardinal Granvelle sent to him from Rome a medal of himself (perhaps a wax model) by Domenico de' Compagni, with instructions to make five large and twelve small silver reproductions of it.

A very favourable specimen of Jonghelinck's work, both in the portrait, which is sympathetic and refined, and in the reverse composition, which is graceful and technically fine, although not original in conception, is the already-mentioned medal of Antonis van Stralen (Plate 23.5), burgomaster of Antwerp in 1565.

Simonis has collected, on seventeen plates, a great number of medals other than those which are signed or have been mentioned already, which he would assign to Jonghelinck. To some of them Stephen H. (of whom presently) has a better claim; such are the medals portraying the painter Antonis Mor. A number, such as those three-quarters-facing of the Count of Egmont and of Philippe le Beau, seem to have not the remotest connexion with Jonghelinck's style; the latter, it is true, is found combined with a reverse by him, but it is to be suspected that this is merely an example of the common trick of the *sur-*

mouleur. A careful study of the material might lead to a more satisfactory delimitation of the artist's work.[337] But, in spite of the enthusiasm which Simonis expresses for Jonghelinck, the study is not likely to attract any critic of artistic sympathies. Jonghelinck is a clever court artist, highly accomplished, unoriginal, mechanical, and dull. Among Italian medallists he would rank with such minor masters as Giampaolo Poggini, from whom indeed, since he doubtless came into contact with him, he perhaps drew more inspiration than from Leone Leoni.

A much more admirable and at the same time sympathetic medallist than Jonghelinck, produced by the Low Countries in the second half of the sixteenth century, was the mysterious artist who has since the eighteenth century been miscalled Stephen of Holland.[338] His signature is STE·, STE·H·, STE·H·F·, or STE·H·FEC. The connoisseur, George Vertue, who guessed that he was a Dutchman, thought that the H was the abbreviation of 'Hollandus', which he supposed to be the Latin for 'Dutchman'. Now Vertue knew only of works done by him in this country, on which he might well have described himself as Stephen the Dutchman. But years before he came to this country he had been signing works in his native land in exactly the same way. To call himself Stephen the Dutchman on a medal of a Utrechter made in Holland would have been pointless. For us to continue to call him Stephen of Holland is therefore mere foolishness, if we regard the name as an interpretation of his signature. Vertue thought that 'Stephens' was his surname, and seems to have been inclined to identify him with Richard Stephens, a sculptor. This is undoubtedly wrong. Richard was born in Brabant about 1542, came to England about 1568 'for religion', and lived there more or less continuously until 1589 or later. The Radcliffe monument of the first three Earls of Sussex in Boreham Church, Essex, is his work. Of the other artist, Stephen H., we know no personal details. But his signed and dated medals and pictures—for he was a painter evidently of some merit—show that in 1558 and 1559 he was working in Utrecht; from 1559 to 1561 chiefly in Antwerp; in Poland in 1561 and 1562; in England in 1562 and 1563. In 1564 he was back in Utrecht. Then he disappears; for the evidence that he was working at the Polish court in 1571 and 1572 is of no value.

There is something extraordinarily attractive about his medals of homely people, such as Mary Dimock (Plate 23.4), Richard and Dorcas Martin (Plate 23.6), and the Dutch lady Engelken Tols (Plate 22.6). The portraits are as charmingly intimate as any you will find in the best period of Dutch painting. And medals like those of Floris Allewyn (Plate 22.5) or Jacobus Fabius (Plate 22.7), while no less intimate, and masterpieces of modelling and handling of texture, show that he understood how to give dignity to a portrait. There is every good reason to attribute to him the medal of the famous Utrecht painter, Antonis Mor, but the portrait is not one of his best.[339] As an instance of his reverses, we may take the charming and unconventional group of Charity (Plate 23.7) on the reverse of a portrait of Hans van den Broeck. Stephen was considerably influenced by the Italian masters—I remember discovering his medal of Fabius among the Italian series in the British Museum, before the signature on it was noticed. But though he may be Italianate, he never loses his freshness and directness of vision; he is not a pupil of the Italian Academy. His medals are always cast.

His paintings were Holbeinesque. Two are still in existence at Lumley Castle, namely one of John, Lord Lumley, dated 1563, and one of Jane Fitzalan, Lumley's first wife. Two others, of the twelfth Earl of Arundel, Henry Fitzalan, and one of Lamoral, Count of Egmont, which were also at Lumley in 1590, seem to have disappeared. It is possible that if the two extant pictures could be cleaned and studied, a new fixed point in the study of Tudor portraiture might be established.[340]

Simonis, who has brought together the majority of the medals of foreigners by Stephen, attributes to him portraits of Henry VIII and Adrian VI which have certainly nothing to do with him. The same must be said of the medal of Pietro Piantanida, a purely Italian work, perhaps Milanese, school of Cellini.[341]

The misleading interpretation of this artist's signature as 'Stephen of Holland', coupled with the fact that his first known medals seem to have been made in Utrecht, has led to the assumption that he was a native of that part of the Netherlands. The assumption is by no means justified. Artistically, we must rather look for his origin in the school which is responsible for that little group of medals, produced between 1552 and 1555, which has been mentioned above in connexion with Cornelis Floris.[342] Stephen may very well have been a native of Flanders or Brabant, and it would be desirable to search the archives there, rather than in Utrecht, in order to discover something of his history.

An artist, known only from his signature ALEXANDER P.F., cast in 1578 a medal of Jehan Baptiste Houwaert, a poet and historian of Brussels. It is a clever portrait and finely executed.[343] A most improbable suggestion has been made by Pinchart, that Alexander is the wealthy goldsmith whom Dürer met at Antwerp during his visit there in 1520–1, no less than fifty-seven years before the date of the Houwaert medal.[344]

The Florentine Giuliano Giannini[345] may be mentioned here, for completeness' sake, since what work of his is known seems to have been executed entirely in the Netherlands, and is not in the least Italian in style. He seems to have been in Antwerp as early as 1560, but it is doubtful whether he settled there before 1581. In 1599 he was old, feeble, and without means of subsistence. His medals, which represent Ottavio Farnese, his wife Margaret of Austria, Alessandro Farnese, and the Duke of Alva, are dry and uninteresting.

The only other Netherlandish medallist of the sixteenth century whom we need mention is Coenrad Bloc.[346] Little or nothing is known of him save what can be gathered from his medals, which bear dates from 1575 to 1602. He is supposed to have been born about 1550, probably in Ghent; and he worked in the Netherlands, Germany, and France. In 1594 he was commissioned to make portrait-medals of the Stadtholder-General of the Netherlands. He produced numerous able portraits, some cast, others struck, of reigning personages and other people of importance; that of Pomponne de Bellièvre, Chancellor of France in 1599, shows his characteristic finish (Plate 23.8). It is a brilliant piece of casting, almost indistinguishable from a struck medal.

In the seventeenth century, which does not concern us, a very well-defined school of medallists sprang up in the Low Countries. But up till then the development of the medal was, as we have seen, somewhat fitful and sporadic. It produced one work, the Erasmus, which takes rank among the finest in existence; but that stands quite alone. The history of the art in this part of the world provides an interesting contrast with what we have seen in Italy, with its highly developed and locally differentiated schools, and in Germany, with its systematically organized craft.

VII

French Medals

In France[347] the medal from almost the beginning of its career was, if not in bondage to, yet in close touch with, the officials of municipalities or of the central government. Naturally documents are more plentiful relating to holders of office connected with the mint than to artists working in a private capacity, so that we know more of the history of the former. Still, although there are a number of private medals of considerable merit, most of the good work was done to official commissions. It is quite possible that that good work would have been better still, had it been otherwise inspired; but a country has the medallists it deserves, and we must therefore suppose that there was no keenly discriminating taste for this kind of art in France. The influence of Italy, after the sixteenth century had set in, was not salutary; for, as usually happens, it is not the more vigorous but the more academic elements in a foreign style that are seized upon by imitators.

At the time of the famous exhibition of French Primitives in Paris some twelve years ago, it was flippantly remarked that with Flemish paintings on the one side, and Italian on the other, it was only a small residuum of pictures that could be claimed as really French. The criticism was an exaggeration, but called attention to the uncertainty of the artistic borderline between France and her neighbours in the fifteenth century; an uncertainty very marked in medals.

However this may be, it must be remembered that it is with a great French patron that the remarkable development of art in the beginning of the fifteenth century is associated. That school of illuminating, which, whether we regard it as North French or as Flemish-Burgundian, at any rate shows the northern artists far in advance of their Italian contemporaries, that school which produced the most famous illuminated manuscript in the world, the Très-riches Heures, had for its chief patron the Duc de Berry. And it was for him, as we have seen,[348] that goldsmiths, probably of Flemish-Burgundian origin, made those medals of Heraclius and Constantine, which were the pioneers of the Renaissance medal (Plate 24.*1*).[349] What is more, the duke actually had a portrait-medal made of himself; for an inventory of 1416 describes one in the following terms: a circular gold jewel, having on one side the Virgin and Child under a canopy supported by four angels, and on the other a 'demy-ymage', i.e. a bust or half figure, in the semblance of the duke, holding in his hand a gold tablet; the which jewel the duke bought from his painter Michelet Saulmon. Whether Saulmon made it, we do not know; but it is quite likely that he did. If it was on the scale of the Heraclius and Constantine, and not something small, like a coin, we may conclude that a most important stage in the history of the medal has been obscured by its loss. A still earlier portrait 'jewel', by the gold-smith Jacquet of Lyon, is mentioned in a fragmentary document of 1401–3.

Though these are lost, we are fortunate in possessing examples of a remarkable series of historical, not personal, medals, relating to the wars between the English and French, and the gradual expulsion of the former from French soil, between 1451 and 1460. There are no less than nine varieties of these medals, which may be dated to 1451, 1454, 1455, and 1460; for all but one of them bear chronogrammatic inscriptions, in which the letters having a numeral significance add up to the year of issue. It is obvious, however, at a glance that they are entirely the work of coin-engravers; they are struck from dies, and the elements in their design are all borrowed from contemporary coins.

Little more than enlarged coins, again, are the four medals of Louis XI (1461–83) relating to the foundation of the Order of St. Michael on August 1, 1469. Of two of these the Paris Cabinet possesses what are called *piéforts*, or trial impressions struck on abnormally thick blanks. There are also in existence more or less medallic pieces struck during the same reign for Gaston de Foix, Charles duc de Guyenne (brother of Louis XI), Jean II duc de Bourbon, and François Phébus, King of Navarre; all with the exception of the last have figures, equestrian or seated, of the persons concerned, while the last shows Christ in the garden with Mary Magdalen.

We must not forget that during the reign of Louis XI the Italian medallists Laurana and Pietro da Milano had been working in the south of France. But, although Laurana even made a medal of Louis himself, French artists remained at this period impervious to Italian influence. One can understand that the rather slovenly technique of these two Italians cannot have appealed to the French craftsmen. However that may be, to the end of the century French art not unhappily preserved its independence.

With the reign of Charles VIII we enter on the period of the medal, properly speaking, as distinct from the bastard coin. We must discount a medal of Aymar de Prie, dated 1485, which is doubtless a 'restitution' of later date; but a cast medal of Charles de Bourbon, Archibishop of Lyon, dated 1486, is contemporary, and French rather than Italian work (Plate 25.*1*). Nicolas Rondot, to whom and to F. Mazerolle we owe most that we know about the history of French medals, definitely attributes it to Louis Le Père, of whom we shall hear later. For this attribution there appears to be not a shred of evidence, documentary or stylistic.[350]

We now, in the last decade of the fifteenth century, come to a group of extremely interesting pieces, the most interesting perhaps in the whole French series. These are complimentary medals presented by loyal cities of France to their rulers on the occasion of royal visits. We have already seen (p. 103) how Nuremberg presented a medal to Charles V on a similar occasion.

In March 1494 (1493 in the old style) Anne of Brittany made a state entry into Lyon. The city on this occasion presented her with a golden lion holding a cup containing 100 gold medals. It is worthy of notice that the word 'medaille', or rather 'metaille', is now for the first time used of such pieces in French documents. Both lion and medal were designed by Jean Perréal, the queen's painter; the execution was entrusted to the goldsmith Jean Le Père, who was assisted by his father Louis Le Père and his brother-in-law Nicolas de Florence.[351] These last two engraved the dies and the Lyon mint struck the medal. (Nicolas de Florence, it must be noted, is not Nicolò di Forzore Spinelli, the famous Florentine medallist.) This medal of Anne and her husband is a charming piece (Plate 25.*2*). The obverse bears, on a field sown with fleurs-de-lis, the bust of Charles VIII, crowned and wearing the collar of St. Michael, with the inscription FELIX FORTVNA DIV EXPLORATVM ACTVLIT 1493. On the other side is the queen's bust, on a field of lis and ermines, and the inscription R.P. LVGDVNEN. ANNA REGNANTE CONFLAVIT, with the lion of Lyon in the margin below the bust. The lingering touch of Gothic in treatment and detail is one of the reasons for the attractiveness of this, the first struck portrait-medal in the French series; for struck it is, the word CONFLAVIT referring to the preparation of the gold out of which it was made, not to the process of making. The piece was reissued in 1502 and 1514.

In the same year 1494, on July 29, the queen entered Vienne, with the little dauphin, Charles-Orland, who afterwards died at the age of three. This entry is commemorated in a piece (Plate 24.*4*) which shows on one side the queen seated, holding a sceptre, and supporting the quaint little dauphin, who stands on her knee. On the reverse are the arms of France and Dauphiné, quarterly, suspended to an eradicated tree and supported by two dolphins. The inscriptions are ET NOVA PROGENIES CELO DEMITTITVR ALTO 1494, from Virgil's fourth Eclogue, and VIENNA CIVITAS SANCTA MARTIRVM SANGVINE DEDICATA, in a semi-Gothic lettering. It has been noted that the style of this piece is very seal-like, and the fact that the British Museum possesses a double matrix, with the two designs *in cavo*, back to back,[352] is supposed to confirm the theory that the existing specimens are merely reproductions of a seal. But the question is not so easily decided. In the first place, the piece in the British Museum is cast, whereas all genuine seal-matrices are cut. True, there exist many forged reproductions of matrices, made by casting. I do not suggest that the double matrix in the British Museum is a false reproduction of a seal, because, in the second place, the inscriptions on it are quite unsuitable to a seal. Thirdly, it may be asked whether there is any other instance of a seal bearing on one side the figure of a royal personage, and on the other the arms of a city, and what sort of authority it could be supposed to convey. Fourthly, such a thing as a double matrix for a seal, with the two designs back to back, is, to say the least, extraordinarily unpractical; I will not say absurd, lest an undoubted instance should be found to contradict me. But seeing that seal and counter seal have to be impressed on opposite sides of the wax at the same time, it is difficult to see what purpose, so far as sealing is concerned, this double matrix could serve. No, this matrix cannot have been a seal. It must have been made from a medal in relief. To make it so, it was necessary to take two wax impressions from the original medal, and placing these impressions back to back, to use this joined piece as a model from which to cast what we now have. In spite of the fact that the thickness of metal between the deepest concavities on either side is so minute, that it is difficult to think that it can represent the thickness of the two wax impressions, I am assured by an expert caster that this is not impossible. The use for which the matrix, however made, was intended, is somewhat of a mystery. It does not seem to belong to that class of *in cavo* medals which, as I have shown elsewhere,[353] were used by bookbinders as stamps. Failing other explanations, I would suggest that the artist, having made this double matrix, used it to make *repoussé* shells or wax models, from which specimens of the medal could be cast by the *cire-perdue* or by the ordinary process. But it must be admitted that the matrix for wax models would have been more convenient if made in two halves hinged together.

The two known specimens of the medal corresponding to this matrix are both cast, though writers who should know better talk of the medal as having been struck. Neither French nor any other die-engravers were capable at the time of producing a die of this size (about three inches) *and depth* capable of standing the strain of striking.

There is no contemporary record of this piece; but we fortunately know the details regarding two other complimentary pieces issued five or six years later. Louis XII had now succeeded Charles VIII on the throne and as husband of Anne.

In 1499 the famous sculptor Michel Colombe made designs for a gold medal to be presented to Louis XII on his entry into Tours. The dies were engraved and sixty such pieces struck by the goldsmith Jean Chapillon; and one of the gold pieces has survived and is in the Paris Cabinet (Plate 25.3). The portrait is again admirable, though hardly so masterly as on the Vienne medal already mentioned. The design of the reverse is a porcupine, with a crown above, and the three towers, for Tours, below. The porcupine, which was fabled not only to prick you when you handled it, but to shoot out its quills at you from a distance, had been adopted as a device, with the motto *cominus et eminus*, by the king's grandfather, Louis d'Orléans.

The city of Lyon surpassed itself on the second entry of Queen Anne, which took place in March 1500. This time the gold medal offered to the royal pair, or more especially to the queen, measured about four and a half inches in diameter (Plate 24.3). It was modelled by Nicolas Le Clerc and Jean de Saint-Priest, and cast by the jewellers Jean and Colin Le Père.[354] We have, as before, busts of the king—an extraordinarily cruel and sensual face, while Charles's had been only weak—and of the queen, on heraldic fields, with loyal inscriptions, and the lion of Lyon below the busts. But there is a distinct advance from the Gothic towards the Renaissance conception of the subject.

Two years later, the citizens of Bourg-en-Bresse, not to be outdone, presented a sumptuous medal to Margaret of Austria, on the occasion of her entry as Duchess of Savoy, on August 2, 1502. It was made by a local goldsmith, Jean Marende, and two versions exist, one probably embodying his first idea, and represented by a single specimen. The other, of which many specimens survive (Plate 24.2), shows the busts of Margaret and her husband Philibert the Fair, confronted, issuing from a wattle-palisade, on a field sown with Savoy knots and marguerites. There is not much modelling in the portraits, but the result is very decorative. The same is particularly true of the shield of arms which forms the design of the reverse.[355]

Specimens of this medal exist with the field enamelled. It is clear that the flat, broad treatment of the relief is admirably suited for decoration in that material which would serve to enhance the images.

We have thus arrived at the sixteenth century, and it must be admitted that we shall find nothing among later French medals to compare in the least degree in interest with those that we have already discussed. A certain number of the medals which seem to belong to Giovanni Candida (p. 71–2) have been claimed as French work; but if they are not Candida's, they are such slavish imitations that it is not surprising to find no others shading off from them to a more independent French style. There is, however, a group of medals, all dated 1518 with one exception—and that is of 1524—which betray to a certain degree the influence of Candida. These pieces, which are certainly Lyonnese, since the persons represented are, most or all of them, of that district, have been on purely circumstantial evidence attributed to one Jéronyme Henry, a goldsmith who worked at Lyon from 1503 to 1538. The medal of Jacques de Vitry is a typical specimen (Plate 26.2). There is evidently something Flemish in them, and this has been explained by the influence of Claus Sluter's work at Dijon in two articles by J. Tricou.[356]

Jacques Gauvain[357] is closely allied to this 'artist of 1518'. He lived for more than thirty years at Lyon, was for a few years engraver to the mint at Grenoble, and died after 1547. His own portraits of himself are characteristic (Plate 26.3). We have also from his hand a medal of the Dauphin François, one of the three (the other two representing Queen Eleonora and the Cardinal Duprat) which were presented to these persons on their entry into Lyon in 1533. An attempt has been made to claim for him two medals of Italians, Bartolommeo Panciatichi (1517) and Tommaso de' Guadagni (1523), who were associated with Lyon. These medals certainly refer to the erection of family chapels in the church of the Jacobins at Lyon, and may have been made in that city. The medal of Panciatichi is obviously from the same hand as one of Bernardino Francesconi of Siena[358] referring to the foundation of the Palazzo Francesconi at Siena in 1520; but the artistic connexion between these two and the Guadagni piece is much less clear. Perhaps the artist who made the medal in 1517 for the Florentine Panciatichi was recommended by him to the Sienese Francesconi in 1520; but that he was a Frenchman remains to be proved, while the resemblance of his work to Gauvain's seems to be extremely faint.

The influence of Candida is further visible, though but slightly, in a little medal with portraits of a man and woman. The busts are not named, the

inscriptions being merely the mottoes TAIRE OV BIEN DIRE and SANS VARIER; but
they have been identified, on inadequate grounds, with Pierre Briçnnonet (one
of Candida's subjects) and Anne Compaing. There is, however, little doubt that
de Foville is right in saying that this medal is by the same hand as a pretty piece
representing Regnault Danet and his wife Marguerite (Plate 26.*1*);[359] and it is a
fair presumption that both are by Danet himself, since we know him to have
been working as a goldsmith in Paris from 1529 to 1538.

Two other medals may perhaps be mentioned here before we proceed to the
official series of the sixteenth century, although they are usually classed among
Italian medals. One is the delightful portrait, usually found in silver, of Marguerite de Foix, Marchioness of Saluces (Plate 25.4).[360] It was struck in 1516, and
bears letters which may be a signature, J.J.C. These have been identified with
one Johannes Clot, who is known to have been working at Genoa about that
time. He is described as a German, but if he made the medal, he must have been
quite out of touch with the art of his own country. The work seems to stand
midway between the contemporary art of Milan and that of France, as represented for the time being by Caradosso and Candida; but it has an engaging
quality of its own. The other medal, bearing the same signature, is less successful; it represents the busts of Marguerite and her husband Louis confronted, and is dated 1503.[361]

François I (1515–27) cannot count, so far as medals are concerned, as a
patron of native French art. He preferred Italian artists; we all know that he
employed Benvenuto Cellini. Less famous men in his service were the gem-
engraver and medallist Matteo dal Nassaro of Verona,[362] who worked for the
king from 1521, or perhaps even as early as 1515, until 1539 (Plate 25.5); and
Benedetto Ramelli. Neither of them, compared with his Italian contemporaries,
ranks very high, though Ramelli's large medal of François I, cast in 1537, is
distinctly showy.

Henri II, on the other hand, took a keen interest in the work of his official
engravers.[363] In 1547 he instituted the office of *tailleur général des monnaies*,
appointing to it Marc Béchot, who may have been a pupil of Matteo dal Nassaro.
Four years later he sent Guillaume de Marillac to Augsburg to inquire into
certain new machinery for striking coins. As a result, this new machinery was
installed in the Maison des Étuves, which, from the mill that worked the rollers,
got the name of the Mint 'du Moulin'. From its inception the Monnaie du Moulin
was used for *pièces de plaisir*, i.e. medals or jetons. After 1551 very few of these
were struck with the hammer.

The new institution, we need not be surprised to hear, was very badly received by the officials of the old mint. There were constant quarrels, lasting for a century, between the Cour des Monnaies and the people of the Monnaie du Moulin. About the same period elapsed between the first introduction of the improved machinery into England and the final supersession of the old process of striking with the hammer. One would confess to a good deal of sympathy with the conservatism of the Cour des Monnaies if one knew that it was prompted by a feeling that the mechanical improvement was not an artistic gain; but it is to be feared that it was merely due to professional jealousy, as in England.

Henri appointed the famous engraver Étienne de Laune[364] in 1552 to be engraver to the new mint. He held office for but a very short time. His prettiest work, however, is to be found in some small hammer-struck medals of Henri II (Plate 25.6). They are very graceful and delicate. His medal of Antoine de Navarre is a good specimen of the highly accomplished style of his medals struck with the mill (Plate 25.7). Even the new machinery was not yet capable of striking medals much larger than five-shilling pieces, so that fortunately the art of casting did not fall into abeyance.

But, after Étienne de Laune, there is astonishingly little in the products of the French mint which rouses our enthusiasm, until the sixteenth century is over. It may be mentioned that in 1558 Guillaume Martin made dies for coins of the Dauphin François II and his bride Mary Stewart, one of which is distinctly medallic in character; and, indeed, there exists an enlargement of it to the scale of 52 mm. Some at least, however, of these enlargements are struck from 'restored' dies, which are actually in the French mint. That is true of the bronze specimen in the British Museum, often cited as a contemporary portrait; and the silver specimen in the same collection appears to be a cast, not a strike at all. One begins to doubt whether the original die, from which all these derive, was as early as 1558. However that may be, from the prototype of this medal, or from one of the coins which represent the busts of the couple on a smaller scale, was evidently derived a large cast medallion, on which the busts are separated and placed on opposite sides. The only specimen of which I am able to judge, Lord Currie's, shows very coarse work, but has evidently been chased considerably after casting. The type is earlier than 1578, when it was engraved in an edition of Rouille's *Promptuarium Iconum*. The bridal medalet of 1558 probably also served as pattern for the rare gold ducat of the same year, which reads on the reverse 'Horum tuta fides'.

The struck medals of the second half of the sixteenth century are typical of the French Renaissance. They are thoroughly accomplished, but the art is so distinctly a court art that it leaves us very cold. It clearly reflects that worship of the classics which so profoundly influenced the French literature of the day. Brucher's medals of Charles IX (1560–74) are among the best of their kind, but extraordinarily uninteresting; Alexandre Olivier's curious medal of the Massacre of St. Bartholomew, on the other hand, has a seal-like effect which attracts attention, although his workmanship, despite this, is usually very poor (Plate 25.8).

In 1572 Charles, who was also enlightened in matters of art, instituted the office of Controller-General of Effigies, and appointed to it the distinguished sculptor Germain Pillon.[365] This was done, it need not be said, in the face of opposition by the Cour des Monnaies. Even when at last the officials accepted the appointment, they continued to give Pillon as much trouble as possible. His business was to provide wax models for the puncheons which were to be used by the mint workmen for making dies. One can imagine how little real effect the appointment of a good artist to such a post can have on the ultimate coin, since his wax model has first to be copied on the puncheon by an inferior engraver, and then the die made by means of the puncheon, and doubtless the lettering and perhaps all the reverse design added by another hand. It is possible that Pillon made the coronation medals of Henri III without the intervention of another engraver. But the pieces on which his fame as a medallist rests are the Valois Medallions. The attribution of these to him is conjectural, but is not belied by comparison with his work as a sculptor. They are large cast medallions, without reverses, attaining, some of them, as much as 171 mm. in diameter, and they represent Henri II (Plate 24.5), Catherine de Médicis, Charles IX, Elizabeth of Austria, and Henri III; and with these royalties must be placed a similar medallion of the Chancellor René de Birague.[366] They were all made between about 1573 and 1577. Good specimens are practically untouched castings with no sign of being worked on with a graver. They are clever, and thoroughly French; if there is any fault to be found with them, it is in a certain superficiality and monotony of conception which reminds one of Clouet's portraits.

An undoubted (in fact, the only signed) work of Pillon's is the cast medal of the poet Philippe Desportes, which is signed G.P. and dates from about 1577; a sympathetic, delicate portrait, and much more attractive than the more ambitious medallions (Plate 26.6).[367]

Germain Pillon died in 1590, and with him we have almost exhausted the medallists of French origin in the sixteenth century who can be regarded as more than ordinary craftsmen. Of the two Danfrie, father and son, both named Philippe, the elder became *tailleur général* in 1582 and died in 1606; the son was Controller-General of Effigies in 1591, *tailleur général* in 1599, and died in 1604. The elder is dry and uninteresting; the younger is not dull, but his method of exciting interest is by verging on caricature. The skilful but rather ludicrous medal of Henri IV as the new Hercules is an instance (Plate 26.8); it refers to the king's conquest of Bresse and Savoy in 1602.

Among the French medallists who did not fill any official position there is one, Jacques Rouaire, who is known to have worked as a goldsmith at Troyes from 1520 to 1571. The solitary piece which bears his signature is indeed jeweller's work and gives the impression that the original, from which existing casts have descended, may have been *repoussé* (Plate 25.9). It represents—so far as can be made out from the inscription—the busts superposed of Henri II, Charles V, Julius Caesar, and Lucretia. So remarkable a conjunction can only be explained, I think, as the production of the fancy of a decorative artist. The Fame of the reverse is an astonishingly clever piece of chasing.

Of the medals which are not attributed to any known artists, one of the most interesting, were it certainly of the time, would be the portrait of Diane de Poitiers. All the struck examples, however, with which I am acquainted are evidently of comparatively modern date, being made from 'restored' dies, i.e. dies which are either old ones re-worked, or modern reproductions. It may be doubted, indeed, whether there was any original medal on which they were based. The reverse, with Diane as her goddess namesake triumphing over prostrate Cupid, and the motto 'omnium victorem vici', is in the style of the eighteenth century rather than the sixteenth.

Italy provided her contingent of medallists to France in the second as in the first half of the sixteenth century. Besides Anteo and Giovanni Paolo,[368] both quite mediocre artists, we have one Jacopo Primavera,[369] of whose personality nothing whatever is known, except his appearance; and that we have in a portrait medal by his own hand. His medals are entirely French in feeling, which may justify us in dealing with him here; but they are at the same time Italian in execution, an admirable illustration of the artistic relations between the two countries at the time. He must have been working from about 1568 to 1585. A florid but pleasing portrait of a young woman of ample proportions, called Helena Nisselys, is sometimes found attached to Jacopo's portrait of himself.

She was probably his wife; indeed, she bears on her sleeve a monogram which is probably to be interpreted H(elena) N(isselys) V(xor) P(rimaverae). For us Primavera has a special interest because he made medals of both Queen Elizabeth (Plate 26.4) and Mary Queen of Scots (Plate 26.5). We do not know that he ever saw either of them; but it is too much to say, as Mr. Lionel Cust does in his work on the portraits of Mary Queen of Scots,[370] that it is certain that Primavera did not work in England. We simply know nothing of his movements, and merely conjecture that he worked in France from the fact that all his portraits, except those of the rival queens, of himself and Helena Nisselys, and one or two others, represent Frenchmen. Mr. Cust goes further, and assigns both the Elizabeth and the Mary medallions to the early years of the seventeenth century. He gives no reason for his theory of so late a date, except that he has proved that so early a date as 1572—which was the date suggested by Scharf— is not supported by the evidence. We may say at once that, since Primavera's activity, as shown by his other medals, does not extend much, if at all, beyond 1585, the seventeenth-century date for these medals is absolutely out of the question. Their style, apart from all other considerations, is enough to prove this. It is unfortunate that Mr. Cust cut the medal of Mary out of his list of con- temporary portraits, for the result has been that subsequent writers, like Andrew Lang, have not thought it worth while even to mention it.

I have said that Scharf's date of 1572 for the medal is not proven. It was based on two assumptions. The first was that Primavera's medals of Elizabeth and Mary were made about the same time. They may have been, but there is nothing to prove it. The second was that the reverse which is sometimes found attached to the Elizabeth medal, of a hand shaking a serpent off its finger into a fire, as St. Paul did at Malta, really belongs to it. The reference of this design is, as other medals of Elizabeth show, to her recovery from small-pox in 1572. But this reverse was never made for this portrait, and is not by Primavera, or of Italian workmanship at all. It was attached by a later caster. Therefore it does not help us to date the portrait. I may say, however, that Chabouillet, in his study of Primavera, comes to the conclusion that Elizabeth cannot have been much more than forty years old when the medal was made, which would date it to about 1573. But he is perhaps reckoning without the vanity of the English queen, whose portraits were apt to flatter her. Still, even if we accept the date 1573 for the Elizabeth, it does not, as I say, bind us to that year, or near it, for the Mary. We may date the Mary ten or twelve years later, if we please; for it is clear that it represents her at an age when her first beauty was past; but we cannot regard it as much later than the year of her death. The only original specimen known to me is in the British Museum; but numerous later copies exist.[371]

Primavera is less interesting in his portraits of men than of women. Like Pastorino, who was a much more able artist of the same type, he becomes tedious when he is unable to rely on purely feminine attractions.

The year 1600 is doubtless a quite arbitrary lower limit to impose upon the Renaissance. In France, however, so far as the history of the medal is concerned, it actually marks an epoch; for just about this date Guillaume Dupré began to work.[372] One cannot leave the history of the French medal, which has been working up to this artist, in whom it found its highest technical achievement, without a word about him. It is of course absurd, except in point of pure technique, to compare him, as some writers have seen fit to do, with the greatest Italian medallists. In conception or in composition he does not rival even Leone Leoni, much less the really great men of the fifteenth century. But his technique, particularly his treatment of surface texture, is so marvellous, that one receives continual pleasure from his medals, despite the banality of his ideas. Sometimes, however, even his skill fails to carry off a bad subject, as in the large medallion of Henri IV and Marie de Médicis with the Dauphin Louis XIII. One feels that this pompous ineptitude must have been dictated to him. His medals are nearly always cast, but so finely cast that it is easy to mistake them for struck pieces. He was nominated Controller-General of Effigies in 1604, and obtained possession of the post in 1606, but he had little influence on the coinage. He died in 1642 or 1643. The medals illustrated, of the Maréchal de Toyras, the Doge Marcantonio Memmo, and Marie de Médicis (Plate 26.9, *10*, *11*), are typical of his brilliant style.

During the first half of the seventeenth century France boasted many other admirable medallists besides Guillaume Dupré. Nicolas Briot has special interest for Englishmen, since he worked in this country during the reign of Charles I and the Commonwealth; but his activity was mainly concerned with coins. Jacob Richier is known by but a single medal, of Marie de Vignon, cast in 1613, which marks him out as a very original and piquant artist (Plate 24.6). But the greatest name, after Dupré, is certainly Jean Warin or Varin.[373] He is the most able of a number of artists bearing the same surname, of whom Claude comes next to him in reputation. Jean's portrait of Richelieu (Plate 26.7) is brilliant in its bold handling of the relief. Claude Warin, on the other hand, is anything but brilliant; the only piece which, while it can certainly be claimed by him, shows anything but a certain conscientious solidity of characterization, is the medal of Jean Salian (Plate 24.7). He produced a series of heavy imaginary portraits of Aristippus, Cicero, Giulio Romano, &c., which lack even that power of characterization which he shows in the Salian or in his medal of Cardinal Mazarin. Nevertheless a whole group of singularly charming and deftly-handled portraits of Englishmen and women of the time of Charles I have been attributed to Claude, rather than to Jean. The attribution is very disputable. But the consideration of this problem may fittingly be postponed until we come to these medals in the English series (pp. 157–8).

And the English and Scottish series will occupy us next, since the medals of Spain during the period which concerns us consist almost entirely of the works of Italian artists such as Leone Leoni and Jacopo da Trezzo, who have already been dealt with elsewhere. We may perhaps mention here, although he belongs to a rather late period, the Florentine bronze sculptor Rutilio Gaci,[374] who signed four or five medals. The earliest commemorates the marriage of Philip III with Margaret of Austria on April 18, 1599. Another medal of the same pair is dated 1609; a third commemorates the accession of Philip IV in 1621; a fourth gives the portrait of himself and his wife Doña Beatriz de Rojas y de Castro, in 1615; and, fifthly, he signed an undated medal of one Alexander Rodulphius. He is a graceful, but not original artist; his only reverse design is a mere adaptation of one by Trezzo. Spain never evolved an independent school of medallists.

VIII

England and Scotland

We have been able to place at the head of the foregoing sections of this sketch such titles as 'Italian Medals', 'German Medals', 'French Medals', and we have only used the phrase 'Medals of the Netherlands' for lack of any adjective more euphonious than 'Netherlandish'. But we now come to a section in which it would be misleading to use the adjective English or Scottish without a warning. Our country never had a real school of native medallists until long after the Renaissance was over and forgotten; even in the seventeenth century, when we can boast of the Simons, English artists of repute were few. Thus the Introduction to the *Medallic Illustrations of the History of Great Britain and Ireland*,[375] a work which is the chief source of the present chapter, is justified in saying, in a phrase apparently suitable especially to the Irish portion of the book, that 'the history of English medallists is in a great degree the history of the medallists of other countries'. That work is a list, invaluable for the historian, of medals and counters or jetons of all sorts and sources, by no means necessarily or even professedly contemporary with the events to which they refer. They are brought together promiscuously for the sake of the light which they directly or indirectly throw on events or personages connected with British history. The effect which is produced on any one who tries to arrive at an idea of the medallic output of England and Scotland down to the end of the sixteenth century, by the sequence of medals described in this book and in Cochran-Patrick's *Medals of Scotland*, is consequently quite bewildering; it is hard to shake off the impression that there are no medals by British hands, except a few which are not of the time to which they claim to belong. That is the result of using a book for a purpose for which it was not primarily intended.

What is now wanted is a survey of those medals which were made in England or Scotland, either by native British artists, or by aliens who worked in the country over a period of years, and who may be, if not claimed for a British

Notes to this chapter begin on p. 186

school, yet regarded as working in association with it. In the very summary sketch which follows, it is of course impossible for us to ignore all the foreign work, but it is possible, and we shall try, to lay special stress on what may be native to this island. Unfortunately, for all the earliest period, there is an almost complete dearth of documentary evidence as regards the medals. We are dependent entirely on the medals themselves. Recently a great deal of useful material has been brought together by Miss Helen Farquhar.[376] Thanks also to Mr. Henry Symonds's researches,[377] we now have a summary of the records of the English mint engravers of the Tudor and Stuart periods; we shall see what use we can make of his work.

In England there is nothing remaining to us that can be called native before the reign of Henry VIII. We have already had occasion to mention certain medals of this king by foreign hands. Thus there is one which goes back to Hans Daucher; two others are evidently in the manner of Hans Schwarz, if not by him. Close to these in pose, though not in treatment, is the rare little cast silver medal, with the Tudor rose on the reverse, executed some time between 1521 and 1541, and probably, to judge from the age of the portrait, nearer the earlier than the later limit (Plate 27.1). This bears no technical relation to the work of any foreign school, and we shall probably not be far out in regarding it as a reduced version, by an English modeller, of the larger medal in the style of Hans Schwarz, which it follows very closely in details of pose and dress (Plate 19.4).

Another piece, which represents Henry in the prime of life, and not with the bloated features which are most familiar to us, is the unique lead casting in the British Museum from a wood or hone-stone model (Plate 27.2). It is extraordinarily like in treatment to a medal of François I of France—the resemblance is assisted by the personal likeness of the two monarchs—and is perhaps of similar, non-English origin.

Of Henry in later years there are, however, at least two medals which we may regard as of English origin. One of these is a small struck piece with a half figure holding sword and orb, and on the reverse the British lion with his forefoot on the orb (Plate 27.3). It dates from about 1542, and the obverse recalls certain German thalers of the time; but this is not enough to prove a German origin. Nor will any one be inclined to doubt the native origin of the rare medal which commemorates the recognition of Henry as supreme head of the Church (Plate 28.1). The portrait is in profile to right, coarsely and clumsily executed, but with considerable liveliness. The inscription describes Henry not only as King of England, France and Ireland, but as Defender of the Faith and under Christ Supreme Head on earth of the Church of England and Ireland. The reverse bears merely translations into Hebrew and Greek of the same legend, and the date 'Londini 1545'. We shall return to this piece later.

Among the other medallic portraits of Henry, there is a large one with a very characteristic representation of the king—in fact the Henry VIII of the English stage (Plate 29.2). It has been said that it may be derived from a painting by Holbein. But except in the costume—which is more or less the same as in dozens of portraits of the king, not only by Holbein but by other less famous artists—it resembles none of Holbein's various paintings of Henry. Perhaps it comes nearest to the Duke of Devonshire's portrait, or that in the Galleria Nazionale at Rome, but it is still far removed from the type. And even if it reproduces the type, it has retained none of the painter's refinement and dignity. The statement in the *Medallic Illustrations* that it may be of German origin is doubtlesss based on the supposed relation to Holbein. But there is no German medallist whose work it resembles. Before leaving it we should not omit to mention that some critics have doubted whether any of the known specimens are as early as the time of Henry. Their doubts, however, do not seem to be justified.

It is evident, in any case, that the picturesque element in Henry VIII (helped by the real importance of his part on the international political stage) attracted the medallists of other countries than England.

Of his wives, only one appears on a medal. That is Anne Boleyn. Unfortunately the one extant specimen is so hopelessly battered about the nose that what may once have been an attractive portrait has become the most pitifully grotesque of caricatures. The piece was made, as the inscription says, in 'The moost happi anno 1534', and Anne wears the dress which she is described as wearing at her coronation in that year. There is no other inscription, but A(nna) R(egina) is in the field.[378]

A year later, were it but genuine, we should have to place the medal of Sir Thomas More;[379] for the reverse design, a felled cypress, with the axe sticking in the stump, and the motto SVAVIVS OLET, evidently refers to his execution. Unfortunately, the piece is a forgery, as will be obvious to any one accustomed to the late sixteenth- and seventeenth-century 'restorations' of medals. Both work and device betray its late origin. On the other hand, Thomas Cromwell, who followed More to the block five years later, is represented on a medal dated 1538, to which no suspicion attaches (Plate 28.2). It is cast in silver, chased and gilt, and known only in the unique specimen in the British Museum. Cromwell is described as Secretary to the King 'AN(no) 38' (which must mean 1538, and not the thirty-eighth year of his age). On the reverse is his shield and the Garter; his election to that dignity dates from 1537. The medal has had an earl's coronet attached to it; this may have been done considerably later, or perhaps when Cromwell became Earl of Essex in 1539. The piece is the work of an excellent craftsman, and the effect of the reverse, with the waved surface of the shield, is very pleasing. The portrait, however, is commonplace, and by no means compares with those on the better of the medals of Henry VIII.

Owing to the dearth of records already alluded to, it is not possible to attribute any of the medals of Henry VIII with certainty to any known persons. But in one case we are, I think, justified in making a conjecture. As I have said, thanks mainly to the researches of Mr. Henry Symonds, we know something about the engravers of the coins at this period. Some of the persons who held the title of graver under Henry VIII were clearly not working artists, but men of position who employed the real gravers. But others were actually working gravers. Now among the medals we have discussed is one bearing a very official character, the 'Supreme Head of the Church' medal of 1545. We shall see that it is evidently by the same hand as another official medal, the coronation medal of Edward VI. Again, on November 5, 1544, Henry Bayse or Basse was appointed chief graver—*capitalis sculptor ferrorum monete*. In 1546 an under-graver, Robert Pitt, was appointed, and soon afterwards a second, John Lawrence. These three continued to hold office together until 1549, when Basse, who was old and failing, retired. I think it is a warrantable assumption that Basse (who was alone in office when the first medal was made) is responsible wholly for that first medal, and at least for the design, such as it is, of the second; in the latter case one of his assistants may have executed the work.[380]

This coronation medal of Edward VI (Plate 28.*3*)—the first coronation medal in the English series—is, I believe, only known in cast specimens. The reverse bears the translation into Greek and Hebrew of the inscription on the obverse, exactly on the analogy of the medal of Henry. There is another coronation medal with a half-figure of the young king in armour, holding sword and orb, and with the double inscription on the reverse—a more ambitious but less successful production. For the portrait on the smaller medal, in spite of its rather primitive workmanship—primitive indeed in comparison with what the other schools across the water were capable of in 1547—is distinctly expressive and pleasing, and creditable to Basse or his assistants.

The only other medal of any importance of this reign is an oval leaden cast with a bust of the king, holding his gloves in his right hand (Plate 29.4). The name is engraved only, not cast in the original; also, it describes him as EDVARDVS V instead of VI; but the features are sufficiently like the undoubted portraits of Edward VI to justify us in accepting the identification. The only known specimen is unfortunately not very sharp, but the composition and conception of the portrait are very pleasing. It is a much better work than another uninscribed medal which is known in a good many late casts, with the king's bust to right. This, I believe, belongs to a series, of which a medal of Henri III of France is another member; indeed, this model itself, with slight alterations, was made to serve for portraits of François II and Charles IX.[381]

The reign of Mary Tudor is illustrated by no single medal of any importance whatever that can claim English origin. There are a number of pieces made by foreign artists, notably Jacopo da Trezzo and Jonghelinck, which give us portraits of Mary or her husband, and in this reign as in others there are counters or jetons which find a place in the *Medallic Illustrations*; but the former are discussed elsewhere, and the latter do not come within our scope. When we reach the reign of Elizabeth there is still, at the beginning, little of native origin.[382] The curious little Phoenix medalet looks like a counter; but it occurs in lead casts, which would not be very practical for use as counters. On the obverse is a Phoenix in flames; on the reverse a youthful bust of Elizabeth facing (Plate 27.5). The inscription begins on the obverse SOLA PHOENIX OMNIA MVNDI and ends on the reverse ET ANGLIAE GLORIA. This has been rendered 'The single Phoenix is all in all and the glory of England'. Just possibly 'omnia' is to be taken in the sense of 'omnino', and 'sola' goes with 'mundi' in the sense of 'unica mundi', but in any case it is a clumsy legend. We know that the Phoenix was adopted by Elizabeth as her badge. There is a variety of the piece which omits the words OMNIA MVNDI; this occurs in copper and is struck. Now, in 1560, when Elizabeth recalled all the base coins in circulation and improved the standard of the silver coinage, the event was commemorated on a little medalet which represents Justice, holding scales and sword, with the motto BENE CONSTITVTA RE NVMARIA. At this time Derick Anthony was chief graver to the mint, having been appointed in 1551; and he must have been responsible for the designs of the Phoenix medalet, even if one of his assistants executed them. When he had to issue this new piece commemorating the reform of the coinage, he was content to strike the portrait side with the die of the copper variety of the Phoenix medalet. The resultant piece—the unique specimen is in the

Hunterian Museum—thus reads on the portrait side ET ANGLIAE GLORIA, although there is no beginning to the phrase. Anthony also used similar designs for another little piece of which the occasion of issue is not known, but omitted the inscriptions, which he replaced by floral wreaths.

The reform of the coinage and the introduction into the mint at the Tower of London of the new machinery of the mill and screw for striking coins were probably the occasion of another tiny silver medalet, which has on the obverse a Tudor rose crowned, between E R, with the inscription E'. D'. G'. ROSA SINE SPINA, and on the reverse a shield with the cross of St. George and TVRRIS LONDINENSIS. It is possible that this is a silver representative of the gold pieces which Elizabeth herself is said to have struck when she visited the Tower on July 10, 1561, to inaugurate the arrangements for the new coinage.

1562 saw the visit to this country of the medallist Stephen H., whom we have already discussed in connexion with the Low Countries (pp. 127–8). Unfortunately it would seem that there was no Englishman capable of profiting by his example. The medals which he executed in this country are for the most part extremely rare; some of them are unique, and of few, if of any, have specimens found their way to collections in the Low Countries.[383]

We must pass over a curious little medal of 1564 referring to the Daundy family, and come to the oval piece which commemorates the queen's recovery from small-pox in 1572 (Plate 27.4). The apparently unique specimen in the British Museum is cast in silver and chased. To a curiously naïve, girlish portrait of Elizabeth is added a reverse with that type of a hand shaking off a serpent into the fire, which I have already mentioned in connexion with Primavera's medal of the queen. The mottoes—the queen's name is not given at all—are, on the obverse, POSVI DEVM ADIVTORIVM MEVM ('I have made God my help', a variation of the inscription on English groats); on the reverse, SI DEVS NOBISCVM QVIS CONTRA NOS. The adaptation of the motto from the coinage is in keeping with the fact that the portrait is very close to that on some of the early milled coins of the reign. The reverse which was attached to the Primavera medal, with a similar design but a different inscription and on a larger scale, may just possibly be by the same hand; at any rate, it is not by Primavera—who rarely if ever made reverses—and it fits the obverse ill in point of size. Was this reverse, or that of the smaller medal, the earlier design? It is difficult to say, and indeed is not of great importance.

Passing over a little medalet which has been conjectured also to belong to 1572, with patriotic inscriptions (QVID NOS SINE TE round the portrait of the queen, and QVID HOC SINE ARMIS round a castle on a mount) we come to the Phoenix badge,[384] cast in silver and chased, which is usually assigned to 1574 (Plate 28.4). On the obverse a Latin couplet laments that virtue infused with so much beauty should be subject to mortality; on the reverse the happiness of the Arabs whose Phoenix is renewed by death is contrasted with the misery of the English, whose Phoenix is the last in the land. The British Museum specimen has the date 1574 engraved on it. It is probable that this date, which is certainly a subsequent addition, was engraved by some one who knew that the medal had been assigned to the year 1574, as it was by Luckius[385] in 1620, and by Evelyn, who doubtless followed Luckius. Other specimens, such as those illustrated by the authors just mentioned, have no date on them. Now Luckius had a passion for giving precise dates to undated medals, and in this case, quite without ostensible reason, he says that the medal was 'a votive medal of the estates of the kingdom of England, made in honour of their Queen Elizabeth, after the winning of certain noble victories against the Spaniard about the year of Christ 1574'. He may have been going by some tradition, but one would like to know what were the victories over Spain of which he was thinking. It seems more reasonable to give the badge to 1572, when the queen's recovery from small-pox and the execution of the Duke of Norfolk, though they marked certain dangers successfully overpassed, showed how perilous was her position. Whatever its date, as the medal is cast from a wax model we cannot easily compare it with the official coinage of the time, or form any idea whether it is the work of one of the mint engravers.

A remarkable group of medals of Sir Richard Shelley, Knight of Malta and Grand Prior of England in that Order, must not detain us, since they are clearly not English work; some were probably made in Italy in 1577, while at a later date a northern artist, Bernard Rantwic, made an inferior and lifeless re-cast of one of them, which he signed with his own name.

In 1580, or soon afterwards, we come to the first of those engraved silver plates, of which the portraits by Simon van de Passe are the most famous examples. This plate, however, shows us not a person but a map of the eastern and western hemispheres, illustrating the voyage of Sir Francis Drake, from December 1577 to September 1580.[386] Four or five examples of this plate map are known, and a close examination of them makes it certain that they are each separately engraved by hand, and not, as is sometimes said, stamped in imitation of engraving. Doubtless some transfer process was employed as a guide in engraving. It is not possible with certainty to attribute the piece to an engraver;

but Mr. Miller Christy has pointed out its close resemblance to the map, engraved by one 'F.G.' (possibly Francis Gaulle or Gualle) for the 1587 Paris edition of Peter Martyr's *de Orbe Novo*. A statement in *Purchas his Pilgrimes* that the plot of Drake's voyage was cut in silver by Michael Mercator may perhaps mean merely that Mercator drew the map which 'F.G.' engraved.[387]

The question may be raised here whether pieces of this kind can properly be called medals. The technique is of course quite different from that of medals, whether struck or cast; but the object, which is to commemorate an event or a person, usually by a portrait, on a small portable piece of metal, is so clearly identical that we may at least give them the benefit of the doubt. The fact that metal, usually silver, is the material, may suffice to meet the objection that a miniature might with almost equal reason be claimed as a medal. And use and custom, which include these pieces amongst collections of medals, may be allowed to have some weight in the argument. The question is, however, of an academic nature, except for curators of collections.

Passing over a medal with the queen's bust and the royal arms, each enclosed in the Garter, of which the date is uncertain, we come to the medals commemorating the return of the Earl of Leicester from the Low Countries (Plate 28.5)[388] A large number of medals and counters refer to this unfortunate affair. In 1585 Leicester was appointed Lieutenant-General of the Queen in command of her army in Belgium, and on his arrival in 1586 he was made Governor-General of the United Provinces. By 1587 he had become thoroughly unpopular; the States superseded him and he returned to England. The medals, which it would seem were made by order of himself or his friends, and presumably in England, represent in various ways a sheep-dog leaving his ungrateful charges—'non gregem sed ingratos invitus desero.' The medal is not a great work of art, although in the portrait on one variety the artist seems to have caught the sitter's air of ineffectual self-complacency.

We have now reached the year of the Spanish Armada. In addition to numerous counters, and to pieces produced in the Low Countries, there are a certain number of oval medals apparently of English workmanship, which are generally associated with the defeat of the Armada and with the successful passage of the queen's government through the manifold perils that threatened it. It must be said at once that the reference of the legends which they bear is quite general, and may or may not be to the events in question. The fact that they are in many cases fitted with loops for suspension, while one in silver in the British Museum preserves the original chain attached to it, has suggested that they were given as naval rewards.[389] One would like it to be so, and perhaps some day the proof will be found. But if we may argue from the reign of James I, when the Exchequer Issues show that large numbers of medals and chains were given by the king to distinguished persons of all sorts, both British and foreign, it would seem that these were not specially naval decorations. One of the group shows Elizabeth's bust in left profile, in very rich attire, with a large ruff closed in front (Plate 28.8). It used to be thought that the wearing of the ruff open in front began to be fashionable in 1588—the queen was painted in such a ruff in that year—and that, since the other medals of this group all show the open ruff, that with the closed ruff is the earliest. Doubt is now thrown on this chronological test.[390] However that may be, on the reverse of this medal with the closed ruff is the Ark floating on the waves, with the motto SEVAS TRANQVILLA PER VNDAS.[391] This would seem to be an obvious allusion to danger escaped upon the seas; and we must not forget that Lord Howard of Effingham's flagship was called the *Ark Royal*. A leaden cast of the bust, without the inscription, and clumsily placed on a circular flan, exists, but cannot count as an independent variety, for it is simply made by casting from some specimen of the complete medal. The other medals of this group have for reverse type a bay tree growing on an island among the stormy waves; the winds blow and lightning issues from the clouds, but NON IPSA PERICVLA TANGVNT (Plate 28.7). The bay was supposed to be a prophylactic against lightning, falling sickness, and other evils. The smaller varieties show the queen's bust very nearly facing, inclined slightly to the left; on the larger ones—some specimens of which, including that in gold in the British Museum, have been suspected—the bust is completely facing and the queen holds orb and sceptre. These medals, particularly the larger ones, have a sort of barbaric splendour which distinguishes them from anything else of their kind. Artistically, however, the smaller piece is easily the superior of the others. They are all, of course, cast and chased; indeed, the chasing is chiefly responsible for the richness of their effect. The field of the larger gold specimen in the British Museum is damascened with roses, enhancing its splendour. The queen's name is not indicated, except on the reverse of the smaller variety by the letters ER; and all alike bear on the obverse the hexameter DITIOR IN TOTO NON ALTER CIRCVLVS ORBE. The word '*circulus*' has been supposed to refer to the English crown, as now established in power and wealth equally with any crown in Europe. But why the legend should refer not to the portrait but to the crown, which is comparatively inconspicuous, and yet so inadequately described by the word '*circulus*', I find it hard to understand, though I can suggest no other interpretation which is not liable to serious objection. (See, however, p. 167.)

These medals of Queen Elizabeth are in some respects the most interesting in the English series. We do not know for certain who made them, but Miss Farquhar has put forth the very plausible suggestion that they, or at any rate the smaller one, may be the work of the famous miniaturist Nicholas Hilliard, who, under James I, held a patent as principal drawer of small portraits and embosser of the king's medals of gold, and who, under Elizabeth, engraved her second great seal in 1586. In any case, one feels that they cannot be the work of a foreigner, so thoroughly English in spirit and conception are they.[392]

We may place in 1588 or the succeeding years what is perhaps the most pleasing of all the portrait-medals of Elizabeth (Plate 28.6). It is merely a half figure, facing, holding orb and sceptre; but the relief and light and shade are dexterously handled, and the slight inclination of the head to one side gives a liveliness to the portrait which we miss in some of the more stately presentments of the imperious lady. It is a thin plate of silver, apparently *repoussé*, i.e. beaten into a mould, jeweller's-fashion, and not cast from a model, although casts reproducing it do exist. It does not appear to be by the same hand as any of the Armada medals.

Of the innumerable counters and medals which are described in the *Medallic Illustrations* in connexion with the last years of Elizabeth, the majority were made in the Low Countries. English, however, and apparently by the same hand, are two enigmatic pieces dated respectively 1601 and 1602. The earlier has the queen's bust with the unexplained legend VNVM A DEO DVOBVS SVSTINEO; on the reverse the crowned monogram of the queen, and the words AFFLICTORVM CONSERVATRIX. A smaller piece with the same types replaces the legend on the two sides by the words THE PLEDGE OF A PENNY, which has prompted the suggestion that this smaller variety is a pattern for copper coinage, and the larger a pattern for a sixpence. The piece of 1602 (Plate 27.6) is again larger, and has the queen's bust, treated in flat, coin-engraver's style, with a quotation from the ninety-first Psalm: 'a thousand shall fall beside thee and ten thousand at thy right, O Queen Elizabeth.' On the reverse is a quaintly unclassical Minerva, trampling under her feet a dragon and a snail; she points with one hand to these creatures, who represent the queen's enemies—identified generally with the powers of evil,—and with the other to a celestial crown sustained in the clouds by a pair of hands between the sun and moon. The motto is to be rendered: 'An eternal crown awaits the chaste'. The coin-like style of these two pieces suggests that they were made at the mint, where Charles Anthony[393] was then chief graver, having replaced his father Derick in 1599. They bear sufficient resemblance in style to the silver crown of 1601 to warrant this attribution. By the same hand, one may guess, is the pretty little medalet of Anne of Denmark (Plate 27.8), generally supposed to be her coronation medal, with the motto ASTVTIA FALLAX, INNOCENTIA TVTIOR, and that of Henry Prince of Wales, with the motto FAX MENTIS HONESTAE GLORIA (Plate 27.7). Charles Anthony held office until 1615, so this piece also falls within his period.

At the very beginning of the reign of James I comes a piece (Plate 28.9), not properly a medal, but what is called a besant, or piece offered up at certain Church festivals. The name is of course derived from the Byzantine gold solidus, and is extended here to a gold coin of much greater value. James on his accession ordered dies for besants for himself and his queen; but all that is left of them is an impression of one side of James's piece. The king is kneeling in prayer before an altar, the four crowns to which he has succeeded lying before him. The legend is a quotation from the 116th Psalm: 'What shall I render unto the Lord for all his benefits toward me?' The descriptions of the other side, and of both sides of the queen's besant are preserved; and the impression, which is all that remains to us, shows that we have lost one of the most pleasing pieces in the whole English series. It is practically certain from documentary evidence that Charles Anthony was responsible for this also; and it shows the same decorative instinct that is patent in the other medals which we have mentioned. The attribution of the besant to Charles Anthony or the under-graver John Dycher has already been suggested by Col. Sandeman[394]; but John Baptist van Landen, not Dycher, was under-graver at the time of James's accession.

James, as already stated, granted a patent to Nicholas Hilliard, in respect of the making of miniatures and gold medals of the king. This was not until 1617; but since Hilliard had already been famous as court miniaturist for many years before James's accession, we may assume that he also enjoyed the privilege of making medals of the king before the grant of this patent. There is a struck medal of 1604, commemorating the Peace with Spain, which has been attributed to Hilliard; the resemblance of the portrait to some of Hilliard's miniatures of the king is close, as Miss Farquhar has remarked. But it is hard and characterless, and the execution leaves much to be desired. It bears no relation in style to any of the Armada medals. The attribution to Hilliard must remain quite conjectural for the present, since any medallist might copy a miniature; the piece certainly has none of the miniaturist's delicacy.[395]

It is not possible here to deal with the medals of the seventeenth century in any detail; but just as in France we should not have been justified in stopping short in our survey without casting a brief glance at Guillaume Dupré, so here, even at the risk of leaving the Renaissance far behind, we must follow the history of the medal up to the middle of the seventeenth century, in order to catch a glimpse of the greatest of English medallists, Thomas Simon. After all, in England the Renaissance is defined for us by the progress of literature rather than of the fine arts; and many of the great Elizabethan writers lived far on into the century. Thus Shakespeare and Beaumont died in 1616, Fletcher in 1625, and Francis Bacon in 1626; but Ben Jonson lived until 1637 and Massinger until 1640. The real epochal line is given by the outbreak of the Civil War. From the standpoint of development, though not of course in point of excellence, the medallists of England from about 1625 down to about 1660 correspond to the Italians of the sixteenth century. The freshness and naïveté which had lent attraction to the Elizabethan and Jacobean works had been succeeded by a sophisticated and technically much more accomplished art.

Among the persons most frequently represented on medals during the reign of James I are Frederick Count Palatine and his wife Elizabeth, the daughter of James I. They were married on February 11, 1613, and one of the most pleasing medals of the time is an oval piece with their busts, signed by the artist 'I.D.B.' Unfortunately, 'I.D.B.' cannot be claimed for the English school; for the only other pieces known to be by him are two signed medals, dated 1602 and 1623, representing Electors of Trèves. He was therefore probably a German. None of the other medals of the pair—and besides others commemorating their marriage there are many relating to Frederick's election and coronation as King of Bohemia in 1619—is of any particular distinction.

Another Jacobean medal, though of personal rather than artistic interest, must be mentioned here (Plate 28.10). It represents Nicholas and Dorothy Wadham, the founders of Wadham College, Oxford, and is traditionally said to have been struck when Mrs. Wadham died in 1618, her husband having died nine years before. But she does not look like a woman of eighty-four years. There is a pleasing simple piety about the two homely portraits and the legend WHEN CHRIST WHO IS OVR LIFE SHAL APPEARE WE SHAL APPEARE WITH HIM IN GLORY. Small skulls, it will be noticed, form part of the decoration of the borders. The piece consists of two shells, struck and soldered together in the manner particularly affected by Dutch medallists; but there is no reason to suppose that it is not English work.

It was in James's reign that Simon van de Passe[396] came to England. He was born in 1595, and was the son of Crispin, who had already engraved portraits of English personages as early as 1592. Since a line-engraving by him of Henry, Prince of Wales, bears the date 1612, he must have begun his career as young as seventeen. He may have visited England in the next year, but until 1615–16 he worked chiefly at Utrecht. A line-engraver on copper of high repute, he won a unique position as the maker of exceedingly charming portraits engraved, though not for printing purposes, on thin silver plates. Usually a portrait, or group of portraits, appears on one side, a coat of arms on the other. One plate, representing Charles as Prince of Wales, is dated 1616, on which ground it has been supposed that most of his portraits of members of the royal family date from that year. There is one—perhaps the finest of all his works in this method—of Queen Elizabeth; two of King James, one wearing a hat (Plate 27.*10*), the other bare-headed; one of Queen Anne; two of Prince Charles, one with a reverse representing him on horseback,[397] the other with a coat of arms; a family group of King James, Queen Anne, and Prince Charles; a charming group of Frederick Count Palatine, the Princess Elizabeth, and their infant son Frederick; one of Prince Maurice of Orange; and one of the Infanta Maria of Spain, the princess whom such strenuous attempts were made to marry first to Prince Henry and then to Charles. There are also one or two portraits of private persons, including a recently discovered and unidentified piece in the British Museum, which, from the arms on the back, would seem to be connected with some one of the family of Ramsey. (Plate 32.*4*).

These are all engraved on silver. The description of their technique as 'stamping in imitation of engraving' is as erroneous as it was in the case of the Drake medal. The matter has been thoroughly threshed out elsewhere, and it is unnecessary to discuss it in detail here. Suffice it to say, in the first place, that it would have been excessively difficult, if not impossible, to make dies for the purpose of stamping such pieces. Since the whole design in the finished plaque is engraved, the lines on the die would all be standing up like knife-edges. Among the numerous punches for die-making which have survived from the seventeenth century—and it is with punches, not with sunk dies, that we must compare the hypothetical dies for Passe's plaques—there are some on which, had it been possible, such fine upstanding lines might well and usefully have been cut. For instance, on the Lowestoft medal of 1665, a masterpiece of low relief. But we have two of Roetiers' punches of that medal, and he has left the fine lines of the shrouds and other rigging of the ships to be engraved subsequently on the finished die. Secondly, assuming that the necessary die could have been made, the expert striker of coins assures us that the fine network of raised lines would hardly survive a single operation; these delicate knife-edges would be crumpled up or broken away. Finally, although the resemblances between the various specimens of one portrait are amazingly close, prolonged examination reveals minute differences. And here again the expert engraver will tell us that by long practice the craftsman, using a transfer as guide, becomes able to make copies of a design which seem to be almost microscopically indistinguishable.[398]

Besides the plaques there exist large quantities of card counters in more or less the same style. Some of them are almost worthy of Passe, but the majority are of much coarser and later workmanship. I believe that nearly all these, like as they usually are to each other, were also separately engraved like the plaques, although some of the poorer specimens appear to be cast.

Passe's plaques, at any rate, remain unrivalled as specimens of this technique, most astonishing examples of conscientious and yet by no means mechanical craftsmanship. He must have employed a number of pupils; and it is instructive to compare two such specimens as those of the James I in the British and South Kensington Museums, and see how the brilliancy of light and shade and relief which is discernible in the one has been lost in the other, where the whole design has, so to speak, gone to pieces.

As early as 1620 Passe seems to have gone to Denmark, where he remained in the king's service until his death in 1647. His place in England was taken by his brother William, but whether the latter worked in silver is uncertain.[399]

The two leading medallists of the earlier part of Charles I's reign in this country were both Frenchmen; but one of them comes under the category of those who worked so long in England as to have become naturalized into the English school. Nicolas Briot, who had made certain improvements in the machinery for striking coins and medals, and failed to obtain recognition in his native country, came to England in 1625, and began almost immediately to enjoy the king's patronage. But his first medal made in this country (Plate 29.3) is a large cast portrait of Théodore Turquet de Mayerne, a distinguished Swiss Physician with an interest in the occult sciences (hence the 'Hermetic' symbols on the reverse of his medal). Mayerne had been physician to Henri IV, Louis XIII, and James I of England, and was now in the service of Charles. He doubtless introduced Briot to his new patron. In spite of a certain heaviness of conception, it is a fine dignified medal; and it is instructive to compare it with

Briot's struck pieces, which seem to sacrifice the largeness of style, of which the Mayerne medal shows him to have been capable, to neatness of execution. The coronation medal of 1626 (Plate 27.9) is an instance; but work on such a small scale is only compatible with largeness of style in the hands of a really great artist, and Briot was not that. The 'Dominion of the Sea' medal (Plate 29.1) perhaps shows him at his best. He is hardly responsible for the smug expression of his sitter, though he may be for the calligraphic rendering of his beard. But the treatment of the ruff and clothes shows a rare mastery of texture, and the ship on the reverse is spirited and alive. This medal was a manifesto, in accordance with Charles's assertion through the British minister at the Hague, 'that the King of Great Britain is a Monarch at sea and land to the full extent of his dominions. His Majesty finds it necessary for his own defence and safety to reassume and keep his ancient and undoubted right in the dominion of these seas.' The claim has an added significance in our own day.

Briot continued in the service of the king; his relations with the parliament have been made the subject of special study by Miss Farquhar, who claims to have vindicated his loyalty to Charles.[400] He died in December 1646. His influence on the technique of the English coinage was undoubtedly great and beneficial.

I have already alluded briefly, in the French section of this sketch, to the medals of Jean and Claude Warin. There are two medals of Englishmen by the latter which are signed and dated. The earlier[401] represents John Prideaux, Regius Professor of Divinity at Oxford from 1615 to 1641 afterwards Bishop of Worcester. It is dated 1638 and signed c WA. The other, obviously by the same hand, represents Sir Thomas Bodley, the founder of the famous library. Bodley had died in 1612, but the medal was made in 1646, as an entry in the Library Accounts for that year shows. 'Mr. Warren' was then paid 2s., the same amount being received by the painter of Sir Thomas's portrait; let us hope that this did not represent their total remuneration. The medal is signed merely WARIN. Thus we find Claude Warin in England in 1638 and 1646; and as a matter of fact the French authorities have been unable to find any trace of him in France from 1631 to 1646.

Now we have an exceedingly brilliant group of medals, chiefly of persons about the court of Charles I, which differ *toto caelo* from the somewhat lifeless but cultivated style of Claude Warin, as shown in the two medals just mentioned, and in others which belong to the French series. The most important is an unsigned medal of the king's chamberlain Thomas Cary (Plate 29.7),[402] a magnificent baroque piece of modelling and composition, fit to rank with any other medal of the seventeenth century. This is dated 1633. To the same year belong medals, similar in handling though less remarkable, of Margaret Cary and Richard Weston, Earl of Portland; in 1634 the same hand portrayed William Blake, Chirographer of the Court of Common Pleas, and his wife Anne (Plate 29.5 and 6); in 1635, Endymion Porter; in 1636, Sir William Ducy; and at an uncertain date, Charles I himself.[403] These all (except the Thomas Cary) bear the signature VA or VARIN or WARIN without any baptismal initial. There is also a medal of Cary signed like all the others, but so weak in treatment that it looks like the work of an imitator or pupil; its weakness is not the heavy stolidity of Claude Warin's style. In the *Medallic Illustrations* all these medals are ascribed to Jean Warin; so is the Bodley. The resemblance to the Prideaux medal, which has only recently become known, indicates, as I have said, that the Bodley is by Claude, not Jean, Warin; and the French critics attribute the whole of the series of medals of Englishmen and women from 1634–6 also to Claude. If he made them, then in 1638, when he certainly made the Prideaux, he had changed his style, utterly and for the worse. Can they be attributed to Jean Warin? The unsigned Cary is entirely worthy of him, and shows many points of affinity to his style; it may have been intended to have a signed reverse like his medal of Richelieu. I am inclined to think that more than one member of the Warin family (or firm, if we may call it so) may have been responsible for some of the medals which are signed with the surname alone. But if Claude had anything to do with these English pieces it must have been in a quite subordinate capacity. He may have accompanied and assisted a more original artist, who, retiring about 1636, after the completion of the medal of Ducy, left Claude to his own devices, to produce the medals of Prideaux and Bodley. This would then explain the apparent discrepancy in the styles attributed to the two Warins.

Thomas Rawlins is responsible for a large proportion of the coins, medals, and badges made towards the end of Charles's reign. A great many of these are of very indifferent quality; but the portraits of Charles I and the young Prince Charles on the 'Forlorn Hope' badge are beautiful (Plate 27.11). In its actual form this badge is made of two plaques joined together; but on the original from which the portrait of the prince is taken the authorship of Rawlins is attested by a signature. If he made this portrait, he was capable of making the equally beautiful badge of Prince Rupert (Plate 27.12). But—possibly because his services must have been in great demand—the mass of his work does not rise to this level.[404]

The last English medallists whom we shall consider are also the finest craftsmen that this country can boast. Abraham and Thomas Simon were born about 1622 and 1623 respectively, of Guernsey parentage—so that even in these medallists there was doubtless foreign blood, although they were born in England.[405] The portrait of Abraham by Lely, engraved in mezzotint by Bloetelinck, seems most decidedly to indicate Jewish origin. Thomas, the more famous of the two, was instructed by Nicolas Briot, became joint-graver to the Royal Mint in 1645, was chief-graver from 1649–60, and died of the plague in 1665. Doubtless his most admired work is the trial-crown which he made and submitted to Charles II in 1663, with the petition, stamped on its edge, that Charles should compare it with the Dutch work of the time—viz. the work of John Roettiers. Charles had the bad taste to prefer Rottiers' work. Simon, it must be remembered, had served the Commonwealth. The Petition-Crown is technically the most perfect piece in the series of English coins; there is indeed nothing in any series that can be said, in the words of the petition, to be 'more truly drawn & emboss'd, more gracefully order'd and more accurately engraven'. But these are the claims of the craftsman rather than the artist, and, without seeking to disparage Simon's coins and struck medals, one finds far more to admire in the cast medals of private persons, of which he and his brother produced a goodly number from 1644 to 1664. A typical one of early date is the portrait of John de Reede, who came as ambassador in 1645 from the States-General of Holland to mediate between king and parliament, and was made a knight and then a baron by the king. This is not signed, but is clearly Abraham's or Thomas's work. Almost contemporary (1646) is the Sir Sidenham Pointz (Plate 30.1), one of the parliamentarian commanders, by Abraham Simon. Fifteen years later we have the beautiful medal of General Monk, signed T.S. and dated 1660 (Plate 30.3); and as specimens of Thomas's latest style we may take the exquisite portraits of Dorcas Brabazon, 1662 (Plate 30.2), and of the Earl of Southampton, of 1664 (Plate 30.4). The fine directness of these portraits, combined with their marvellous delicacy of modelling and chasing, is unequalled in the seventeenth century. There is no affectation about them. The artist, knowing his own limits, did not as a rule, in this series, attempt reverse designs, but was content with an inscription. They are the English analogue of the medals of Hagenauer of some 120 years earlier; and they are finer and subtler than the German's work.

George Vertue, in his book on Thomas Simon (1753, p. 25), has a characteristically vague sentence, in which he speaks of the numerous medals which were made at the time of the Civil War: 'many having been performed by *Thomas Simon* the Engraver of Medals, and some others from Models in Wax, after the Life, by *Abraham Simon*, and cast in Gold and Silver; whose Fame was in high Repute, at the same time with his Brother, who often highly repaired his Works'. If this means anything, it means that all the medals concerned, which are not struck but cast from wax models, are from models by Abraham Simon, whether signed by Abraham or by Thomas; and possibly Vertue understood that those which are signed by the latter were the pieces which Thomas had 'highly repaired', i.e. chased and finished. Vertue had access to certain documents, and was the repository of certain traditions, which we can hardly trace now. The general opinion about these cast medals seems to be that though Abraham was more especially famous as a wax-modeller, and Thomas as an engraver and chaser, and though some medals may be joint productions, yet both men probably were individually responsible for certain medals from start to finish. If we had a wax model signed by or demonstrably made by Abraham and a cast therefrom signed by him or by Thomas, the answer to the riddle would be easier; but, so far as I can see, the materials for a judgement are not so obvious. The wax models[406] in the British Museum attributed to Abraham Simon correspond to no medals at all; the medals signed by Thomas are fully as fine in conception and design as those signed by Abraham, but we do not know whether he or Abraham made the models for them; and I must say frankly that to me the medals signed by Abraham and those signed by Thomas are quite indistinguishable in point of style.[407]

Though the cast and chased portraits by the Simons are undoubtedly the finest achievements by any English artists in medallic portraiture, it must not be supposed that the struck pieces from dies engraved by Thomas take any lower relative rank, i.e. among the work of English die-engravers. The fine medal commemorating the naval actions of 1653 (Plate 30.5) is a masterpiece; the shipping is treated with a skill worthy of contemporary Dutch medallists, and the composition of the other side, out of very simple elements, is admirable. There is less to be said for his other works, such as the Dunbar medal of Cromwell (Plate 30.7); if the design is not happy, we may perhaps lay some of the blame on Cromwell himself, who decided what should be represented. The work is extraordinarily minute; but it is no true praise to say that to appreciate its beauty you must use a glass. Minuteness and delicacy of finish are again the chief qualities of the coronation medal of Charles II (Plate 30.6). In these Thomas Simon stands easily in the first rank of die-engravers of any time and any country.

But we have only considered the work of the Simons in England, as that of Dupré in France, because they represent the culmination of the technique of the art in their several countries, though they fall, strictly speaking, well outside the period with which we are concerned. In that period it is, as we have seen, difficult to find any distinct line of development among English medals; the achievements of the official die-engravers, the Basses or the Anthonies, are very modest. It is idle to pretend that the English medal in the sixteenth century can rank with its fellows on the other side of the Channel.

SCOTLAND

Two of the most important medals connected with Scotland[408] have already occupied us; there are indeed in existence few if any medals of their class more interesting than that of Archbishop Schevez and Primavera's portrait of Mary Stewart. It is possible that, if it were still extant, equal or greater interest would attach to what is supposed to have been a medal of James III. This piece was let into the Chef of St. John Baptist at Amiens, and disappeared during the French Revolution. We know it from a description by the famous seventeenth-century scholar Ducange; it was of gold, about $2\frac{1}{3}$ inches in diameter, and weighed as much as 6 or 7 pistoles. In spite of its size, I doubt whether it was a medal; for the inscription on it described it as 'new coin of James III', etc. (MONETA NOVA). It also gave the name of the mint (Berwick) and the king's motto IN MI DEFFEN. The king was represented enthroned. On the reverse was St. Andrew and the motto SALVVM FAC POPVLVM TVVM, as on various of James's ordinary gold coins. It is supposed that the coin may have been presented by James to the shrine either in 1475, when he visited it under safe-conduct from Edward IV, or in 1478, when he received a safe-conduct for the same purpose but did not go.[409]

The piece was surprisingly large, even for an exceptional coinage of those days. One would like to be certain that it was not one of those pieces of mystification, the work of Prag goldsmiths of the sixteenth century, which have provided us with medals or large coins of Pedro the Cruel, of Elizabeth of Hungary, and of the Empress Eleonara, and also with a marriage medal which, curiously enough, has found its way into the English series and been associated—quite groundlessly—with Henry VII and Elizabeth of York.[410] If it was genuine, it may, as Miss Farquhar suggests, have been a besant or offering penny, like that of James VI which is partly preserved. But it is useless speculating without even an engraving to assist us. Mr. Cochran-Patrick has noted that the king's name is followed by TERTII, which does not occur on the coins, and that he is called REX SCOTIE, whereas, on all coins between the death of David I and the accession of James VI to the throne of England, the title is REX SCOTORVM. These irregularities, however, only show that it was an exceptional piece.

The medal of Archbishop Schevez, cast in 1491, has, I think, been satisfactorily placed with the two medals of Quintin and Christine Metsys among the series of the Low Countries.[411]

Far from satisfactory, on the other hand, is the curious piece which represents King James IV; on the reverse, on a rock in the midst of the sea, is a column supporting a janiform head, with the motto 'Utrunque'. It is engraved in the *Sylloge* of Luckius, and therefore was in existence before 1620. But it may be doubted whether any of the known specimens (they are all cast) goes back to within a century of the date (the eve of Flodden) to which Luckius assigns it. The spirit of the motto and device, the poor casting and rough workmanship, all point to the neighbourhood of 1600. The maker has tried to preserve a certain touch of Gothic in the letter $\bar{\text{A}}$ of his inscription; and he was probably attempting to do the same in the n of the reverse, though he has made a letter more like a seventeenth-century cursive than a Gothic capital. Possibly an original struck specimen, if there ever was one, would produce a more favourable impression; at present, what is extant has all the characteristics of a forgery of the seventeenth century, as which, indeed, it is put down in the *Medallic Illustrations*.[412]

With the struck medalet of John Duke of Albany, Regent of Scotland (Plate 30.8), we at last get into touch with something certain. Like the earliest French medals, it is entirely coin-engraver's work. It bears on one side, on a cross, the shield crowned of the arms of the duke impaling those of his wife, a French heiress of the family of La Tour d'Auvergne. On the reverse is the Holy Dove standing upon a shield of the duke's arms within a collar of the Order of St. Michael. The motto is SVB VMBRA TVARVM (ALARVM being oddly omitted), and the date 1524. The two[413] known specimens (in the Hunterian Museum and the Paris Cabinet) are both struck in gold, which came from Craufurd Moor. In 1524 Albany, unable to control the Scottish nobles, threw up his position and retired to France. But the medal was made before this happened, and we may assume, failing further evidence, that, such as it is, it is the work of native talent. There is, or was, a variety of the piece, with a cypher-monogram of the duke's name and an enigmatic legend on the obverse, instead of the shield.

The reign of James V (1513–42) is illustrated by no contemporary medals, nor is there anything from the first ten years of Mary's reign. In 1553 was struck a beautiful little piece (Plate 30.9), which, though it was probably not a medal, but a pattern for a coin, may be mentioned here for the sake of the engaging portrait of the queen that it bears. It is generally supposed that it was struck from dies engraved by John Acheson, engraver to the Scottish mint, not in Scotland but in Paris. For in the register of the Paris mint is a licence to him to engrave dies with the queen's effigy. The next piece with the queen's portrait is the small medal which has already been mentioned, commemorating the marriage of Mary to the Dauphin François in 1558. In this or the next year we must place, if genuine, a strange medal, of which no specimen seems now to be extant.[414] On the obverse, below a crown, are the busts of François (now King) and Mary face to face, surrounded by three circles of inscriptions; on the reverse the arms of France and Scotland quarterly, crowned, between a French star and a Scottish thistle, again in three circles of inscription. These inscriptions are in part strangely blundered and enigmatical; one of them, for instance, is HORA NONA DOMINVS IHS EXPIRAVIT HELLI CLAMANS ('at the ninth hour the Lord Jesus gave up the ghost, crying *Eli'*). Another is CIVITAS PARISIIS REGIORVM, which seems to defy translation. It is impossible to pronounce on the question whether this medal was of the time; but if it was, we may doubt whether it was of an official character, much less an official coronation medal, as some have supposed. Judging from Anderson's engraving, the piece which he described was struck; it has a resemblance, probably superficial, to the French medals of a century earlier commemorating the expulsion of the English from France.

Although they bear no portraits, the two medals to which we now come are of considerable interest from other points of view. In 1560 was struck a medalet or jeton (Plate 30.*11*) bearing on the obverse the arms of France modern dimidiated, impaling Scotland and England quarterly, with the inscription MARIA D. G. FRANCOR. SCOTOR. REG. ETC. On the reverse are two crowns (France and Scotland) and above them in clouds a third crown outlined with stars. The inscription is ALIAMQVE MORATVR, the date 1560. Is this other crown which Mary awaits a celestial crown—the starry one represented—or is it the crown of England? Some have thought that ETC. in the legend of the obverse indicates her claim to the English crown; and one cannot see any other explanation of it, although the ETC. has been misplaced after REG. instead of before it. The misplacement may have been wilful, as to put the ETC. in its right place would have been too patent an allusion. In the same way, the starry crown may have been intended to supply an answer to awkward questions which might have been raised by the inscription on the reverse. Such a half-concealed manifesto throws a curious light on the relations with England at the time.

We do not know whether this piece was made in Scotland or in France; more probably in the latter. But of the medalet of George Lord Seton, Mary's 'loyal and magnanimous' follower, and his wife Isabella (Plate 30.*10*), we know that it was struck in Scotland, even if the dies were made elsewhere. The Records of the Privy Council of Scotland contain the following entry under January 6, 1562:

> In presence of the Lords of Secrete Counsale, comperit Michaell Gilbert, burges of Edinburch, and producit ane pile and ane tursall maid for cuneyeing of certane pecis of gold and silvir, the pile havand sunken thairin foure lettris, viz. G S I H, linkand within utheris, and the circum-scription thairof berand 'nemo potest duobus dominis servire'; the tursell havand thre crescentis with ane thirsell closit within the samin writtin about 'un dieu, un loy, un foy, un roy', togidder with twa punscheownis, the ane berand the saidis letteris G S I H linkit as said is, and the uther berand the saidis crescentis and thirsell inclosit as said is; with the quhilkis pile, tursell, and punscheownis he cunyeit certane pecis of gold and silver, quhilkis being swa producit wer in presence of the saidis Lordis deliverit to Andro Hendersonn, wardane of the cunyehous, to be kepit be him unusit or prentit with in tyme cuming.

This Michael Gilbert is known as a goldsmith employed by Queen Mary. Mr. Cochran-Patrick regards it as uncertain whether he was a medallic artist, and evidently inclines to the view that he used dies made in France. Why, it is hard to understand. There is nothing particularly French in the appearance of the piece, nothing that a goldsmith of ordinary skill could not have produced. The mistake DVOBIS for DVOBVS might have been made anywhere; but I doubt whether a Frenchman would have engraved DICV for DIEV. We may surely allow this piece to be wholly Scottish in origin.

Three years later, in 1565, a medal of extremely rude workmanship is supposed to have been struck, in two versions, to commemorate Mary's marriage with Darnley. The two versions differ only in the portraits, which are crowned on the one, uncrowned on the other, Mary's hair being also differently dressed. But this second version has simply been made from the other by remodelling; that is to say, a wax model, which had been constructed from the first version, was altered in the details already mentioned, and a new specimen cast.

It is necessary to observe, however, that the lettering and modelling of both these pieces engender grave suspicion that they are not of the time. They are probably later forgeries based on the rare silver ryal of the same year, which has the busts uncrowned, and Darnley's name preceding the queen's.

Passing over the medal of Mary by Primavera, already described above, (p. 140) we come to the reign of James VI. His marriage to Anne of Denmark in 1590 is supposed to be commemorated on a piece which may be described rather as curious than by the more enthusiastic epithets which have sometimes been bestowed on it (Plate 29.8). The way in which the two busts and the crown are plastered on to the field, and the representation of the queen as about twice the size of her husband, are extremely quaint and even comical in their effect. The achievement of Scotland on the reverse, with the time-honoured motto IN DEF(E)NCE, is rich, not to say florid, but in a style quite alien to the obverse, and possible modelled by a different hand.

There is nothing but the comparative youth of the portrait of James to fix this medal as early as 1590. Another medal, however, actually dated in that year, represents James in armour and laureate; on the reverse is the Scottish thistle and the motto NEMO ME IMPVNE LACESSET. It is rather rough, almost primitive, in workmanship.

After the accession of James VI to the English throne there appears little that is of artistic interest among distinctively Scottish medals; and pieces like Briot's Scottish coronation medal of Charles I are naturally classed, for our purposes, with his English work. But we must not omit, for the sake of its pathetic appeal, a curiously interesting medal which has been supposed to represent Mary Stewart—which it certainly does not—or Darnley's mother, Lady Margaret Douglas, or Lady Arabella Stewart. Whoever the lady is, her half figure, in a curious headdress, is surrounded by the inscription O GOD GRANT PATIENCE IN THAT I SVFFER VRANG. On the reverse are two rhyming inscriptions: in the centre QVHO CAN COMPARE VITH ME IN GREIF. I DIE AND DAR NOCHT SEIK RELEIF; around, HOVRT NOT THE ♥ QVHOIS IOY THOV ART. In the margin, at the beginning of this latter inscription, are two hands touching, one of them holding a heart; they have been described as a male and a female hand, but on the scale on which they are rendered it is difficult to see how this distinction, probable as it is, can be discerned. The identification of the lady with the unfortunate Lady Arabella, who was imprisoned by James in 1611 and died in the Tower of London in 1615, rests on the inscriptions, which are supposed to apply to her separation from her husband and her sufferings during her imprisonment. The two hands and the heart are thought to refer to her marriage with William Seymour a year before her imprisonment. Now all this will not bear examination, even if the portrait resembled the authenticated portraits of the lady in question, which it does not. Doubtless the Lady Arabella suffered wrong; but the points of the two inscriptions on the reverse are, first, that the lady is dying from some injury from which she *dares* not seek relief— which hardly describes unjust imprisonment—and, second, that she appeals to her husband or lover not to hurt her heart. This has no relation to the circumstances of the Lady Arabella; and the identification must remain uncertain. The lady in this resembles other persons who while desiring to remain anonymous have themselves portrayed by medallists and accompany their portraits with plaintive rhymes. She reminds us of the Italian—some have identified him with Cesare Borgia, though the legend is surely inappropriate—on whose medal we read VOLGI GLI OCHI PIATOSI AI MIE[I] LAMENTI PO[I]CHE FORTVNA VOLE CHE COSI ISTENTI; or of that other with his lament IL RIMEDIO CH IO TENTO PIV MI NOCE; or Simon's anonymous sitter (tradition identifies him with M. de Martinay) who exclaims sadly IE NE VIS QV' A REGRET 1647.

It should be mentioned that all known specimens of the medal supposed to represent Arabella Stewart seem to be modern casts, deriving doubtless from a seventeenth-century original.

We have wandered far from Italy in our pursuit of the medal, and it may seem that there is not much relation, except in externalities, between these Scottish pieces of the seventeenth century and the productions of the Italian medallists of the fifteenth. Yet the last note we have struck is that of personality breaking out through anonymity, and it will be remembered that at the beginning we insisted on the principle that personality was of the essence of the medal. It is possible that, in the course of this sketch, criticism which may seem to some rather severe has been levelled at very praiseworthy artists; but I think it will be found, on consideration, that such criticism has been directed upon one of two defects. Either, on the one hand, the artist has appeared to sacrifice the personality of his sitter to technical display, or to ignore it because he seems incapable of appreciating anything but the craftsman's side of his business. Or, on the other, he has seized in the personality of the sitter, or imported into it, nothing but less noble, less refined elements; aiming at realism, he has missed the good in his subject. It seems to me that the study of the medal is peculiarly valuable to critics of art, because it presents certain problems in a concentrated and very definite form. The rant which may be mistaken for eloquence, the rhetoric which—to borrow a distinction drawn by that fine critic, Edward Dowden—has at its back vanity rather than an enthusiastic personal character and a faith, the brute force which simulates a powerful individuality, all these are easily detected; and a prolonged study of medals makes the eye keen to discriminate between the sincere and the affected in the major arts. One should not, of course, forget that the true object of criticism is to discern the good (because it is the good that really matters even if it does not always survive), and not merely to censure the bad; but the two operations are complementary and are combined in the process of discrimination. And there is plenty of room for such discrimination, even in Italian art of the best period. Doubtless it will be urged that originality may take forms which to the hidebound traditionalist or academician appear coarse and even obscene. The answer is that never has any art of which those qualities appear to be the essence enjoyed more than a brief season of success, and that those who can only recognize originality in a complete break with tradition had better not meddle with criticism. Sainte-Beuve assigned to the Théâtre Français the rôle of opposing 'le grossier, le facile et le vulgaire'. An art, even a minor one, with a long tradition behind it, may play something of the same part in artistic criticism.

NOTE. Mr. Charles Johnson suggests that the motto on the Armada medals (*Ditior in toto* . . . , Plate 28,7) refers to Waller's verses 'On a Girdle':

> It was my heaven's extremest sphere,
> The pale which held that lovely deer;
> My joy, my grief, my hope, my love,
> Did all within this circle move.
>
> A narrow compass, and yet there
> Dwelt all that's good and all that's fair;
> Give me but what this ribband bound,
> Take all the rest the sun goes round.

So too, for the courtier-medallist, the border of the medal, or the inscription itself, encloses 'all that's good and all that's fair'—the image of England's queen.

Notes

1 The *New English Dictionary* derives the word *medal* from *metallum*, through assumed popular Latin type *metallea* and Romance *medallia*, and the known Italian *medaglia* and French *médaille*. Ernest Babelon, on the other hand (*Traité des Monnaies grecques et romaines*, 1901, i, col. 6 f.), is inclined to accept the mediaeval interpretation of *medalia* or *medallia* as the 'half coin', *medietas nummi*; but, though the word certainly was used of the *obolus* or half-denarius, this is probably only a popular etymology.

2 See *Burlington Magazine*, vol. xxx (March 1917), p. 104, on the definition of the plaquette.

3 See the remarks on this subject in Fabriczy, *Italian Medals*, pp. 16 f.

4 *Dialogo dell' Imprese militari et amorose.* Written about 1550, and printed at Rome, 1555. In 1556 Lodovico Domenichi republished it at Venice, adding a *Ragionamento* of his own. In 1559 it appears again, at Milan, together with a *Discorso* by Ruscelli; and in the same year Rouille of Lyon reprinted the joint work of Giovio and Domenichi. Other well-known works were Gabriel Symeoni's *Le sententiose Imprese et Dialogo*, Lyon, 1560, and Lodovico Dolce's *Imprese nobili et ingeniose di diversi Prencipi*, &c., Venice, 1566. A very full study of the whole subject will be found in the appendix to A. Salza's monograph on Luca Contile (Florence, 1903), pp. 205–252; but, admirable as this study is, more use might have been made of the medallic evidence. J. Gelli's ill-arranged and garrulous *Divise, Motti, Imprese di Famiglie e Personaggi Italiani* (Milan, 1916) is, for the same reason, of little use to the student of medals. See K. Giehlow, 'Die Hieroglyphenkunde des Humanismus in der Allegorie der Renaissance', *Jahrbuch der Kunsthistorischen Sammlungen des allerhöchsten Kaiserhauses*, XXXII, i, 1915, pp. 1–232. L. Volkmann, *Bilderschriften der Renaissance, Hiero-glyphik und Emblematik in ihren Beziehungen und Fortwirkungen*, Leipzig, 1923. There is a complete bibliography for emblems in three works by J. Landwehr, *Emblem Books in the Low Countries, 1554–1949*, Utrecht, 1970; *German Emblem Books, 1531–1888*, Utrecht, 1972; *French, Italian, Spanish and Portuguese Books of devices and emblems, 1534–1827*, Utrecht, 1976. A proper use of medal reverse types is made by G. de Tevarent, *Attributs et symboles dans l'art profane, 1450–1600*, Geneva, 1959, *Supplément et index*, Geneva, 1964; E. Wind, *Pagan Mysteries of the Renaissance*, 2nd. ed. London, 1968.

5 *Lett. fam. del. Comm. Ann. Caro*, ed. Seghezzi, Padua, 1748, iii, p. 190.

6 See *Archiv für Medaillen-und Plakettenkunde*, i (1913–14), p. 4.

7 See 'Classical Influence on the Renaissance Medal', in *Burlington Magazine*, vol. xviii (February 1911), pp. 259 ff. R. Weiss, 'The study of ancient numismatics during the renaissance (1313–1517)', in *Numismatic Chronicle* 1968, pp. 176–87.

8 J. Guiffrey, *Inventaires de Jean Due de Berry*. 2 vols. 1894–6. J. von Schlosser, *Die ältesten Medaillen und die Antike* in Vienna *Jahrbuch*, xviii, 1897. On the Heraclius and Constantine medals see also my note in the *Numismatic Chronicle*, 1910, p. 110. See also R. Weiss, 'The medieval medals of Constantine and Heraclius', in *Numismatic Chronicle*, 1963, pp. 129–44. R. Weiss, 'Le origini franco-bizantine della medaglia italiana del Rinascimento', in *Venezia e l'Oriente fra tardo Medioevo e Rinascimento* (ed. A. Pertussi) in the series *Civiltà Europea e Civiltà Veneziana, Aspetti e Problemi, 4* (Fondazione Giorgio Cini) Venice/Florence 1966, pp. 339–50.

9 Fonds latin 14,360.

10 *Corpus* nos. 1–4. L. Rizzoli, 'L'opera di G. F. Hill sulle medaglie italiane del Rinascimento e

l'origine padovano della medaglia', in *Atti e Memorie del'Istituto Italiano di Numismatica*, VII, 1932, pp. 128–41 (re-arranging the medals as published in the *Corpus* and recording a piece not noticed by Hill). L. Rizzoli, 'Ritratti di Francesco il Vecchio e di Francesco Novello da Carrara in medaglie e affreschi padovani nel secolo xiv', in *Bollettino del Museo Civico di Padova*, XXV, 1932, pp. 104–14. F. Cessi, 'Una medaglia di Francesco Novello da Carrara coniata in un sesterzio Antoniniano', in *Padova*, 1965, fasc. 11–12, pp. 9–11, publishes a medal similar to *Corpus* no. 2 which is struck on a Roman imperial coin.

11 *Notebooks*, p. 107.

I

12 On the technique of casting and striking the chief early authorities are Benvenuto Cellini, *Oreficeria* (best edition by Milanesi, 1857), and Vasari, Introduction to his *Lives* (cap. ii on Sculpture). Both authors are unfortunately much more interested in striking than in casting. Of the former there is a spirited translation by C. R. Ashbee (*The Treatises of Benvenuto Cellini on Goldsmithing and Sculpture*, 1898). The translation of Vasari's chapter in L. S. MacLehose's *Vasari on Technique* (1907) is, so far as work on medals is concerned, quite misleading, owing to confusion in the use of technical terms. The sketch of the subject by W. J. Hocking in the *Numismatic Chronicle*, 1909, pp. 56 ff. is useful. For the methods of casting in general, without special reference to medals, Mr. H. Wilson's *Silverwork and Jewellery* (2nd ed., 1912) chapters xxxi and xxxii should be consulted. For extant portraits modelled in wax, as models for medals or as independent works of art, reference may be made to Habich's article on Antonio and Alessandro Abondio in Helbing's *Monatshefte*, i (1901), pp. 401 ff.; my description of models in the *Burlington Magazine* vol. xv (1909), pp. 31 ff., and vol. xxiv (1914), pp. 212 f.; Menadier's publication of the Berlin models in *Amtliche Berichte*, 1910, pp. 314 ff.; and (for the famous series of portraits at Breslau) M. Zimmer in *Schlesiens Vorzeit in Bild und Schrift*, Breslau, 1887, pp. 591 ff., and Courajod in *Gazette des Beaux-Arts*, vol. xxix (1884), pp. 236 ff. In the Arthur Sambon Collection was a model which, if genuine (I do not condemn it, for I have not seen it), must be the earliest surviving thing of the kind, for it professes to be the model for the Florentine medal of Filippo Strozzi (Sambon Sale, Hirsch, Munich, 1914, lot 11). Otherwise, the earliest model in existence seems to be Mr. Henry Oppenheimer's Negroboni (see p. 24 and n. 13 below).

The observations which are printed here on certain questions relating to the methods by which medals were produced do not pretend, I need hardly say, to be either authoritative or exhaustive. They offer nothing new to the working medallist; but these questions constantly present themselves to the student of medals, and it may be useful to put into print such answers as I have been able to collect in the course of a fairly long study of the subject. The craftsman will doubtless find much to criticize; and for such criticism I shall be only too grateful. Meanwhile, if some of the uninitiated may be reminded by these notes that there are more ways than one of producing a medal, and that it is no less slovenly to talk of all medals as being 'struck' than it would be to describe etchings as woodcuts, some good will have been done. The substance of the present chapter has already appeared in the *Burlington Magazine*, vol. xxxi (November and December 1917).

See E. J. Pyke, *Biographical Dictionary of Modellers in Wax*, Oxford 1973. The wax model from the Sambon collection was re-published by J. Babelon, 'Un medaillon de cire du Cabinet des Médailles. Filippo Strozzi et Benedetto de Majano', in *Gazette des Beaux Arts*, 1921, pp. 203–10. For a wax model attributed to Pisanello (*sic*) see the auction catalogue of the R. Gaettens collection, *Auktions-Katalog XXI*, 1 April 1966, Gaettens, Lübeck, lot 4, plate XXI (in colour).

13 *Burlington Magazine*, vol. xv (April 1909), pp. 31 f. *Corpus* no. 537. The model is now in the Metropolitan Museum, New York.

14 Vienna *Jahrbuch*, xiii, pp. 55 f. esp. p. 65.

15 Kenner did not know at the time he wrote that Leone signed his smaller medal of Charles (with the reverse *Salus Publica*) actually on the truncation of the bust. See the *Burlington Magazine*, vol. xv (May 1909), p. 97. But in such a place the signature does not strike the eye.

16 *Burlington Magazine*, vol. xxiv (October 1913), p. 39.

17 *Burlington Magazine*, vol. xxxi (November 1917), p. 181, c on the plate.

18 *Burlington Magazine*, vol. xiv (January 1909), p. 216; *Numismatic Chronicle*, 1910, p. 368.

19 Brit. Mus., *Sel. Ital. Medals*, Plate 20.1. *Corpus* 330. See note 89 below.

20 *Burlington Magazine*, loc. cit., vol. xxxi (Nov. 1917), p. 182, A and D on the plate. *Corpus* nos 880, 881.

21 The medal of Giuliano has been condemned by Armand as a 'restitution' of later date than the sixteenth century (ii, p. 94, note on No. 4). If so, that of Leo X must also be condemned; for the two are obviously by the same hand. Armand, however (i. p. 159, 10), thinks the latter may be by Francesco da Sangallo. I agree with Fabriczy (*Italian Medals*, p. 143) in thinking that the medal of Leo X is the best of that Pope, and that both pieces are of sixteenth-century origin. A third medal, that of Cardinal Antonio Ciocchi del Monte of Montesansavino, belongs to the same group and to the same author. *Corpus* no. 882.

22 So Habich, *Jahrb.* xxxiv, p. 5; in apparent contradiction, however, to xxvii, p. 258.

23 See the translations by Lady Herringham (1899) or Mottez (Paris, 1911). The best translation is that of D. V. Thompson, 2 vols., Yale, 1933.

24 *Burlington Magazine*, vol. xxiv (January 1914), p. 211. *Corpus* no. 1050. See note 187 below.

25 See N. Rondot in *Revue Numismatique*, 1895, pp. 403–16. For any cast not made from the original model, the word 'aftercast' seems to be the most convenient term. The German term is *Nachguss*, the French *surmoulage*.

26 A fairly typical sixteenth-century die is that of the medal of Giov. Guidiccioni which is preserved in the Museum of the Society of Antiquaries of Scotland in Edinburgh, and has been published by Hocking in their *Proceedings*, xlix, 1914–15, p. 324. Cellini says that both dies of medals were called by the same name, *tasselli*, whereas in the case of coins the lower die was called *pila*, the upper *torsello* (English *pile* and *trussel*).

27 To be carefully distinguished from *matrices* in our sense of the word.

28 See the diagram in Ashbee's translation of Cellini, p. 76.

29 On the introduction of the mill into France and England, see the sketch by Hocking, *Numismatic Chronicle*, 1909, pp. 66 ff. On Eloy Mestrell, who struck the first milled coins in the Tower of London, see also Symonds, *Numismatic Chronicle*, 1916, pp. 69 ff.

30 I may perhaps refer to my pamphlet *On Medals* (Civic Arts Association, 1916) for a discussion of the principles of modelling for cast and struck medals respectively.

31 Burlington Fine Arts Club, *Catalogue of Italian Sculpture*, &c., 1912, p. 136 and Plate LXVII. (Now in the British Museum.)

32 Sotheby's Sale Catal., July 17, 1902, lot 378.

33 A selection from them is illustrated in the *Burlington Magazine*, vol. xxxi (1917), p. 213.

34 The King of Italy's *Corpus Nummorum Italicorum* gives the signature on this coin as C.M. I seem, however, to distinguish a G in the first letter.

35 'Templum hoc init. habuit temp. Prior. Sor. Hypp. Cath. Ruffo MDCLXVII'. On a Maltese cross, a shield (surmounted by a coronet): per pale (1) Ruffo; (2) per fess, in chief Papal keys and umbrella, in base the Buoncompagni dragon.

36 It has the shield of Alexander VII (1655–67), over which St. Peter and St. Paul hold the Papal tiara, and is evidently for the unsigned medal of 1662 illustrated by Bonanni, p. 641, No. xviii. The collection also contains models for the medals given by Bonanni, ibid., Nos. xi and xix, both by Gaspare Morone.

37 The observation is due to Baron de Cosson. G. F. Hill, 'Some lead Italian medals', in *Archiv für Medaillen-und Plakettenkunde*, V, 1925/26, pp. 20–5. R. Weiss, 'Nota sugli esemplari plumbei di medaglie Rinascimentali', in *Italia Numismatica*, 1964, pp. 71–2.

38 For much of the information which follows, when other references are not given, I am indebted to the late Mr. S. W. Littlejohn; it is based partly on the traditions of the metal-worker's craft, partly on his examination of the medals themselves. I have also to thank Dr. Otto Rosenheim for some valuable criticism from the scientific chemist's standpoint. Being neither craftsman nor chemist, I offer the remarks which follow with great diffidence, and shall be glad to receive criticisms. As regards printed authorities: some hints are given by Pomponius Gauricus, *de Sculptura* (written 1504), c. ix; see the translation by Mr. Eric Maclagan in the Introduction to the Burlington Fine Arts Club Catalogue, *Italian Sculpture* (1912), p. 16. H. Brockhaus's translation (Leipzig, 1886) must be used with great caution. H. Lüer's *Technik der Bronze-Plastik* (pp. 16–18) deals sketchily with the subject. A number of recipes for artificial colouring are said to be given by Wuttig in a work published at Berlin in 1814; but this is inaccessible to me. Some information from the chemical side is to be found in the article by

H. Kühl, 'Die Bildung der Patina', *Kunstgewerbeblatt* of the *Zeitschr. für bildende Kunst*, May 1913, pp. 150–3. An admirable account of various modern methods (mainly Japanese) of patination and colouring is given in Mr. H. Wilson's *Silverwork and Jewellery* (2nd ed., 1912), chapter xlv; this should be read in supplement to the remarks that follow.

The Brockhaus edition of Pomponius Gauricus has been replaced by that annotated and translated by A. Chastel and R. Klein in the series *Hautes Études Médiévales et Modernes, 5*, Geneva/Paris (Droz) 1969. The discussion of finishes appears at pp. 230–2. For the conservation of copper alloys and of lead see B. Mühlthaler, *Kleines Handbuch der Konservierungstechnik*, Bern & Stuttgart, 1967. The standard English handbook is H. J. Plenderleith and A. E. A. Werner, *The Conservation of Antiquities and Works of Art*, London, 1972.

39 Greek pitch is 'powdered resin (white pine) from which the oil has been evaporated over hot water' (Ashbee, *Treatises of Cellini*, p. 157). The manuscript in question is said to be in the library of St. Mark's at Venice.

40 *Sigillum* means a small figure, as in classical Latin, or at any rate only a 'casting'; not, as Brockhaus takes it, a seal-impression, which would make nonsense here. (Ed Chastel and Klein, p. 232 and n. 47.)

41 Wilson (op. cit., p. 368) gives the warning that over-heating of bronze sweats the tin on to the surface of the metal.

42 Wilson gives, after Spon, various other recipes for the use of oxide of iron and plumbago, in combination with each other or with other materials (pp. 378 f.).

43 Brockhaus's translation of 'ex palearum, si prius emaduerit, suffumacione' by 'durch Anrauchen von Erzschlacken in ganz nassem Zustande' is sheer nonsense; grammar prevents our referring *emaduerit* to the *paleae*, and *paleae* must mean chaff, not bronze-dross, since the latter would not produce fumes. *Paleae*, in fact, seem to be the equivalent of the pine-needles, resinous shavings, or rice straw, the fumes from which are used for colouring metal by the Japanese. (Ed. Chastel and Klein, p. 232 and n. 47.)

44 Gauricus recommends salted vinegar. An elaborate Japanese formula is given by Wilson, p. 371. See also note 38 above for the Chastel and Klein edition of Gauricus.

45 The late Professor A. H. Church recommended a solution of hard paraffin-wax in benzoline. It does not dissolve easily; but a weak solution may be applied twice or thrice in rapid succession to the medal, which should be gently brushed or wiped previously. Thirty grains of paraffin-wax (cut into thin shavings) per measured ounce of benzolene should be left to dissolve, being shaken occasionally, for a day or two. Mr. R. P. Bedford, who communicates this recipe, adds that after treatment the metal should be left for about twenty-four hours, so that the benzoline may evaporate, and should then be polished with wads of cotton-wool or a soft brush.

46 *Forty-fifth Annual Report of the Deputy Master and Controller of the Mint*, 1914, p. 53. J. C. Rich, *The materials and methods of sculpture*, Oxford/New York 1947, pp. 199–211, on patination and finishes.

47 F. Rathgen, *The Preservation of Antiquities* (Eng. trans., Cambridge, 1905). See now Plenderleith and Werner cited at note 38 above.

48 For methods, see H. Wilson, op. cit., chapter xxix.

49 One would expect 'boiled', as indeed Brockhaus translates; but the text gives 'perfrigi'.

II

50 For the general outlines of Pisanello's life I may be allowed to refer to my *Pisanello* (Duckworth, 1905), which is fully illustrated and has a bibliography up to that date. (The 'reissue' dated 1912 was brought out without my knowledge and is quite unrevised.) Since 1905, however, much has been discovered especially by Giuseppe Biadego (*Atti del R. Instituto Veneto di Scienze*, &c., 1907–8, t. lxvii, pp. 837–59; 1908–9, t. lxviii, pp. 229–48; 1909–10, t. lxix, pp. 183–8, 797–813, 1047–54; 1912–13, t. lxxii, 1315–29); several dates in the artist's life have been fixed, and his name shown to be not Vittore (as Vasari has it) but Antonio. For the painter's career see Hill in Thieme-Becker 27, 1933, pp. 92–3. B. Degenhart in *Dizionario biografico degli italiani* 3, 1961, pp. 571–4; *idem, Encyclopedia of World Art*, 11, 1966, cols. 369–75. To those summary accounts of Pisanello may be added the monographs on his career by Hill, London 1905; B. Degenhart, Turin 1945; E. Sindona, Milan 1961; R. Chiarelli, *L'opera completa del Pisanello*, Milan 1972; G. Paccagnini, *Pisanello alla corte dei Gonzaga*, Venice 1972; G. Paccagnini, *Pisanello*, London 1973. The latest work on the drawings by Pisanello is Maria Fossi

Todorow, *I disegni del Pisanello e della sua cerchia*, Florence 1966. G. F. Hill, *Drawings by Pisanello*, Paris/Brussels 1929, has been re-issued (New York 1965). It remains valuable both for the scale and quality of its reproductions, but it should be noted that of the 71 drawings given by Hill, only 35 are accepted by Fossi Todorow as autograph works by Pisanello. (See also note 63 below.)

On Pisanello's medals, supplementary to Hill, *Corpus*, pp. 6–13, are G. F. Hill, 'On some dates in the career of Pisanello', in *Numismatic Chronicle*, 1931, pp. 181–96; G. F. Hill, 'A lost medal by Pisanello', in *Pantheon*, 1931, pp. 487–8; M. Salmi, 'Appunti su Pisanello medaglista', in *Annali dell'-Istituto Italiano di Numismatica*, 4, 1957, pp. 13–23; R. Weiss, *Pisanello's medallion of the Emperor John VIII Palaeologus*, London (British Museum) 1966.

51 Once in the Paris Cabinet. Wroth, British Museum *Catalogue of Imperial Byzantine Coins*, vol. i, Frontispiece. (See the monograph by Weiss, note 50 above).

52 *Corpus* no. 19. Kress no. 1.

53 See J. de Foville in *Revue Numismatique*, 1909, pp. 406–10. *Corpus* no. 20. Kress no. 2.

54 M. Fossi Todorow, *I disegni del Pisanello e della sua cerchia*, Florence, 1966, no. 67.

55 *Corpus* no. 21. Kress no. 3.

56 *Corpus* no. 23. Kress no. 5.

57 *Corpus* no. 22. Kress no. 4.

58 L. Simeoni, *Nuovo Archivio Veneto*, xiii (1907), p. 158. Signor Giuseppe Biadego has kindly re-examined the frescoes and confirms Simeoni's identification of the portrait. The medallions are at the sides of two windows in the Cappella Guantieri. On the left of the side window is Leonello, on the right of the same window is Pisanello; on the left of the end window is Palaeologus; on the right of the same window there may have been a fourth medallion, but it is no longer visible. Now about forty years before Simeoni, Crowe and Cavalcaselle (*Hist. of Painting in North Italy*, ed. Borenius, ii, p. 164) said the persons represented were 'John Palaeologus, Lionel of Este, Sigismund Malatesta, and the freebooter Piccinino'. Possibly they mistook the Pisanello for Piccinino, owing to a superficial similarity in the headdress. If so, not much weight can be placed on their identification of the portrait of Sigismondo Malatesta. If they are right, we must date the smaller of the two medals of this man before 1443. But, as there is a superficial resemblance between certain portraits of Malatesta and of Leonello (such as that on

the medal with the reverse of the old and the young man seated below a sail), I think it is more probable that here again Crowe and Cavalcaselle made a mistake, and that the portait now lost was a second Leonello.

59 *Corpus* no. 34.

60 *Corpus* no. 36. Kress no. 16.

61 *Corpus* no. 39.

62 *Corpus* no. 40.

63 Hill, *Pisanello*, frontispiece. Hill, *Drawings by Pisanello*, 1927, pl. LXIII, no. 70. Fossi Todorow, no. 16 (as a product of the the Neapolitan workshop). The drawing is, however, autograph, for only Pisanello would have troubled to alter the date.

64 *Corpus* no. 43.

65 G. F. Hill, 'A lost medal of Pisanello', in *Pantheon*, 1931, pp. 487–8.

66 *Burlington Magazine*, vol. xii (Dec. 1907), pp. 147 f.; *Sel. Ital. Medals*, Plate 14.2. *Corpus* no. 74.

67 *Corpus* no. 75.

68 *Burlington Magazine*, vol. xix (June 1911), p. 138. *Corpus* no. 76.

69 *Corpus* nos. 78–90. Kress nos. 31–4.

70 Hill, *Portrait Medals of Italian Artists*, p. 32. *Corpus* no. 87. Kress no. 32.

71 Friedländer, Plate XI; Heiss, *Niccolò*, &c., pp. 32–6. At Venice there is a puzzling medal of Diva Maria Anna of Siena, with Lixignolo's signature on the reverse (*Le Gall. Naz. Ital.*, i, Plate XIII. 3). The medal of Ant. Salvalaio, which professes to be by Petrecino, is a forgery based on his medal of Gianfrancesco Pico della Mirandola. On Petrecino, see further Gruyer, *L'Art Ferrarais*, pp. 609–11, *Corpus* pp. 26–7. Kress p. 13. On Lixignolo see *Corpus* p. 26, Kress p. 13.

72 *Corpus* no. 96. Kress no. 36. The font is mentioned in documents as an Este device, described as *el batesmo* (see Venturi, in *Rivista Storica Italiana* ii, p. 733).

73 See, for instance, Motta, *Arch. Stor. Lombardo*, xvi (1889), pp. 403–9; Venturi, *Atti e Mem. Deput. Prov. Rom.*, vi (1888–9), pp. 377 ff.; H. Cook, *Burlington Magazine*, vol. xxvii (1915), p. 98. *Corpus* pp. 28–9.

74 *Corpus* no. 102. Hill there gives the medallist as Lodovico Coradino.

75 *Corpus* no. 104, attributed to Coradino.

76 *Corpus* no. 141.

77 Hill, Pisanello, pp. 255 ff. *Corpus* pp. 37–43. Rimini exhibition catalogue, 1970, *Sigismondo Pandolfo Malatesta e il suo tempo*, pp. 105–23, 'Le

medaglie malatestiane'; pp. 139–41, no. 71 (Matteo's medal with the facade of S. Francesco); pp. 168–76, 'Ritrovamenti di medaglie nel Tempio malatestiana'. P. G. Pasini, 'Note su Matteo de' Pasti e la medaglistica malatestiana', *La Medaglia d'arte. Atti del primo convegno internazionale di studio, Udine 1970*, Udine, 1973, pp. 41–75.

78 *Corpus* no. 189.

79 *Corpus* no. I130.

80 Burl. Fine Arts Club, *Exh. of Ital. Sculpture* (1912), Plate LXII. 8. *Corpus* no. 173.

81 *Corpus* no. 190, Kress no. 67.

82 *Sel. Ital. Medals*, Plate 10. 3. *Corpus* no. 183. Kress no. 66.

83 Heiss, *L. B. Alberti*, pp. 7–15; Hill, *Pisanello*, pp. 192 f.; *Portrait Medals of Italian Artists*, pp. 29 f. K. Badt, 'Drei plastische Arbeiten von Leone Battista Alberti', in *Mitteilungen des Kunsthistorischen Institutes in Florenz*, 8, 1957/58, pp. 78–87. J. Pope-Hennessy, *The Portrait in the Renaissance*, Bollingen Series vol. XXXV, London/New York 1966, pp. 66–8. For the Dreyfus example of the plaque see J. Pope-Hennessy, *Renaissance Bronzes from the Samuel H. Kress Collection*, London 1965, no. 1.

84 On these two see *Corpus* pp. 15–19. Ivo Uzorinac, 'Francesco Laurana (Frano Vranjanin)', *Numizmatičke Vijesti* 12, no. 23, 1965, pp. 21–43. J. Pope-Hennessy, *Italian Renaissance Sculpture*, London, 1971, pp. 67–8, 314–17.

85 *Corpus* no. 52.

86 *Corpus* no. 65. Kress no. 27.

87 *Corpus* no. 60.

88 Thieme-Becker 7, 1912, p. 538. *Corpus* p. 80. Kress no. 102. A painted portrait of the Sultan Mohammad II, identified as the work of Costanzo and preliminary to the medal, is published by Basil Gray, 'Two portraits of Mehmet II', in *Burlington Magazine* 61, 1932, pp. 4–6. The second drawing published by Gray is described as a copy after the portrait by Gentile Bellini. F. Babinger, 'Un ritratto ignorato di Maometto II, opera di Gentile Bellini', in *Arte Veneta* xv, 1961, pp. 25–32, however, claims (p. 26) that version to be perhaps by Costanzo. It is attributed to Nakkas Sinan Bey in *Apollo*, xcii, no. 101, 1970, p. 3, fig. 1.

89 *Corpus* no. 330. See p. 25 above.

90 Sambon, *Riv. Ital.* iv (1891), p. 481 n. 22 and vi (1893), p. 79. Hill agrees in the *Corpus* with Sambon's identification of the sitter as Frederick III of Aragon.

91 *Corpus* pp. 47–9. Kress pp. 17–18.

92 *Corpus* no. 193.

93 *Corpus* pp. 50–51. Thieme-Becker 32, 1938, p. 419. Hill, 'Francesco Gonzaga and Bartolommeo Montagna', *Burlington Magazine* 40, (1932), pp. 197–8.

94 *Corpus* nos. 204, 205.

95 Friedländer, p. 128, Plate XXIII.

96 Bode (*Zeitschr. f. bildende Kunst*, November 1904, p. 37) objects to the identification with Bandello's heroine, because the dress points to the period about 1475. But what was the date of the tragedy of Giulia of Gazzuolo? Some time during Lodovico Gonzaga's tenure of the bishopric of Mantua (1483–1510) is, I believe, all that we can say. Perhaps it took place quite early in that period. The argument from the dress—especially as we are dealing with a girl of lowly station in a little provincial town, not with a Florentine—amounts to very little.

97 See the careful monograph by H. J. Hermann, in *Jahrb. Kunsthist. Samml. d. A. H. Kaiserhauses*, xxviii (1910), pp. 201–88. *Corpus* pp. 51–4. Kress pp. 18, 19. *Dizionario Biografico degli Italiani* 1, 1960, pp. 580–82.

98 *Corpus* pp. 55–60. Kress pp. 19–20. To the bibliography in the *Corpus* may be added R. Weiss, 'The medals of Pope Julius II (1503–1513)', in *Journal of the Warburg and Courtauld Institutes* 28, 1965, pp. 163–82, with, at p. 172 note 86, reattributions of medals between Giancristoforo Romano and Serbaldi. The earliest medal of Isabella d'Este by Giancristoforo was commissioned in February 1495 according to a letter published by C. M. Brown in 'Gleanings from the Gonzaga Documents in Mantua', in *Mitteilungen des Kunsthistorischen Institutes in Florenz* 17, 1973, p. 158.

99 There is a mystery about this medal. For the documents referring to it, see A. Luzio, *La Galleria dei Gonzaga venduta all' Inghilterra nel 1627–8* (1913), pp. 192 ff. The medal was completed by 1498. In 1507, however, Jacopo d'Atri wrote to the marchesa about a medal of her by Giancristoforo as if it were a new thing. As Jacopo knew her intimately, he can hardly be referring to the old medal. Again, in November 1505 Giancristoforo was charged, when passing through Fossombrone, to give a specimen of his medal of the marchesa to L'Unico Aretino; this again can hardly have been the medal made seven years before. Luzio thinks that the second version is to be recognized in the gold specimen at Vienna. But he is under the impression that the medal was struck

from dies, whereas it was cast; and the differences between the Vienna and other specimens are quite trifling, of the kind that is constantly found in different copies of a cast medal, and in no sense sufficient to justify its being regarded as a new version. The new version, whatever it was, that was made in or before 1505, has therefore not been identified. Luzio's erroneous theory seems to have been put forward earlier independently by Fabriczy (*Ital. Medals*, p. 52, note). *Corpus* no. 221. Kress no. 76.

100 These have been attributed to Serbaldi. See note 98, above.

101 *Corpus* no. 233.

102 *Corpus* no. 232.

103 *Ital. Medals*, pp. 51 ff.

104 *Gazette des Beaux-Arts* 39, 1908, pp. 385–93.

105 *Corpus* pp. 61–3. A bronze figure of a nude woman is attributed to Cavalli by Middeldorf in J. Pope-Hennessy and A. Radcliffe, *The Frick Collection* Vol. III, *Sculpture, Italian*, New York 1970, p. 102.

106 The large model for the testoon of the emperor and empress, which has been attributed to him, was made from the designs of Ambrogio de Predis: see *Bollett. d'Arte*, September 1914, pp. 300–1. *Corpus* p. 61.

107 *Burlington Magazine*, vol. xx (January 1912), p. 202. *Corpus* nos. 246–9.

108 *Revue de l'Art ancien et mod.*, xxxii, 1912, pp. 281 ff.

109 Friedländer, Plates XII, XIII; Venturi in *Arch. Stor. dell' Arte*, i, pp. 385–97; Heiss, *Sperandio*; J. de Foville, *Sperandio* (1910) and in *Revue Numismatique* 1912, pp. 430 f. I have published three drawings and an otherwise unknown medal of Giustiniano Cavitello in *Burlington Magazine*, vol. xvi (October 1909), p. 24, and vol. xix (June 1911), p. 38. *Corpus* pp. 89–104. Thieme-Becker 31, 1937, pp. 359–60. Kress pp. 26–8. For drawings by Sperandio see also A. E. Popham and P. Pouncey, *Italian Drawings . . . British Museum*, London, 1950, no. 252. *Recent Acquisitions, Sculpture, Drawings, Prints*, National Gallery of Art, Washington DC., 1974, p. 48, no. 13.

110 *The Times Literary Supplement*, April 20, 1916, p. 181.

111 *Ital. Medals*, p. 89.

112 Reproduced in de Foville's monograph.

113 It would ill become us to do so, seeing that at that time English connoisseurs (with the exception of Sir Hans Sloane) had apparently not realized, as Goethe had, the importance of Italian medals. E. Gans, *Goethe's Italian Medals*, San Diego (Calif.), 1969, p. 6.

114 *Corpus* pp. 70–74. The leather impressions of the lost medal of Federigo of Urbino are described in the *Burlington Magazine*, vol. xx (January 1912), p. 200.

115 *Corpus* pp. 13–14. I. Uzorinac, 'Paulus de Ragusio', *Numismatika* nos. 2–4, 1934–6, pp. 106–21, Kress p. 11.

116 *Corpus* pp. 76–9. A. S. Weller, *Francesco di Giorgio*, Chicago, 1943.

117 *Corpus* no. 307, now in the British Museum.

118 For the *Discordia* relief see J. Pope-Hennessy, *Catalogue of Italian Sculpture in the Victoria & Albert Museum*, London, 1964, no. 282 as by Francesco di Giorgio.

119 *Corpus* pp. 138–9. *Dizionario Biografico degli Italiani* 7, 1965, pp. 589–91.

120 *Burlington Magazine*, vol. xxiv (January 1914), p. 211. *Corpus* no. 541.

121 *Corpus* p. 108, no. 410.

122 See *Burlington Magazine*, vol. xviii (October 1910), pp. 19 f. *Corpus* p. 108, no. 411.

123 *Corpus* p. 107.

124 *Corpus* pp. 108–9.

125 *Corpus* pp. 110–12. Kress pp. 29–30. *Dizionario Biografico degli Italiani* 11, 1969, p. 269.

126 H. Janson, 'The putto with the Death's Head', *The Art Bulletin* 19, 1937, pp. 423–49.

127 *Corpus* no. 432.

128 *Corpus* pp. 115–21. Kress pp. 31–2. P. Grotemeyer, 'Drei Medaillen von Camelio', *Münchner Jahrbuch der Bildenden Kunst* 12, 1937/38, pp. x–xi. W. Schwabacher, 'En unkendt Renaissancemedaille af Camelio', *Konsthistorisk Tidskrift* 13, 1944, pp. 92–5. (See Plate 31.4 for an unpublished medal of Cleopatra.)

129 *Corpus* pp. 123–6. Kress pp. 32–3. Hill, 'Fra Antonio da Brescia', *Miscellanea di Storia dell'Arte in onore di Igino Benvenuto Supino*, Florence, 1933, pp. 483–5. *Dizionario Biografico degli Italiani* 3, 1961, pp. 540–41.

130 *Revue Numismatique* 1912, pp. 419–28. See *Corpus* p. 123, n. 1.

131 Rizzini, *Illustrazioni dei Civici Musei di Brescia*, p. 28, nos. 179, 180. *Georg Habich zum 60. Geburstag*, Munich, 1928, p. 10. *Corpus* p. 124 n.; no. 583.

132 *Italian Medals*, p. 78.

133 *Corpus* pp. 126–30, where the identification of the medallist as Maffeo Olivieri is supported. Kress p. 33. Thieme-Becker 26, 1932, pp. 6–7. A. Morassi, 'Per la ricostruzione di Maffeo Olivieri', *Bollettino d'Arte* 30, 1936, pp. 237–49.

134 *Jahrb. K. Preuss. Kunstsammlungen*, 1909, pp. 81 ff.

135 *Burlington Club Catal. of Winter Exhib.*, 1910–11, p. 50.

136 Bode in *Zeitschr. f. bild. Kunst*, xv (1904), p. 40; *Burlington Magazine*, vol. xii (1907), p. 149. *Corpus* pp. 121–2. Kress p. 32.

137 Turin, *Corpus* no. 549.

138 *Corpus* pp. 142–8.

139 *Burlington Magazine*, vol. xv (May 1909), p. 97. *Corpus* no. 583.

140 *Corpus* pp. 148–53. Kress pp. 35–7.

141 *Corpus* pp. 154–7. Kress no. 184.

142 Venturi, *Storia dell' Arte Ital.*, vi. p. 801.

143 *Corpus* no. 610. Kress no. 186.

144 *Corpus* no. 612. Kress no. 187.

145 *Bull. de l'Art anc. et mod.*, 15 févr. 1914.

146 Hill, 'Giovanni Zacchi and the Bolognese School', *Burlington Magazine* 25, 1914, pp. 335–41.

147 Hill, 'Nicolo Cavallerino et Antonio da Vincenza', *Revue Numismatique*, 1915, pp. 243–55. Kress pp. 89–90.

148 *Corpus* pp. 168–74. Kress pp. 38–9. P. Bondioli, 'Per la biografia di Caradosso Foppa', *Archivo Storico Lombardo* 75/6, 1948/9, pp. 241–2. C. C. Bulgari, *Argentieri, gemmari, e orafi d'Italia, Parte, Prima, Roma*, vol. 1, Rome, 1958, p. 246.

149 *Corpus* no. 635, where the medal is attributed to Ambrogio da Clivate.

150 In the *Corpus* Hill denies the attribution of any of the coins or coin-like medals to Caradosso.

151 *Corpus* nos. 653, 654.

152 *Corpus* nos. 655, 656. A portrait plaque of Trivulzio is attributed to Caradosso in D. W. H. Schwarz, 'Ein Bildnisplakette des Gian Giacomo Trivulzio', *Schweizerische Landesmuseum in Zurich, Jahresberichte* 66, 1957, pp. 39–57.

153 Hill, *Portrait Medals of Italian Artists*, pp. 41 f. *Corpus* no. 659. Kress no. 194. R. Weiss, 'The medals of Julius II', *Journal of the Warburg and Courtauld Institutes* 28, 1965, pp. 163–82 (at pp. 169–72).

154 *Corpus* no. 662. Hill does not recognise any of the extant medals of the sitter as the work of Caradosso. The struck medal mentioned is given to Cavalli, see *Corpus* nos. 267, 268.

III

155 Hill, 'The Roman medallists of the renaissance to the time of Leo X', *Papers of the British School at Rome*, ix, 1920, pp. 16–66.

156 F. Mazio, *Serie dei coni di medaglie pontificie . . . esistente nella ponteficia zecca di Roma*, Rome 1824, admits to all of the abuses mentioned by Hill. Mazio gives an account of the dies for medals which had been in private ownership, and were then newly ordered into one series. He gives prices for the restruck medals. A Supplement to Mazio was published in Rome in 1884, concerned with the nineteenth century papal medals.

157 *Corpus* pp. 191–5, the name given as Guacialoti. Kress p. 41.

158 *Corpus* nos. 747–9.

159 *Corpus* no. 751.

160 *Corpus* no. 742.

161 This fact was first observed by the late Lieut. P. H. C. Allen. *Corpus* no. 745, cf. no. 756.

162 *Atti e Memorie dell' Istituto Ital. di Num.*, ii (1915), p. 260. *Corpus* nos. 755, 753.

163 *Corpus* pp. 195–201. Kress pp. 41–2.

164 On the renaissance practice of using foundation medals see R. Weiss, 'Un umanista veneziano Papa Paolo II', *Civiltà Venezian, Saggi 4*, Venice 1958, pp. 69–81.

165 J. de Foville in *Revue Numismatique*, 1912, pp. 103 ff. Hill does not repeat in his *Corpus*, at no. 909, the suggestion that the medal of Cosimo I de Medici may be by Cristoforo. The identification of the sitter in the painted portrait as Cristoforo is also rejected, see *Corpus* p. 196 and note to no. 910*bis*.

166 *Atti e Mem. dell' Ist. Ital. di Numism.*, ii, pp. 257 ff. *Corpus* no. 755. Kress no. 211.

167 *Ital. Medals*, p. 157. *Corpus* no. 754. Kress no. 210.

168 See *Numismatic Chronicle*, 1910, pp. 340–69, where all the known varieties of the medals of this Pope are described and illustrated. See also Weiss, n. 164 above.

169 *Corpus* pp. 202–3.

170 *Corpus* pp. 201–2.

171 *Corpus* no. 775. Kress no. 215. R. Weiss, 'Un umanista veneziano Papa Paolo II', *Civiltà Veneziana, Saggi 4*, Venice 1958, pp. 58–9 shows the artist to have been more probably Emiliano Orfini.

172 Habich pp. 82–3. *Corpus* pp. 205–11. Kress p. 43.

173 *Corpus* no. 812. Hill's *Corpus* records six medals of Toscani by Lysippus, nos. 808–13. On no. 810 see R. Weiss, 'Une médaille à demi connue de Lysippus le jeune', *Schweizer Münzblätter*, Jahrgang 10, Heft 37, May 1960, pp. 7–10. On the sitter, see R. Weiss, 'Un umanista e curiale del Quattrocento- Giovanni Alvise Toscani', in *Rivista di Storia della Chiesa in Italia*, 12, 1958, pp. 321–33.

174 *Corpus* no. 806.

175 Habich pp. 83–7. *Corpus* pp. 211–21. Kress. pp. 43–5. Hill gives the two portraits to Candida in the *Corpus*, nos. 822, 823.

176 The Dreyfus specimen is *Corpus* no. 823a; Kress no. 222.

177 *Corpus* nos. 828, 829.

178 E.g. Mazerolle, *Médailleurs français*, i, p. xi.

179 Hill, *Portrait Medals of Italian Artists*, p. 32. *Corpus* no. 905.

180 *Corpus* pp. 238–43. Kress pp. 48–9. *Dizionario Biografico degli Italiani* 9, 1967, pp. 580–82.

181 *Corpus* no. 915. Hill, 'The portraits of Giuliano de Medici', *Burlington Magazine* 25, 1914, pp. 117–18.

182 *Ital. Medals*, pp. 109 f. *Corpus* no. 311, ascribed to Francesco di Giorgio.

183 *Corpus* no. 312, ascribed to Francesco di Giorgio.

184 *Corpus* nos. 907, 908, where the attribution to Benedetto or his circle is repeated.

185 *Corpus* no. 1087, as Jacopo della Sassetta.

186 *Corpus* pp. 243–80. Kress pp. 49–56.

187 *Burlington Magazine*, January 1914, p. 211. *Corpus* no. 1050. The specimen is unique, and was acquired by the British Museum from the T. W. Greene sale, see *British Museum Quarterly*, 8, 1933–34, p. 116, plate XLI.b.

188 *Corpus* no. 962.

189 A gold privy-seal matrix of Charles the Bold, Duke of Burgundy, 1467, cut by a Spinelli, is no. 145 in the Berne exhibition catalogue *Die Burgunderbeute und Werke Burgundischer Hofkunst*, 1969, but is not by the medallist.

190 The Memling portrays neither Spinelli nor Candida, according to M. J. Friedländer, *Early Netherlandish Painting*, VI, Part I, Leyden 1971, no. no. 71, who suggests rather that the sitter is a collector because either of the two artists would have displayed one of his own works. Roberto Weiss once suggested (in conversation) that the sitter might be a member of one of the two Florentine families of Diotisalvi Neroni or Del Nero, the coin being a punning allusion to the family name. K. M. McFarlane, *Hans Memling*, Oxford, 1971, pp. 40–41, also suggests that the sitter might be a Neroni.

191 E. Solmi, in *Raccolta Vinciana*, vii. (1912), p. 138.

192 *Corpus* no. 945, Kress no. 262.

193 *Corpus* nos. 1014, 1015.

194 The specimen was acquired by the British Museum from the T. W. Greene sale, see *British Museum Quarterly*, 8, 1933–34, p. 116, plate XLI.a.

195 *Corpus* no. 1023.

196 *Corpus* no. 957.

197 *Corpus* no. 1018. Kress no. 286. The reverse type appears on two chairs from the original furnishing of the Palazzo Strozzi, one now in the Museo Horne, Florence, and one from the Figdor collection now in the Metropolitan Museum, New York. Nickel suggests that the reverse design is a rebus on the family misfortunes of the Strozzi. (See F. Rossi, *Il Museo Horne a Firenze*, Florence, 1966, no. 142. H. Nickel, 'Two falcon devices of the Strozzi: an attempt at interpretation', *Metropolitan Museum Journal* 9, 1974, pp. 229–32.)

198 *Corpus* nos. 1089 (as Gioacchino Turriano), 1088.

199 *Corpus* no. 1079.

200 *Corpus* pp. 276–9. A terracotta roundel of Savonarola by one of the sons of Andrea della Robbia is in the Musée des Beaux Arts, Lille. See Kress no. 282.

201 *Corpus* no. 971. Kress no. 267.

202 *Corpus* no. 927.

203 *Burlington Magazine*, vol. xxii (December 1912), p. 132. *Corpus* no. 1086.

204 *Burlington Magazine*, vol. xxvii (September 1915), p. 236. *Corpus* no. 1036.

205 *Corpus* no. 1092.

206 C. W. King, 'The emerald vernicle of the Vatican', *Archaeological Journal*, 27, 1870, pp. 181–90. G. F. Hill, *The Medallic Portraits of Christ: the False Shekels; the Thirty Pieces of Silver*, Oxford, 1920. *Corpus* nos. 162 (Kress no. 57), 895–904, 1040. G. Habich, 'Zum Medaillen-Porträt Christi', *Archiv für Medaillen-und Plakettenkunde*, II, 1920/21, pp. 69–78 (a review article on Hill's monograph). A. R. S. Kennedy, 'The medals of Christ with Hebrew inscriptions', *Numismatic Chronicle*, 1921, pp. 134–42.

207 Hill and Habich disagreed on the source of the portraits, see the note to *Corpus* no. 904. Habich claimed that the Berlin panel was copied from the

medal type, and that the type was neither characteristically northern, nor connected with the emerald intaglio. J. Shearman, *Raphael's Cartoons in the Collection of H.M. the Queen*, London, 1972, p. 50, n. 34, argues that the medal does derive from the cameo, and that the effigy was regarded as a true portrait of Christ.

208 Fabriczy, in *Jahrb. k. pr. Kunstsamml.*, xxiv (1903), pp. 71 ff., and in *Ital. Medals*, pp. 135 ff. *Corpus* pp. 82–7. Kress pp. 24–5.

209 Medals of Ferdinand II of Naples, Angelo Cato, Giov. Gioviano Pontano, &c. *Corpus* nos. 335–43.

210 *Corpus* nos. 344, 345.

211 *Burlington Magazine*, vol. xx (October 1911), p. 23. *Corpus* no. 485, reattributed to Maffeo Olivieri, Kress no. 160. The Foulc collection is now in the Pennsylvania Museum.

IV

212 Burl. Fine Arts Club, *Catal. of Winter Exhib.*, 1910–11, p. 50, no. 2; *Sel. Ital. Medals*, Plate 41. *Corpus* p. 287, no. 1118. The Lovel medallion is in Westminster Abbey. Ulrich Middeldorf has suggested (privately) that the medal may have been made after the death of Federigo, 1482, on a commission from his successor Guidobaldo, who was himself made Knight of the Garter in 1504. For Torrigiano see J. Pope-Hennessy, *Italian Renaissance Sculpture*, London, 1971, pp. 304–5.

213 U. Middeldorf, 'Portraits by Francesco da Sangallo', *Art Quarterly* i, 1938, pp. 109–38 (at p. 138, catalogue of the medals). Kress p. 59.

214 The two are illustrated side by side in *Burlington Magazine*, vol. xxxi (1917), p. 179. *Corpus* nos. 880–84, as the work of the Medallist of the Medici Restoration. Their technique has been discussed in the Introduction (p. 25).

215 *Corpus* no. 1109. Kress no. 314.

216 For his medals, see Plon, *Benvenuto Cellini* (1883); E. Camesasca, *Tutta l'opera del Cellini*, Milan 1955, pp. 35–6; 66–8. F. Panvini Rosati, *Medaglie e Placchette italiane dal Rinascimento al XVIII secolo*, Roma, 1968, pp. 37–8.

217 Armand 1. p. 147.3: 3. p. 59,a. Plon, pp. 202–3. Camesasca, p. 36, plate 3. D,E. G. Mariacher, 'Il ritratto di Francesco I di Tiziano per la corte di Urbino', *Pantheon*, 1963, pp. 210–21, suggested that

Titian's three portraits of the king derive from Cellini's medal. The prime version of the portrait is that commissioned by Aretino and presented to the king in 1539 (H. E. Wethey, *The Paintings of Titian, II The Portraits*, London, 1971, no. 37). An example struck in lead (Plate 31.5) of the obverse of the Francis I medal is recorded in *The Annual Reports of the Fitzwilliam Museum Syndicate*, 1967, plate VI. It has traces of rust-pitting, showing that the die was not used immediately. Another example struck in lead, also uniface, is recorded in the auction catalogue of the Georges Gallet collection, Paris, 28 May 1924, lot 137. Cast versions of the medal are relatively common. The dies for the two medals of Pope Clement VII are in the Bargello, Florence (see F. & E. Gnecchi, *Guida numismatica universale*, Milan, 1903, p. 304, no. 3221 (here Plate 31.2).

218 The Bembo portrait is not now attributed to Cellini, for a discussion of the problem see Kress no. 484b.

219 Hill, *Burlington Magazine*, 18, 1910, pp. 13–14, plate I.A. The Rosenheim specimen was lot 97, plate 1, in the sale of the collection, Sotheby, 30 April 1923, and is now in the British Museum.

220 See Hill, *Burlington Magazine*, 18, 1910, pp. 13, 19. The group of medals is now regarded as simply Milanese work, see Kress nos. 198, 423, 424, and 484b.

221 See H. de la Tour, *Procès-verbaux du Congr. Intern. de Numism.*, Paris, 1900, pp. 382–99, where the works of the two men are for the first time properly distinguished. Hill in Thieme-Becker 9, 1913, p. 408. Grotemeyer, *ibid*, 27, 1933, p. 351. Kress pp. 59–60.

222 Heiss, *Flor.* ii, pp. 96–105; *Burlington Magazine*, vol. ix (September 1906), pp. 408 f. Habich pp. 122–3, plates lxxxiv, lxxxv. Thieme-Becker 26, 1932, p. 289. Kress pp. 60–63 (with full bibliography).

223 See below, p. 90.

224 The wax portrait of Francesco I dei Medici in the Bargello, Florence, conventionally given to Cellini, is now ascribed to Pastorino. See L. Berti, *Il Principe dello Studiolo*, Florence, 1967, pp. 37–40, plate I. A porcelain version of the Pastorino portrait, dated 1586, appears in plate 28.

225 For the Poggini, see Grotemeyer in Thieme-Becker 27, 1933, pp. 187–8. Habich, p. 118, plates lxxx, lxxxi. Kress pp. 63–4. G. Kubler, 'A medal by G. P. Poggini depicting Peru and predicting Australia', *Mitteilungen des Kunsthistorischen Instituts in Florenz*, 11, 1964, pp. 149–52. F. Bartolotti, 'Orazio

Foschi giureconsulto riminese in una medaglia di Domenico Poggini (1589)', *Italia Numismatica* 20, 1969, pp. 215–16.

226 Fabriczy, p. 181. Forrer 2 pp. 190–94; 7 pp. 336–7 is still the most convenient account, with the longest list of works. Thieme-Becker 13, 1920, pp. 91–2. Habich p. 136, plate xcviii. Kress pp. 65–7.

227 Armand, iii, p. 136; *Burlington Magazine*, vol. xxiv (1914), pp. 212, 217, 348. The wax is now in the British Museum. Wax models by Mazzafirri and by Mola are published in the catalogue of the 1912 exhibition by the Burlington Fine Arts Club, *Catalogue of a collection of Italian Sculpture and other plastic arts of the Renaissance*, London, 1912, pp. 136–7, plate LXVII. Hill, in *Burlington Magazine* 31, 1917, pp. 212–15. The waxes are now in the British Museum (see *British Museum Quarterly* 8, 1932/3, pp. 86–7, pl. XXXVI; pp. 129–30, pl. XLIII).

228 Thieme-Becker 25 1931, pp. 27–8. Kress p. 68 (with full bibliography). Panvini Rosati pp. 54–5. D. Steinhilber in 'Berichte der Staatlichen Munsammlungen', in *Münchner Jahrbuch der bildenden Kunst* 20, 1969, p. 244, no. 13, fig. 20 (die for a medal of Ferdinand II de 'Medici of 1628). For Mola as a silversmith see C. G. Bulgari, *Argentieri, gemmari e orafi d'Italia, Parte Prima, Roma,* vol. 2, Rome, 1959, p. 160, plate 13; A. Morassi, *Art Treasures of the Medici*, London, 1964, pp. 30–31, pl. 34; J. F. Hayward, *Virtuoso goldsmiths and the triumph of Mannerism 1540–1620*, London, 1976, pp. 157–8, 321.

229 Ferarès in *Revue Numismatique*, 1910, pp. 196 ff. *Corpus* no. 878.

230 Habich p. 105. Bulgari, *Argentieri . . . Roma,* i, pp. 337–8.

231 *Corpus* no. 699.

232 Thieme-Becker 3 1909, pp. 435–6. C. G. Bulgari, *Argentieri, gemmari e orafi d'Italia, Parte Prima, Roma,* vol. 1, Rome 1958, pp. 151–2. *Dizionario Biografico degli Italiani,* 9, 1967, pp. 166–9. Kress p. 68. Panvini Rosati p. 37. For designs by Perino del Vaga for engraved rock-crystals by Bernardi see John Gere, *Burlington Magazine*, 1960, pp. 13–14; B. Davidson, *Mostra di disegni di Perino del Vaga e la sua cerchia*, Florence, 1966, nos. 13, 14, 41 (designs for rock-crystal and other hard stone engraving).

233 Armand 1, 137.1. Kress no. 484c.

234 I have attempted to reconstruct his work in *Burlington Magazine*, vol. xxix (1916), pp. 251 ff.

235 Thieme-Becker 6, 1912, pp. 313–14. Habich pp. 116–17, plate lxxvii. Kress pp. 68–9. Panvini Rosati pp. 38–9. C. G. Bulgari, *Argentieri, gemmari e orafi d'Italia, Parte Prima, Roma*, Rome, 1958, vol. 1, p. 281.

236 The stone is published by O. M. Dalton, *Catalogue of the engraved gems of the post-classical period* (British Museum), London 1915, no. 403.

237 One of the portrait medals of Cardinal Alessandro Farnese conventionally ascribed to Cesati (Habich, *Med. it. Ren.*, plate lxxvii.8) has been attributed to Guglielmo della Porta. See W. Gramberg, 'Guglielmo della Porta, Coppe Fiamingo and Antonio Gentili da Faenza', *Jahrbuch der Hamburger Kunstsammlungen* 5, 1960, pp. 31–52 (at p. 42, n. 27). M. Leithe-Jasper, 'Eine Medaille auf Papst Pius IV von Guglielmo della Porta', *Mitteilungen des Kunsthistorischen Institutes in Florenz*, 16, 1972, pp. 329–35.

238 F. P. Weber, 'Attribution of medals of Priam, Augustus, and Alexander the Great to the medallist of Pope Paul III, possibly Alessandro Cesati', *Numismatic Chronicle* 1897, pp. 314–17. Hill, 'Classical influence on the Italian medal', *Burlington Magazine* 18, 1911, pp. 259–69. For medallic representations of the Mausoleum see M. Greenhalgh, 'A Paduan medal of Queen Artemesia of Caria', *Numismatic Chronicle* 1972, pp. 295–303. For a contemporary view of Cesati's reputation as a maker of imitation Roman coins see note 240 below.

239 Fabriczy, p. 189. Thieme-Becker 29 1935, p. 60. Habich, p. 11, fig. 44, p. 117, plate lxxix. Kress pp. 69–70. C. G. Bulgari, *Argentieri, gemmari e orafi d'Italia, Parte Prima, Roma*, vol. 1, Rome, 1958, p. 397.

240 Fabriczy, p. 191. Thieme-Becker 4, 1910, pp. 329–30. *Dizionario Biografico degli Italiani,* 12, 1970, pp. 480–83. For Giovan Federico Bonzagni see also Kress p. 70; Panvini Rosati pp. 39–42. Giovan Giacomo Bonzagni enjoyed a great reputation for the reproduction of Roman coins. E. Vico, *Discorsi sopra le medaglie de gli antichi*, Venice, 1555, Cap. xxiii, p. 67, wrote 'Nell'imitatione (per dimostrare la eccellenza loro) facendo nuovi cogni di acciaio, nell'eta mia sono stati eccellenti, Vettor Gambello, Giovanni dal Cavinò Padoano, e suo figliuolo; Benvenuto Cellini, Alessandro Greco, Leone Aretino, Iacopo da Tresso, e Federico Ronzagna Parmigiano. Ma Giovan Iacopo di costui fratello, che hoggi per merito della sua virtù tiene in Roma l'ufficio del

segnare in piombo, ha superati tutti i moderni in
cosi fatte arti: della cui maniera, chi grandemente
non è prattico, resterà facilmente igannato, e le sue
medaglie riceverà per antiche'. The imitative ancient
coins by Gambello (Camelio, see note 128) and of
Alessandro Greco (Cesati, see note 235) have types
which are original inventions by the artists, the
Cavino works (see note 246) however are facsimiles
of Roman coins. The imitations by the Bonzagni,
Cavino's son, Cellini, Leone Leoni and Jacopo da
Trezzo have not been identified.

241 The attribution to Riccio, first disputed, I
believe, in my *Portrait Medals of Italian Artists*, p.
50, has also been challenged by J. de Foville, *Archiv
für Medaillen- u. Plakettenkunde*, i, p. 74 (though I
cannot accept his attribution of it to the artist of
the Venetian medals of about 1550); on the other
hand, Mr. Whitcombe Greene defends it (*Numismatic Chronicle*, 1913, pp. 418 f.). Innumerable
copies of this medal, which were probably made to
affix to copies of the candelabrum, are extant. Frag-
ments of such a candelabrum, with copies of the
medal attached, found their way, it may be observed,
to the Cottbus centre for the official collection of
metallic objects made by the German Government
for war purposes in 1916 (*Berliner Münzblätter*,
xxxvii, 1916, p. 564). *Corpus* p. 140. Kress no. 385.

242 'In casa de Mistro Alvise orevese', (Marcantonio Michiel) *Notizia d'opere di disegno . . . Jacopo
Morelli* (ed. G. Frizzoni), Bologna, 1884, p. 75.

243 A. Ballarin, 'Valerio Belli e la glittica nel
cinquecento', in the catalogue of an exhibition at
Vicenza, 1973, *Il gusto e la moda nel cinquecento
vicentino e veneto*, pp. 133–60 (pp. 145–8, list of
Belli's medals). See Plate 31, . U. Middeldorf,
'Eine Kleinbronze von Valerio Belli', *Pantheon* 34,
1976, pp. 115–16. *Dizionario Biografico degli Italiani*,
7, 1965, pp. 682–4. Kress pp. 72–3.

244 Hill, *Portrait Medals of Italian Artists*, p. 48.
Kress no. 385a.

245 The medal is documented (see Kress no. 386)
and the dies are in the Bargello, Florence. See F. & E.
Gnecchi, *Guida numismatica universale*, Milan, 1903,
p. 304, no. 3221 (Plate 31.*1*). At least two reverse
dies were used (cf. the specimens illustrated here
and in Kress). A struck silver example of the medal
as illustrated here appeared in Sotheby sale Zurich
26/7 Nov. 1975, lot 705.

246 R. H. Lawrence, *Medals by Giovanni Cavino
the Paduan*, New York 1883 (privately printed).
Forrer, 1, pp. 366–73. Thieme-Becker 6, 1912, pp.

236–7. Kress pp. 73–6. Panvini Rosati pp. 46–7.
F. Cessi, *Giovanni da Cavino, medaglista padovano
del cinquecento*, Padua. 1969. G. Gorini, 'Appunti
su Giovanni da Cavino', *La Medaglia d'Arte. Atti
del primo convegno internazionale di studio, Udine
1970*, Udine, 1973, pp. 110–20, 121–2.

247 Forrer 1, pp. 411–12: 7, pp. 549–50. Thieme-
Becker 23, 1929, p. 87.

248 *Numismatic Chronicle*, 1909, Plate xxi.
Franks and Grueber, *Med. Illustrations* (1911),
Plate 182, no. 3; T. D. Kendrick, *British Antiquity*
(1950), pp. 73, 74.

249 *Burlington Magazine*, vol. xii (December
1907), p. 150; *Numismatic Chronicle*, loc. cit.;
Franks and Grueber, *loc. cit.* Plate 182, no. 2.

250 Zielinski in *Atti Congr. Int. Roma*, vol. vi
(1904), pp. 49–54. He probably died in 1573. Thieme-
Becker 25, 1931, pp. 174–6. Kress p. 77.

251 Thieme-Becker, *s.v.* Caraglio; *Madonna Verona*, xi. pp. 83–95.

252 *Sel. Ital. Medals*, Plate 43. 3. Habich p. 109,
pl. lxxiv, 4.

253 Kress pp. 77–8.

254 See Kress pp. 78, 79, nos. 417a,b, for medals
of Tommaso Rangone attributed to Sansovino.
Against this attribution, however, it may be noted
that the Will of Rangone does not mention Sansovino
as author of any of the eight medals of the sitter, see
G. Astegiano, 'Su la vita e le opere di Tommaso da
Ravenna', *Bollettino del Museo Civico di Padova*
1925, pp. 49; 236–60, at p. 240. R. Pasi, 'Le medaglie
del ravenate Tommaso Rangoni detto il Filologo',
Medaglia 3, no. 6, 1973, pp. 6–24 identifies the
artists only as Vittoria and Matteo della Fede.
E. Weddigen, 'Thomas Philologus Ravennas, Gelehr-
ter, Wohltäter und Mäzen', *Saggi e Memorie di
storia dell'arte* 9, 1974, pp. 7–76, suggests that from
the several versions of the Will and other early
documentation the medallists were Vittoria, Martino
da Bergamo, and Matteo della Fede (Matteo Pagano).

255 For a discussion of this medal as by Vittoria,
see Morgenroth no. 125.

256 F. Cessi, *Alessandro Vittoria, medaglista
(1525–1608)*, Trento, 1960.

257 Hill, *Portrait Medals of Ital. Artists*, pp.
77 f. Cessi pp. 62–4.

258 *Archiv f. Medaillen- u. Plakettenkunde*, i,
pp. 73 ff., 122 ff. J. de Foville, 'L'Élève vénitien de'
Riccio', *Archiv für Medaillen- und Plakettenkunde*,
i, 1913/14, pp. 73–81. G. F. Hill, 'A group of Venetian
medals', *ibid.*, pp. 122–6. Habich, pp. 127–8, plate

lxxxix, reattributes some of the group to Danese Cattaneo, including the medals of Elisabetta Quirini and Francesco Commendone.

259 E. Plon, *Leone Leoni*, &c. (Paris, 1887). Habich pp. 130–134. Kress pp. 81–3. Panvini Rosati pp. 48–9. Schottmüller and Hill in Thieme-Becker 23, 1929, pp. 84–7 give a special bibliography for the medals by Leoni, to which may be added F. Kenner, 'Leone Leoni's Medaillen für den Kaiserlichen Hof', *Jahrbuch der Kunsthistorischen Sammlungen in Wien*, 13, 1892, pp. 55–93. P. Valton, 'Médaille de Danaé par Leone Leoni', *Revue Numismatique*, 9, 1905, pp. 496–8. B. G. Proske, 'Leone Leoni's medallic types as decoration', *Notes Hispanic* (Hispanic Society of America) vol. 3, 1943, pp. 48–57. C. C. Vermeule, 'An imperial medallion of Leone Leoni and Giovanni Bologna's statue of the flying Mercury', *The Numismatic Circular* (London) November 1952, cols. 505–9; 'A study for a portrait medallion by Leone Leoni and a note on the media employed by Renaissance and later medallists', *ibid.* November 1955, cols. 467–9. P. Tribolati, 'Due grandi incisori di conii della zecca "cesarea" milanese: Leone Leoni da Arezzo, Jacopo da Trezzo', *Rivista Italiana di Numismatica*, 1955, pp. 94–102.

260 In February and March 1541 he was still receiving a monthly salary from the Papal mint (E. Martinori, *Annali della Zecca di Roma* (Paolo III), pp. 20, 55).

261 Luckius, *Sylloge Numismatum Elegantiorum*, Strasbourg, 1620, p. 67, illustrates an imaginary medal of Doria in which the effigy is based on Bronzino's portrait of Doris as Neptune. The figure holds a rudder, and not a trident, and derives from the engraving in Paolo Giovio, *Elogia virorum bellica virtute illustrium*, Basel, 1577, after Bronzino. See J. Pope-Hennessy, *The Portrait in the Renaissance*, London/New York, 1966, p. 244, p. 324 note 50.

262 Hill, *Portrait Medals of Ital. Artists*, Plate XXVI. C. D. E. Fortnum, 'On the original portrait of Michel Angelo by Leone Leoni', *Archaeological Journal*, xxxii, 1875, pp. 1–15. Kress no. 429. The latest discussion of the medal is given in G. Vasari, *La Vita di Michelangelo* (ed. P. Barocchi), Milan/Naples, 1962, 1, p. 109; 4, pp. 1735–8.

263 Habich gives the medal of Martin de Hanna to Leoni, p. 131, plate xcii, 4, and that of Daniel de Hanna as being in the style of Leoni, p. 131, plate xcii, 1. The latter, with one other, are ascribed to Alessandro Vittoria by F. Cessi, *Alessandro Vittoria Medaglista (1525–1608)*, Trento 1960, pp. 81–3, 117.

264 Hill, *Portrait Medals of Ital. Artists*, p. 71. His name, Nizolla, or Nizzola, is given in a letter to Cosimo I (Armand, iii, p. 114). J. Babelon, *Jacopo da Trezzo et la construction de l'Escurial*, Paris, 1922, pp. 182–234. Habich p. 134, plates xciii, xciv. Thieme-Becker 33, 1939, pp. 392–3. P. Tribolati, 'Due grandi incisori di conii della zecca "cesarea" milanese: Leone Leoni da Arezzo, Jacopo da Trezzo', *Rivista Italiana di Numismatica*, 1955, pp. 94–102. Kress pp. 83–4.

265 For a remarkable specimen in gold see Hill, 'A gold medal of Mary Tudor', *British Museum Quarterly* 1928, pp. 59–60.

266 For Fontana and Pompeo Leoni see Kress pp. 84–5.

267 A. Balletti, in *Rassegna d'Arte*, 1901, pp. 107 f.; 1904, pp. 44–6; 1914, pp. 46–8. Forrer 5, pp. 272–5. Habich pp. 138–9, plate c. Thieme-Becker 29, 1935, pp. 225–6. Kress pp. 85–6 (full bibliography).

268 Forrer 5, p. 500. Habich p. 139, plate c. Thieme-Becker 31, 1937, pp. 14–15. Kress pp. 86–7.

269 Forrer 1, pp. 210–211. Thieme-Becker 5, 1911, p. 428. *Dizionario Biografico degli Italiani* (as Andrea or Giovanni Battista Cambio) 17, 1974, pp. 141–4. Hill, *Burlington Magazine* 29, 1916, p. 59. Habich p. 139, plate c. Kress p. 87. J. de Coo, *Museum Mayer van den Bergh, Catalogus 2*, Antwerp, 1969, no. 2442. For unattributed medals of the school see Hill, 'Notes on Italian Medals XX', *Burlington Magazine* 27, 1915, at pp. 236–42. Morgenroth no. 331. Kress nos. 461–3. De Coo, *ed. cit.* nos. 2440, 2442.

270 *Burlington Magazine*, vol. xxix (May 1916), p. 59.

271 *Burlington Magazine*, vol. xii (December 1907), pp. 141 ff. The conjecture there made that A·A· is the signature of Agostino Ardenti has since been confirmed by R. Burckhardt (*Anzeiger für schweizerische Altertumskunde*, 1918, p. 48). Alessandro Ardenti, on the other hand (a painter of Faenza, of whom Ruspagiari made a medal), is proved by the same writer (ibid., p. 44) to be the author of the medals signed AR, as was also suggested in the *Burlington Magazine*, loc. cit. E. F. Bange, *Die italienischen Bronzen der Renaissance und des Barock*, zweiter Teil; *Reliefs und Plaketten*, Berlin (Staatliche Museen), 1922, nos. 256–9. Hill 'Some Italian medals of the sixteenth century', *Georg Habich zum 60. Geburtstag*, Munich, 1928, pp. 10–13, at pp. 11–12, a medal of Titian.

272 Habich in Helbing's *Monatsberichte*, i, pp.

401 ff.; E. Fiala, *Antonio Abondio* (in Czech), Prag 1909; cp. *Archiv f. Medaillen- u. Plakettenkunde*, i, pp. 97–109, 161. F. Dworschak, in Habich, *Die deutschen Schaumünzen des XVI Jahrhunderts*, ii 2, Munich, 1934, pp. 486–507. F. Dworschak, *Antonio Abondio, medaglista e ceroplasta 1538–1591*, Trento, 1958. Three items are attributed to Abondio by G. Probszt, 'Unbekannte Renaissance-Medaillen', *Numismatische Zeitschrift* 74, 1951, pp. 86–99, nos. 2, 10, 15. Kress pp. 88–9. A figure bronze is ascribed to Abondio in U. Schlegel, 'Einige italienische Kleinbronzen der Renaissance', *Pantheon* 24, 1966, pp. 388–96.

273 *Burlington Magazine*, vol. xxiv (October 1913), p. 39.

274 *Sel. Ital. Medals*, Plate 49. 1. Dworschak pp. 84–5.

275 Habich, loc. cit., and in Thieme-Becker, *Lexikon*, s.v.; *Archiv f. Medaillen- u. Plakettenkunde*, i, pp. 42 ff. Dworschak in Habich *Corpus*, ii 2, pp. 525–34.

V

276 *The Tarn and the Lake*, 1913, pp. 23 f.

277 Hill wrote this chapter in 1914. No attempt has been made now to interfere with or reinterpret Hill's vigorous prejudices concerning German art. The series of articles by Habich mentioned are 'Studien zur deutschen Renaissancemedaille', *Jahrbuch der Königlich Preussischen Kunstammlungen*, xxvii, 1906, pp. 13–69 xxviii, 1907, pp. 181–98; 230–72; xxxiv, 1913, pp. 1–35. These articles were followed by a valuable summary work, *Die deutschen Medailleure des XVI. Jahrhunderts*, Halle, 1916, and superseded by the monumental corpus of German Renaissance medals, *Die deutschen Schaumünzen des XVI. Jahrhunderts*, 2 vols in 4, Munich 1929–34. The corpus is cited in the annotations as Habich *Corpus*. There are two other useful general works, A. Erman, 'Deutsche Medailleure des sechzehnten und siebzehnten Jahrhunderts', *Zeitschrift für Numismatik* 12, 1885, pp. 14–102; and the catalogue of the Vienna cabinet, K. Domanig, *Die deutsche Medaille in Kunst-und Kulturhistorischer Hinsicht*, Vienna, 1907. This book is cited here simply as 'Domanig', the author's other works being named more fully. A. Suhle, *Die deutsche Renaissance-Medaille*, Leipzig, 1950, is principally concerned with the work of Schwarz, Weiditz, Hagenauer and Gebel.

278 These two medals are illustrated by Menadier in *Amtl. Berichte a. d. kön. Kunstsammlungen*, xxix, 1908, pp. 295–8. Habich *Corpus* ii, 2, p. li.

279 But Valentin Maler's most important work is all cast from wax models, not engraved. P. Grotemeyer, 'Gussformen deutscher Medaillen des 16 Jahrhunderts' *Neue Beiträge zur süddeutschen Munzgeschichte*, 1953, pp. 103–16 gives a list of 29 clay models for medals.

280 Habich *Corpus* nos. 1–3.

281 Habich *Corpus* i, 1, pp. 3–7.

282 Domanig, Plate 4. 39; a better specimen in Burlington Fine Arts Club, *Exhib. of German Art*, Plate LIII, no. 2. Habich *Corpus* no. 18. Kress no. 583.

283 Habich *Corpus* i, 1, pp. 13–58; ii, 1, pp. lxxxv–xc.

284 Habich *Corpus* no. 56. H. Grunthal, 'A German medal of Henry VIII of England', *Museum Notes* (American Numismatic Society) 8, 1958, pp. 181–3.

285 Habich *Corpus* i, 1, pp. 23–49; ii, 1, pp. xc–xcviii. Thieme-Becker 30, 1936, pp. 262–3. M. Bernhart, 'Die Porträtzeichnungen des Hans Schwarz', *Münchner Jahrbuch der bildenden Kunst*, xi, 1934, pp. 65–95. P. Grotemeyer, 'Hans Schwarz aus Augsburg als Zeichner', *ibid.* xii, 1937–8, pp. 210–8. A. Suhle, *Die deutsche Renaissance-Medaille*, Leipzig, 1950, pp. 13–28. R. Gaettens, 'Der Konterfetter Hans Schwarz auf dem Reichstag zu Worms 1521'; *Der Wormsgau* 3, 1951, pp. 3–16.

286 On these medals see pp. 122–3. The specimen illustrated, of Henry VIII, from the Bute collection, is now in the British Museum, see *British Museum Quarterly* vii, 1952, p. 11, plate II.4.

287 Habich *Corpus* i.1, pp. 54–69; ii.1, pp. c–cvii. Thieme-Becker 35, 1942, pp. 267–8. A. Suhle, *Die deutsche Renaissance-Medaille*, Leipzig, 1950, pp. 29–35. M. Bernhart, 'Zwei unbekannte Bildnismedaillen der deutschen Renaissance', *Münchner Jahrbuch der bildenden Kunst*, xiii, 1938–9, pp. 87–9. P. Grotemeyer, 'Über einige neue Medaillenmodelle der Renaissance', *Blätter für Münzfreunde und Münzforschung*, 1954, pp. 163–5, (model for a medal of Carl Coquiel). P. Grotemeyer, 'Eine Medaille des Andreas Doria von Christoph Weiditz', *Centennial Volume, American Numismatic Society* (ed. H. Ingholt), New York, 1958, pp. 317–327.

288 Domanig, Plate 11. 100. Habich *Corpus* no. 376.

289 Habich *Corpus* i.1, pp. 70–101; ii.1, pp. cviii–cxvi. A. Suhle, *Die deutsche Renaissance-Medaille*, Leipzig, 1950, pp. 36–51. F. Baillion, 'Une

médaille inédite de Frédéric Hagenauer', *Revue belge de Numismatique* 96, 1950, pp. 195–6. M. M. Salton, 'Ein Buchsbaum-Modell des Friedrich Hagenauer', *Schweizer Münzblätter* vol. 4, no. 14, 1953, pp. 48–9.

290 By Habich, in the Berlin *Jahrbuch* 39 (1918), pp. 135 ff. Habich *Corpus* i, 1, p. 129; ii, 1, p. cxvi.

291 Habich *Corpus* i, 1, pp. 105–6.

292 Habich *Corpus* i, 1, pp. 111–17; ii, 1, pp. ccix–cxxiii.

293 Habich *Corpus* no. 1299, as perhaps by Gilg Kilian Prager.

294 Illustrated in Domanig's *Porträtmedaillen des Oesterreichischen Kaiserhauses* (Wien, 1896), Plate VI, no. 32. Habich *Corpus* no. 785, as by Hans Kels.

295 The three medals are regrouped by Habich, *Corpus* nos. 2200, 2201, 2203, as the work of the monogrammist H.S.K., perhaps to be identified as Hans Schenck.

296 Habich *Corpus* i.2, pp. 140–77. A Suhle, *Die deutsche Renaissance-Medaille*, Leipzig, 1950, pp. 52–62. Kress pp. 112–14. M. M. Salton, 'Ein Steinmodell des Mathes Gebel', *Schweizer Münzblätter*, vol. 1, no. 3, 1950, p. 41 (for a medal of Georg von Embs, Habich *Corpus* no. 1208). W. M. Milliken, 'Four stone models for German Medals', *Bulletin of the Cleveland Museum of Art* 44, 1957, pp. 114, 118–21. (Two of the models are for medals by Gebel, recorded by Habich *Corpus* nos. 973, 1956.)

297 See the Vienna *Jahrbuch*, vol. xvi.

298 Habich *Corpus*, nos. 1014, 985, 1208, 1061 respectively, all of the medals being given to Gebel.

299 Domanig, Plate 10. 78. Habich *Corpus* i.2, pp. 257–60. The two signed medals are nos. 1829, 1831.

300 Habich *Corpus* i, 2, pp. 257–60.

301 Habich *Corpus* ii, 1, pp. 278–88. Thieme-Becker 28, 1934, pp. 123–4.

302 Habich *Corpus* no. 1962.

303 This hymn ('O Veneranda Unitas, O Adoranda Trinitas, per Te sumus creati', &c.) is from the sequence 'Benedicta sit semper sancta Trinitas', found in various manuscripts from the eleventh to the fifteenth century. See W. Baumker, *Das kathol. Kirchenlied*, i, p. 667.

304 Domanig, p. 27 and Plate 21. Habich *Corpus* i.2, pp. 181–98. Thieme-Becker 25, 1931, p. 406. G. Probszt, *Ludwig Neufahrer*, Vienna, 1960. W. M. Milliken, 'Four stone models for German Medals', *Bulletin of the Cleveland Museum of Art* 44, 1957, pp. 114, 118–21. (The model by Neufahrer recorded by Habich *Corpus*, no. 1378.)

305 Domanig, pp. 20 f. and Plate 16. Habich *Corpus* i, 2, pp. 250–4; ii, 1, p. cxx.

306 Domanig, p. 27 and Plates 18 and 19. Habich *Corpus* i, 2, pp. 221–36.

307 It is interesting to note the close affinity in conception and treatment between this medal and some of the latest German productions, such as K. Goetz's large medal on von Tirpitz, which is instinct with the same unconscious humour.

308 Domanig, Plate 18. 165. Habich *Corpus* no. 1632.

309 Domanig, p. 32 and Plate 22. Habich *Corpus* ii. 1, pp. 291, 293–312. Thieme-Becker 36, 1947, pp. 217–8. W. M. Milliken, 'Four stone models for German medals', *Bulletin of the Cleveland Museum of Art* 44, 1957, pp. 114, 118–21 (including the model by Wolff for a medal of Pope Alexander V, as recorded by Habich *Corpus*, ii. 1, p. 311, no. 5). P. Grotemeyer, 'Über einige neue Medaillenmodelle der Renaissance', *Blätter für Münzfreunde und Münzforschung*, 1954, pp. 163–5 (no. 3 is a model for Habich *Corpus* no. 2138, of Christoph von Trebra).

310 Domanig, p. 44 and Plates 30 and 31. Habich *Corpus* ii, 1, pp. 352–81.

311 See above, p. 99. The marks on the truncation of the bust of Panziruolo are really a signature, not an ornament as Habich supposes. Habich properly excludes the medal from the *Corpus*.

312 Habich *Corpus* ii, 1, pp. 422–38.

313 Habich *Corpus* ii, 1, pp. 384–93.

VI

314 *L'Art du Médailleur en Belgique*, 2 vols., Brussels, 1900, 1904. In this chapter, where other detailed references are not given, this book should be referred to. The only other general surveys are J. W. Frederiks, *Penningen*, Amsterdam 1947, and the exhibition catalogue by L. Wellens de Donder, *Médailleurs et Numismates de la Renaissance aux Pays-Bas*, Brussels (Bibliothèque Royale), 1959. The catalogue was also published in Flemish, with the same number order for the materials, but different pagination.

315 *Histoire de la gravure des médailles en Belgique* (Brussels, 1870).

316 V. Tourneur, 'Quentin Metsys, médailleur', *Revue belge de Numismatique* 72, 1920, pp. 139–60. Thieme-Becker 24, 1930, pp. 227–8. L. Smolderen, 'Quentin Metsys médailleur d'Érasme', in *Scrinium Erasmianum*, vol. II, Leiden, 1969, pp. 513–25

(refusing as the work of Metsys all but the Erasmus medal). The medallist was probably born in 1465 or 1466.

317 *Anzeiger für schweizerische Altertumskunde*, N. F., xiii, pp. 42 ff.

318 G. Habich, 'Die Erasmus-Medaille', *Archiv für Medaillen-und Plakettenkunde*, iv, 1923/24, pp. 119–22. A Gerlo, *Erasme et ses portraitistes*, Nieuwkoop, 1969, Cap. I, 'Erasme et Quentin Metsijs'. E. Panofsky, 'Erasmus and the visual arts', *Journal of the Warburg and Courtauld Institutes* 32, 1969, pp. 200–27 (at pp. 214–19).

319 On 'Terminus' see E. Wind, 'Aenigma Termini', *Journal of the Warburg and Courtauld Institutes*, 1, 1937/38, pp. 66–9. Panofsky (cited at note 318 above) pp. 215–16.

320 According to Tourneur the medals all remain the work of Metsys, but Hill's objections have been supported by Smolderen in the monograph cited at note 316 above.

321 Habich *Corpus* no. 303, in the style of Hans Schwarz. The medal effigy derives from Dürer's engraved portrait of Erasmus of 1526, but the name of the medallist is not known.

322 The proof of Metsys' authorship of the medal is only given in a letter from Erasmus to Henry Botteus, 29 March 1528, 'Vnde statuarius iste nactus sit effigiem mei demiror, nisi fortasse habet eam quam Quintinus Antuerpiae fudit aere' (*Opus Epistolarum Des. Erasmi Roterodami* ed. P. S. Allen, Oxford, vii, 1928, p. 376, lines 5, 6: cf. iv, 1922, p. 237, n. 2). The artist was paid more than 30 florins for the medal (v, 1924, p. 470, lines 38, 39). Two letters from Erasmus to Pirckheimer, 8 February and 3 June 1524, mention the preparation of reproductions of the medal for the friends of Erasmus. He complained that the relief on the reverse of the medal was of such bulk that it weakened the quality of the portrait in the casting process, and he recommended that Pirckheimer should have the relief of the reverse lowered, in the process of reproduction, by changing the head of Terminus into a profile effigy (*ed. cit.* v, 1924, p. 397, lines 34–42; p. 470, lines 29–38). Panofsky, *Journal of the Warburg and Courtauld Institutes* 32, 1969, pp. 217–18, and L. Smolderen, 'Quentin Metsys médailleur d'Érasme', in *Scrinium Erasmianum*, vol. II, Leiden, 1969, p. 516, suggest therefore that there may have been two versions of the Massys medal with variant forms of the Terminus device on the reverses. No specimens of the variant are known.

323 K. Goossens, 'Janus Secundus als medailleur', in *Jaarboek 1970 Koninklijk Museum voor Schone Kunsten*, Antwerp 1970, pp. 29–84 (French summary).

324 P. Lelarge-Desar, in *Revue de l'Art anc. et mod.*, 1914, pp. 75 f.

325 This inscription is quoted by Jean Second (*Epist.* i. 7. 46) when he sends a specimen of the medal to Dantiscus.

326 V. Tourneur, 'Jean Second et les Busleyden', in *Rev. belge de Numism.*, 1914, pp. 140–72.

327 Franks and Grueber, *Medallic Illustr.*, Plate 2, No. 6.

328 *Numismatic Chronicle*, 1904, p. 48.

329 *Jahrb.* xxviii, p. 257.

330 Simonis 1, pp. 93–109. J. W. Frederiks, *Penningen*, Amsterdam 1947, pp. 10–19. L. Wellens De Donder, *Médailleurs et Numismates de la Renaissance aux Pays-Bas*, Brussels 1959, pp. 49–51.

331 Simonis 1, pp. 111–23. V. Tourneur, 'Jacob Zagar und die Everard Back-Medaille', *Archiv für Medaillen-und Plakettenkunde* i, 1913/14, pp. 14–20. V. Tourneur, 'Jacques Zagar et la Médaille de Liévin Kaarsemaker', *ibid.* pp. 200–4. Thieme-Becker 36 1947, p. 383. J. W. Frederiks, *Penningen*, Amsterdam, 1947, pp. 10, 20. L. Wellens De Donder, *Médailleurs et Numismates de la Renaissance aux Pays-Bas*, Brussels, 1959, pp. 53–7.

332 See V. de Munter, in *Rev. belge de Numism.*, 1914, pp. 173–80. Kress no. 630.

333 Simonis 2, pp. 43–186. Thieme-Becker 19, 1926, pp. 35–7. V. Tourneur, 'Le Médailleur Jacques Jongheling et le cardinal Granvelle, 1564–1578', *Revue belge de Numismatique* 79, 1927, pp. 79–83. V. Tourneur, 'La Médaille d'Antoine Morillon par Jacques Jongheling', *ibid.* 92, 1940/46, pp. 77–81. Marcel Hoc, 'L'oeuvre de Jacques Jongheling, médailleur anversois (1530–1606)', in the exhibition catalogue, Paris, Cabinet des Médailles, April–May 1949, *Concours de Numismatique*, pp. 127–30. G. Probszt, 'Unbekannte Renaissance-Medaillen', *Numismatische Zeitschrift* 74, 1951, pp. 86–95 (nos. 23, 25 attributed to Jonghelinck). R. van Luttervelt, 'Bij een penning van J. Jonghelinck', *Jaarboek voor Munt-en Penningkunde* 42 1955, pp. 99–102. L. Wellens De Donder, *Médailleurs et Numismates de la Renaissance aux Pays-Bas*, Brussels, 1959, pp. 94–115. L. Wellens De Donder, 'Documents inédits relatifs à J. Jonghelinck', *Revue belge de Numismatique* 106, 1960, pp. 295–305. L. Smolderen, 'Jacques Jonghelinck, waradin de la monnaie d'Anvers de 1572 à 1606', *Revue belge de Numismatique* 115, 1969, pp. 83, 247.

334 All seven of these medals are attributed to Symons by V. Tourneur, 'Jan Symons, médailleur anversois', *Revue belge de Numismatique* 77, 1925, pp. 45–55. For the medal of de Taxis see O. Le Maire, 'La médaille d'Antoine de Tassis', *Revue belge de Numismatique*, 81, 1930, pp. 253–4.

335 M. Bernart, 'Die Granvelle Medaillen des XVI. Jahrhunderts', *Archiv für Medaillen-und Plaketten-Kunde*, ii, 1920/21, pp. 101–19. V. Tourneur, 'La Médailleur Jacques Jongheling et le cardinal Granvelle, 1564–1578', *Revue belge de Numismatique* 79, 1927, pp. 79–93. R. van Lutterveldt, 'Bij een penning van J. Jonghelinck', *Jaarboek voor Munt- en Penningkunde* 42, 1955, pp. 99–102.

336 J. D. A. Thompson, 'The Beggars' Badges and the Dutch Revolt', *Numismatic Chronicle* 1972, pp. 289–94. For the letter from Morillon see Simonis 2, p. 77.

337 It must be admitted that there is a surprising difference in style between the struck and the cast medals which are assigned to him; thus the struck medals of the Governess of the Netherlands and of Alva stand quite apart from the cast medals of Perrenot, Philip II, Viglius van Zwichem, &c.

338 In addition to Simonis, see my article in the *Burlington Magazine*, vol. xii (March 1908), pp. 355, where the absurdity of the traditional name was first pointed out, and his work as painter and medallist in England discussed; also S. Muller in *Tijdschrift v. h. K. Ned. Genootschap voor Munt- en Penningkunde*, xix, 1911. In describing a new medal of Bernhard Walter of Augsburg by the same artist in *Burlington Magazine*, vol. xxxiii (August 1918), pp. 56 ff., I have taken the opportunity of summing up what is really known of him.

The artist's name is Steven van Herwijck. The standard accounts of the artist are V. Tourneur, 'Steven van Herwijck, médailleur anversois (1557–1565), *Numismatic Chronicle* 1922, pp. 91–132; Thieme-Becker 16 1923, pp. 565–6. To these may be added G. F. Hill, 'Two Netherlandish artists in England. Steven van Herwijck and Steven van der Meulen', *Transactions of the Walpole Society* xi, 1923, pp. 29–32. E. Majkowski, 'Steven van Herwijck's serie der Jagellonen-Médaillons en zijn vermeend verblijf in Polen, 1551–1562, *Jaarboek van het Koninklijk Nederlandsch Genootschap voor Munt-en Penningkunde* 24, 1937, pp. 1–37 (showing that van Herwijck did not work in Poland, but made the medals from secondary sources). V. Tourneur, 'Steven van Herwijck et les baillis de l'ordre de Malta à Utrecht', *Revue belge de Numismatique* 93, 1947, pp. 59–66. V. Tourneur, 'La médaille Guilielmus Fabius de Steven van Herwyck', *Revue belge de Numismatique* 94, 1948, pp. 101–4. L. Wellens De Donder, 'La médaille "Venus et l'Amour" de Steven van Herwijck', *Revue belge de Numismatique* 105, 1959, pp. 165–70. L. Wellens De Donder, *Médailleurs et Numismates de la Renaissance aux Pays-Bas*, Brussels, 1959, pp. 82–93. J. van Dorsten, 'Steven van Herwyck's Elizabeth (1565)—a franco-flemish political medal', *Burlington Magazine* 1969, pp. 143–7. (Here Plate 32, 2.) J. G. Pollard, 'The medal of Jan van Gorp by Steven van Herwijck', *Mints, Dies and Currency. Essays in Memory of Albert Baldwin* (ed. R. A. G. Carson), London, 1970, pp. 325–29 (here Plate 31.6).

339 Kress no. 637 (as van Herwijck). Tourneur rejected the attribution to van Herwijck of the medal of Mor, but Hill's view is supported by Pollard (in the article cited at note 338 above) at p. 326.

340 The Lumley portraits are given to Steven van der Meulen in R. Strong, *The Elizabethan Icon*, London, 1969, nos. 66, 67.

341 Kress no. 423. The medal is ascribed to a follower of Abondio, perhaps Milanese, by Habich in 'Staatliche Münzsammlung Erwerbungsbericht' *Münchner Jahrbuch der Bildenden Kunst*, N.F. 9, 1932, p. 61, plate II.4., and to Abondio by Dworschak, *Antonio Abondio, medaglista e ceroplasta 1538–1591*, Trento, 1958, p. 50.

342 Above, p. 124.

343 L. Wellens De Donder, *Médailleurs et Numismates de la Renaissance aux Pays-Bas*, Brussels, 1959, pp. 125–7.

344 Dürer's acquaintance may, however, be the goldsmith Alexander van Brugsal, who is mentioned in 1505–6; and possibly even the Alexander of Brussels who was employed from 1494 to 1509 at the English mint and produced the fine profile portrait of Henry VII on his coins. See H. Symonds, *Numismatic Chronicle*, 1913, pp. 351–3; 1915, pp. 133–4. Hill in *Numismatic Chronicle*, 1924, pp. 254–60. See also note 377.

345 L. Wellens De Donder, *Médailleurs et Numismates de la Renaissance aux Pays-Bas*, Brussels, 1959, pp. 74–6. Kress p. 123.

346 Thieme-Becker 4 1910, p. 119. V. Tourneur, 'Conrad Bloc, médailleur anversois', *Revue belge de Numismatique* 77, 1925, pp. 199–211. F. Mazerolle, 'Coins de médailles de Conrad Bloc', *ibid.* 79, 1927, pp. 95–8. O. N. Roovers, 'Portretten van Johan

Casimir', *Jaarboek van het Koninklijk Nederlandsch Genootschap voor Munt-en Penningkunde* 28, 1951, pp. 121–2. L. Wellens De Donder, *Médailleurs et Numismates de la Renaissance aux Pays-Bas*, Brussels, 1959, pp. 115–25. Kress pp. 122–3.

VII

347 Where other references are not given, the sources for this chapter will be found in F. Mazerolle, *Les Médailleurs français du XVe Siècle au milieu du XVIIe* (1902–4), and N. Rondot, *Les Médailleurs et les Graveurs de Monnaies, Jetons et Médailles en France* (1904). There are other general accounts of the medals discussed in this chapter by J. de Foville in *Histoire de l'Art* (ed. A. Michel), IV, ii, 1911, pp. 679–700; V, ii, 1913, pp. 757–76, and in J. Babelon, *La médaille en France*, Paris, 1948.

348 See above, p. 19 and note 8.

349 R. Weiss, 'The medieval medallions of Constantine and Heraclius', *Numismatic Chronicle* 1963, pp. 129–44. Weiss attributes the original medals to the Parisian workshop of Michelet Saulmon.

350 J. Tricou, 'Médailles de personnages ecclésiastiques lyonnais du xve au xviie siècles', *Revue Numismatique*, 1950, at pp. 178–80, does not repeat the attribution to Le Père but does claim that the medal is of the date that it bears. M. Huillet d'Istria, *La peinture française de la fin du moyen age. Le Maitre de Moulins*, Paris, 1961, p. 27, note 53 suggests however that the portrait type in the medal can be compared with painted effigies only of a later date.

351 J. Tricou, *Médailles lyonnaises du xve au xviiie siècles*, Paris 1958, no. 2.

352 Our illustration is of impressions from this matrix.

353 *Burlington Magazine*, vol. xx (January 1912), pp. 200 f.

354 J. Tricou, *Médailles lyonnaises du xve au xviiie siècles*, Paris, 1958, no. 4. Kress no. 527. For Perréal see G. Ring, 'An attempt to reconstruct Perréal', *Burlington Magazine* 92, 1950, pp. 255–61. M. Huillet d'Istria, 'Au sujet d'articles récents sur Jean Perréal', *Gazette des Beaux-Arts* 40, 1952, pp. 57–63 (82–4). C. Sterling, 'Une peinture certaine de Perréal enfin retrouvée', *L'Oeil* no. 103–4, 1963, pp. 2–15, 64–5. (Sterling notes at p. 5 and note 6 that Perréal did not provide the designs for the medal.)

355 Forrer 3, pp. 567–8. Thieme-Becker 24 1930, p. 85. Kress no. 528.

356 J. Tricou, 'Médailles de personnages ecclésiastiques lyonnais du xve au xviie siècle', *Revue Numismatique* 1950, at pp. 186–9. J. Tricou, *Médailles lyonnaises du xve au xviiie siècle*, Paris, 1958, nos. 9–11.

357 N. Rondot, *Jacques Gauvain*, Lyon, 1887. Thieme-Becker 13 1920, p. 294. J. Tricou, *Médailles lyonnaises*, etc. pp. 14, no. 15. V. Tourneur, 'La médaille de Philibert Guigonard', *Revue belge de Numismatique* 1921, pp. 137–43; cf. *Archiv für Medaillen-und Plakettenkunde*, iv, 1923/24, 173.

358 For Panciatichi see J. Tricou, 'Médailles religieuses de Lyon', *Revue Numismatique* 1951, pp. 115–16; J. Tricou, *Médailles lyonnaises*, etc. no. 7; Kress no. 533. For Guadagni see J. Tricou, 'Médailles religieuses de Lyon', *Revue Numismatique* 1951, at pp. 116–17; J. Tricou, *Médailles lyonnaises*, etc. nos. 12–14, Kress no. 534. For Francesconi see *Corpus* no. 1170; Kress no. 309.

359 Not Marg(uerite) Vérité, as Armand oddly reads the name. De Foville's attribution to Danet is to be found in *Rev. Numism.*, 1910, pp. 392–9. Forrer 1, p. 502; 7, pp. 202–3. *Corpus* no. 847 *ter.* note. Kress no. 540.

360 Armand, ii. 123, 14; iii. 204 c. *Corpus* no. 711. The supposed initials are a version of ETC.

361 *Corpus* nos. 712, 713.

362 H. de la Tour, 'Matteo dal Nassaro', *Revue Numismatique* 1893, pp. 517–61. Thieme-Becker 25, 1931, p. 350. S. Sulzberger, 'Matteo dal Nassaro et la transmission des oeuvres flamandes en France et en Italie', *Gazette des Beaux-Arts* 55, 1960, pp. 147–50. Kress p. 102.

363 W. McA. Johnson, 'Numismatic propaganda in Renaissance France', *The Art Quarterly* 31, 1968, pp. 123–53.

364 Thieme-Becker 9, 1913 pp. 2–3. H. Stöcklein, 'Die Medaillen von E. Delaune in der Staatlichen Münzsammlung München', *Georg Habich zum 60. Geburtstag*, Munich, 1928, pp. 53–62. B. Thomas, 'Die münchner Harnischvorzeichnungen des Étienne Delaune für die Emblem-und die Schlangen-Garnitur Heinrichs II von Frankreich', *Jahrbuch der Kunsthistorischen Sammlungen in Wien* 56, 1960, pp. 7–62 (the article includes at pp. 24–5 medal designs by Delaune for Henri II). The articles on Delaune are continued by B. Thomas, *ibid.* 58, 1962, pp. 101–68: 61 1965 pp. 41–90. W. McA. Johnson, 'Numismatic propaganda in renaissance France', in *The Art Quarterly*, 31, 1968, pp. 123–153 (includes references to Delaune medal designs).

365 J. Babelon, *Germain Pilon*, Paris, 1927, catalogue nos. 81–121. Thieme-Becker 27, 1933, pp. 44–6. J. Babelon, 'Une médaille inédite de Germain Pilon', *Cahiers Numismatique*, June 1964, pp. 4–9 (a medal of Elizabeth of Austria).

366 J. Babelon, 'Le médaillon du Chancelier René de Birague', par Germain Pilon à la Bibliothèque Nationale', *Gazette des Beaux-Arts* 1920, pp. 165–72. (A specimen of the medal of superlative quality, with its original box.)

367 J. Babelon, *Germain Pilon*, Paris, 1927, no. 120, rejects the attribution of the medal.

368 H. de la Tour, *Rev. Numism.*, 1893, pp. 259–78. Thieme-Becker 26, 1932, p. 211.

369 G. F. Hill, 'Quelques médailles italiennes', *Arethuse*, fasc. 30, 1931, at pp. 29–30. Thieme-Becker 27, 1931, p. 403. J. Babelon, *La Médaille en France*, Paris, 1948, pp. 33–4.

370 L. Cust, *Notes on the Authentic Portraits of Mary Queen of Scots*, London, 1903, pp. 121–2. R. Strong, *Tudor and Jacobean Portraits*, (National Portrait Gallery catalogue), London, 1969, vol. 1 p. 215, no. 1918 (noting that the Primavera effigy of Mary Queen of Scots is based on the Hilliard type of 1578).

371 R. Strong, *Portraits of Elizabeth*, Oxford, 1963, pp. 138–40, no. 19 (dated to perhaps 1600). Cf. *Numismatic Chronicle* 1963, pp. 269–71.

372 Mazerolle 1, pp. cxxix-cxxxix: 2, pp. 125–42, giving references to the plates of *Trésor de Numismatique, médailles françaises*, 2ᵉ partie, Paris, 1834, which remains the only convenient source for illustrations of the medals. Forrer 1, pp. 654–60: 7, p. 239. Thieme-Becker 10, 1914, pp. 173–4 (with chronological list of the medals). C. Maumené, 'Le visage royale d'Henri IV, des médailles de Guillaume Dupré aux peintures de Rubens', *Demareteion*, Paris, i, no. 1, 1935, pp. 28–39. J. Babelon, *La médaille en France*, Paris, 1948, pp. 39–43. Kress pp. 105–7.

373 J. de Foville in *Rev. de l'Art anc. et mod.*, xxxiv, pp. 149 ff., with bibliography. F. Mazerolle, *Jean Varin*, Paris, 1932. V. Tourneur, 'Les origines de Jean Varin', *Revue belge de Numismatique* 84, 1932, pp. 65–76. Thieme-Becker 35 1942, p. 161. For Claude Varin see J. Tricou, *Médailles lyonnaises du xvᵉ au xviiiᵉ siècle*, Paris, 1958, pp. 28–55. J. Tricou, 'Deux médaillons inédits de Claude Warin au Musée des Beaux-Arts de Lyon'. *Bulletin des Musées et Monuments Lyonnais*, iii, 1957/61, no. 4 (1960), pp. 311–14. Thieme-Becker 35, 1942, p. 161.

374 Ad. Herrera, in *Boletín de la Soc. Española de Excursiones*, xiii (1905), pp. 57–70. Forrer 5, 1912, pp. 277–80. Thieme-Becker 13, 1920, pp. 23–4.

VIII

375 By A. W. Franks and H. A. Grueber, based on the work of Edward Hawkins. It was published in 1885, and a series of plates in illustration of it was issued by Mr. Grueber for the Trustees of the British Museum in 1904–11. The medals referred to in this chapter are nearly all illustrated in this work. (The two volumes of text, with some line illustrations, were reprinted, London, 1969.)

376 H. Farquhar, 'The Portraiture of our Tudor Monarchs on their coins and medals', *British Numismatic Journal* 4, 1907, pp. 79–143; 'Portraiture of the Stuarts on the Royalist Badges', *ibid.*, 2, 1905, pp. 243–90; 'Portraiture of our Stuart monarchs on their coins and medals', *ibid.*, 5, 1908, pp. 145–262; 6, 1909, pp. 213–85.

377 H. Symonds, 'The English Mint Engravers of the Tudor and Stuart periods, 1485–1688', in *Numismatic Chronicle* 1913, pp. 349–377; 'Alexandre de Bruchsella', *ibid.*, 1915, pp. 133–5; 'The Mint of Elizabeth', *ibid.*, 1916, pp. 61–105; 'The Elizabethan coinages for Ireland', *ibid.*, 1917, pp. 97–125. G. F. Hill, 'Alexander of Bruchsal', *ibid.*, 1924, pp. 254–260. P. Grierson, 'Notes on early Tudor coinage. 4 The origin of the portrait groats' in *British Numismatic Journal*, 41, 1972, at pp. 89–93, shows that the dies were cut by Alexander's successor John Sharp.

378 D. Allen, 'A medal of Anne Boleyn', *British Numismatic Journal* 25, 1945/48, pp. 209–11; cf. p. 340.

379 *Medallic Illustrations*, plate II, no. 8. The medal is studied, as a seventeenth century piece, by J. B. Trapp, '"SUAVIUS OLET": a bronze medal of Thomas More and its motto', *Moreana* 4, November 1964, pp. 39–43; 'The Abate Picinelli, Domenico Regi and Thomas More, a postscript', *ibid.*, 6, May 1965, pp. 45–8.

380 G. F. Hill, 'A medal of Henry VIII as Supreme Head of the Church', *Numismatic Chronicle* 1916, pp. 194–5 (a contemporary description of the medal).

381 *Medallic Illustrations* 1, p. 57, no. 8: The latter is recorded by F. Perry, *A series of English Medals*, London, 1762, plate 2, fig. 5. It is possible that the medal of Edward VI (no. 8) is one of a group

of later antiquarian concoctions, perhaps of the seventeenth or early eighteenth century. It compares closely in style with a group of French portrait medals, as Hill notes in his text: cf. Rondot, plate XIX.2 of 'Anne de Montmorency' with the medal of Henri II, *Trésor de Numismatique et de Glyptique. Médailles francaises . . .* 1ᵉ Partie, Paris, 1836, plate XIV.4 and Engel-Gros collection sale catalogue, Paris, 17 December 1921, lot 106, plate X. If the medal of Edward VI is one of this group, the publication by Perry provides a terminal date for their production. The medal of Henry VIII (*Medallic Illustrations* 1, p. 48, no. 45: here plate 29.2) may also be an antiquarian invention. A group of Italian medallic inventions is noticed in A. S. Norris and I. Weber, *Medals and Plaquettes from the Molinari Collection at Bowdoin College*, Brunswick, Maine, 1976, nos. 201–3.

382 R. Strong, *The portraits of Elizabeth*, Oxford, 1963, pp. 134–40, suggesting some dating for the medallic portraits. To these may be added the newly discovered medal by Steven van Herwijck, see the article by van Dorsten cited at note 383 below.

383 To the English medals should be added J. van Dorsten, 'Steven van Herwijck's Elizabeth (1565)—a franco-flemish political medal', *Burlington Magazine*, 1969, pp. 143–7 (here Plate 32, 2).

384 H. Farquhar, 'John Rutlinger and the phoenix badge of Queen Elizabeth', *Numismatic Chronicle* 1923, pp. 270–93, assigning the medal to Rutlinger and dating it after 1578 (p. 293). R. Strong, *The Portraits of Elizabeth*, Oxford, 1963, p. 134 no. 3 dates the medal to c. 1574.

385 *Sylloge Numismatum Elegantiorum*, 1620, p. 255.

386 See *The Silver Map of Drake's Voyages*, by Miller Christy (1900), and Lord Milford Haven's *British Naval Medals* (1919) p. 1. J. Evans, *Num. Chron.* 1906, pp. 77–89; 348–50.

387 The statement is proved by a remarkable version of the medal (Plate 32.7) engraved on silver and unique in being both signed and dated, 1589. It has on the obverse and reverse maps of Drake's circumnavigation of the globe of 1577–80, and showing the new colony of 'Virginea' and Drake's discoveries in Upper California. On the eastern hemisphere is a cartouche engraved '*Micha: Merca: fecit extat londi: prope templu Gallo: Ano 1589*'. The records of resident aliens in London show Mercator to have been living in the city at that date, near the French Church. The medal was lot 138 in Christie,

London, sale, 4 April 1967, and is reproduced from the electrotype copy in the British Museum. It is now in the Kraus Collection, New York, and is published in H. P. Kraus, D. W. Waters and R. Boulind, *Sir Francis Drake a pictorial biography*, Amsterdam, 1970, pp. 218–20, no. 58.

388 The exquisite portrait of Leicester engraved by Hubert Goltzius on a roundel of gold, and recorded in *Medallic Illustrations* 1, p. 134 no. 90, plate 9 no. 12, as lost, is still preserved in the City Museum and Art Gallery, Birmingham (Accession no. 1532–1885). (Plate 32.5.) The print version of the portrait is O. Hirschmann, *Verzeichnis des graphischen Werks von Hendrick Goltzius*, Leipzig, 1921, no. 199a; J. W. Frederiks, *Penningen*, Amsterdam, 1947, fig. 16.

389 Lediard, *Naval History*, p. 262, says that the queen gave rewards to the Lord High Admiral, Officers and Seamen; also, in a note, that 'several medals were struck in England in Memory of this glorious Victory', but he does not connect any of the medals with the rewards.

390 R. Strong, *The Portraits of Elizabeth*, Oxford, 1963, p. 136 no. 11 (dated c. 1585).

391 On the Armada medal legend FLAVIT JEHOVA ET DISSIPATI SUNT see A. M. De Jong, 'Armada Literatur', *Tijdschrift voor Geschiedenis* 72, 1961, pp. 203–19.

392 E. Auerbach, *Nicholas Hilliard*, London, 1961, pp. 191–3, p. 325 nos. 212, 213 (where the gold medals are accepted as the work of Hilliard).

393 Symonds, *Num. Chron.* 1913, pp. 359–60.

394 *Num. Chron.*, 1896, p. 260.

395 E. Auerbach, *Nicholas Hilliard*, London 1961, pp. 193–4, p. 325 no. 214 (where the medal is described as being probably by Hilliard).

396 The latest discussion of his technique is in my article in *Num. Chron.*, 1915, pp. 230–42; the technique of the counters is discussed by Miss Farquhar in *Num. Chron.*, 1916, pp. 133–93.

397 Lady Evans, 'A silver plaque of Charles I as Prince', *Numismatic Chronicle* 1908, pp. 266–72. *British Museum Quarterly* xvii, 1952, p. 11. The plaque is attributed to Renold Elstrack.

398 The Victoria and Albert Museum has two copies of Passe medallions of James I and the Infanta Maria (M. 49, 50–1914), probably English work of the early nineteenth century, which show how skilfully these pieces could be duplicated by hand engraving.

399 On the later English work see H. Farquhar, 'Silver counters of the seventeenth century', *Numis-*

matic Chronicle 1916, pp. 133–93; 'Additional notes on silver counters of the seventeenth century', *ibid.* 1925, pp. 78–120; L. A. Lawrence, 'On a portion of a set of silver counters exhibiting London criers and their cries', in *British Numismatic Journal*, 1918, pp. 49–55. The form has remarkable vitality in the Low Countries, for which see J. W. Frederiks, *Dutch Silver*, vols. 2, 3. The Hague, 1958, 1960. A representative group is illustrated by J. W. Frederiks, *Penningen*, Amsterdam 1947

400 *Numismatic Chronicle*, 1914, pp. 169–235.

401 Ibid., 1913, pp. 422–6.

402 A variant of the Margaret Cary medal is published in *British Museum Quarterly* i, 1927, pp. 103–4, plate LVIII.

403 The date on the known specimens of the Charles I appears to be 1649; but the medals have been chased, and it would seem that in particular the date has been altered. H. Farquhar, 'Medallions true and false of Mary Queen of Scots and Charles I', *Numismatic Chronicle*, 1913, pp. 246–54, at p. 248.

404 H. Farquhar, 'The Forlorn Hope medal of Charles I', *Numismatic Chronicle* 1930, pp. 316–29 shows that the piece here called the Forlorn Hope badge is not so, and that the appellation belongs to *Medallic Illustrations* 1, p. 302 no. 123, Plate 26 no. 9. The medal here Plate 27.*11*, is not dated by Farquhar, but she does suggest that from its quality it was produced at a more leisurely time than that of the Court at Oxford. The effigy of Prince Rupert is close to the painting by Van Dyck, 1637, now in the Louvre (O. Millar, *The Age of Charles I, Painting in England 1620–1649*, Tate Gallery, London, 1972, p. 130 no. 255). An unique medal by Rawlins, of Edward Wray of Barlings, Lincolnshire, signed and dated 1657, is now in the Fitzwillian Museum, and is illustrated in *Fitzwilliam Museum Cambridge Annual Report, 1964*, p. 7, Plate VI. The medal was first published by Derek Allen in *The Walpole Society* 27, 1938/39, p. 45 note 6, where the medals by Rawlins are also listed, p. 50, Appendix II. (Here, Plate 32.*6*.)

405 H. Farquhar, 'Thomas Simon ''one of our Chief Gravers'' ', *Numismatic Chronicle* 1932, pp. 274–310. 'New light on Thomas Simon', *ibid.* 1936, pp. 210–34. D. Allen, 'Warrants and sketches of Thomas Simon', *British Numismatic Journal* 23, 1938–41, pp. 439–48. D. Allen, 'Thomas Simon's Sketch-Book', *The Walpole Society* 27, 1938/39, pp. 13–53. S. E. Whetmore, 'Notes on Thomas Simon', *British Numismatic Journal* 30, 1960/61, pp. 159–73. H. W. A. Linecar, 'Some aspects of Thomas Simon

and his work', *The Numismatic Circular* 81, 1973, pp. 430–3; 475–6. A. Nathanson, *Thomas Simon, his life and work 1618–1665*, London, 1975. Abraham Simon was born in 1617 and died probably in 1692 (see the Pedigree by C. Anthony attached to the article by Helen Farquhar in *Numismatic Chronicle* 1936, between pages 220–1, and Whetmore, *ed. cit.* p. 168). An unrecorded cast silver medal of a man by Abraham Simon (Sotheby sale, London, 12 June 1974, lot 11) is now in the Fitzwilliam Museum (see *Annual Report of the Syndicate*, 1974, pl. XI g). See Plate 32.*3*.

406 The waxes are illustrated by D. Allen in *The Walpole Society* 27, 1938/39, plate IX.

407 The problem of distinguishing the work of Thomas Simon from that of Abraham is discussed by D. Allen, *The Walpole Society* 27, 1938/39, pp. 22–3, 31–3, and appropriate lists of the medals are given in Appendix I (pp. 46–50). The rare example in gold of a medal signed by Abraham Simon of the Earl of Loudoun, 1646, formerly in the Cochran Patrick collection, is now in the Fitzwilliam Museum, and is illustrated in *Friends of the Fitzwilliam Museum Fifty-Sixth Annual Report, 1964*, p. 3.

408 R. W. Cochran-Patrick's *Catalogue of the Medals of Scotland* (1884) is a useful collection of material, but quite uncritical. Most of the medals concerned will also be found in the *Medallic Illustrations* of Hawkins.

409 The coinage of James III includes an issue of groats and half-groats of *c.* 1485 which have a remarkable naturalistic portrait of the king. See I. H. Stewart, *The Scottish Coinage*, London, 1967, p. 66: nos. 107, 119.

410 M. Bernhart, 'Judenmedaillen', *Archiv für Medaillen-und Plakettenkunde*, iii, 1921/22, pp. 115–23; U. Klein, 'Eine juristisch-numismatische Tübinger Dissertation aus dem Jahre 1755. Ein Beitrag zu den sogenannten Judenmedaillen', in *Beiträge zur Süddeutschen Münzgeschichte*, 1976, pp. 210–44.

411 Above, pp. 118–9.

412 But, as we have seen, unless the specimen engraved by Luckius was a struck specimen, the cast forgery must have been in existence by the beginning of the century.

413 There is none in the Advocates' Library as stated in *Medallic Illustrations*.

414 It is described in Anderson's *Thesaurus*, Pl. clxiv. 13.

Bibliography

This bibliography has been cast in a different form from that given by Hill in the original publication of the book. Hill allowed himself only the sparsest of annotation to his text, and therefore in the Italian section supplemented the lists of general works with a list of monographs arranged in alphabetical order of medallists. For this new bibliography however, the detailed references to monographs are omitted, as the appropriate reference for any given artist can be found through the notes which appear in this edition.

For medallists in general it may be noted here that the entries in L. Forrer, *A Biographical Dictionary of Medallists*, 8 vols., London, 1904–30 (Vol. 1 2nd ed.) are frequently far fuller than those in Thieme-Becker, *et al. Algemeines Lexikon der bildenden Künstler*, 37 vols., Leipzig, 1907–50, and then occasionally (particularly with minor medallists). Thieme-Becker simply gives a summary of Forrer.

The only other general accounts of European medals are J. Babelon, *La médaille et les médailleurs*, Paris, 1927; M. Bernhart, *Medaillen und Plaketten*, 2nd edition, Berlin, 1920, 3rd edition ed. T. Kroha, Brunswick, 1966 (the bibliographical references in the 2nd edition are more useful); G. F. Hill, 'The medal: its place in Art', *Proceedings of the British Academy* xxvii, 1941, pp. 225–45, G. F. Hill, *Guide to the Exhibition of Medals of the Renaissance in the British Museum*, London, 1923. General references for some Italian medallists can also be found in A. Venturi, *Storia dell'Arte Italiana*, and the *Enciclopedia Italiana* (Treccani). The *Dizionario Biografico degli Italiani* at present in its infancy, allows extensive treatment for medallists, but it may be noted that only the more important medallists will appear (e.g. Agostino Ardenti is not in vol. 4).

The only general bibliography for medals, from Pisanello to the twentieth century, is P. Grierson *Bibliographie Numismatique*, Brussels, 1966, pp. 159–69.

The principal periodicals concerned with medals are *Archive für Medaillen- und Plakettenkunde*, 5 vols., 1913–14, 1920–26, *Gazette numismatique française*, 1897–1914, and *Medaglia*, Milan, 1971 ff. The periodical, *Numismatic Literature* published by the American Numismatic Society, New York, has a section which reports articles on historical medals. It may be supplemented by using the appropriate portions of the *Art Index*, *Répertoire d'Art et d'Archéologie* and of the annual bibliographical fascicule of *Zeitschrift für Kunstgeschichte*.

ITALIAN MEDALS

General Works

A. ARMAND *Les médailleurs italiens des quinzième et seizième siècles*, Paris, 1883–87, 3 vols.

Useful additions to Armand appear in G. F. Hill, 'Not in Armand' *Archiv für Medaillen-und Plakettenkunde* ii, 1920/21, pp. 10–28: 45–54.

R. Müller, 'Nachtrag zu Armand', *ibid.* iii, 1921/22, pp. 41–4.

C. A. Ossbahr 'Nachtrag zu Armand' . . . aus dem Königl. 'Münzkabinett zu Stockholm', *ibid.* iv, 1923/4, pp. 93–4.

M. Bernhart, 'Nachtrage zu Armand', *ibid.* v, 1925/6, pp. 69–90 (materials from the collections in Berlin, Vienna and Munich).

G. Probszt, 'Unbekannte Renaissance-Medaillen' *Numismatische Zeitschrift* 74, 1951, pp. 86–95.

T. W. Greene 'Notes on some Italian Medals', *Numismatic Chronicle* 1913, pp. 413–21.

E. BERNAREGGI *Monete d'oro con ritratto del Rinascimento Italiano 1450–1515*, Milan, 1954.

P. DELAROCHE, *et al.* See below *Trésor de numismatique* . . .

C. VON FABRICZY *Italian Medals* (translated by Mrs G. W. Hamilton), London, 1904.

J. FRIEDLÄNDER *Die italienischen Schaumünzen des fünfzehnten Jahrhunderts*, Berlin, 1882.

P. A. GAETANI *Museum Mazzuchellianum, seu numismata virorum doctrina Praestantium*, 2 vols., Venice, 1761–3 (The collection is now in Brescia, see Public Collections, below).

G. HABICH *Die Medaillen der italienischen Renaissance*, Stuttgart-Berlin, 1924.

A. HEISS *Les Médailleurs de la Renaissance* 9 vols., Paris, 1881–92.

   I   *Vittore Pisano*, 1881.

  II *Francesco Laurana, Pietro da Milano*, 1882.

 III *Niccolò, Amadio da Milano* etc., 1883.

  IV *Léon Battista Alberti, Matteo de' Pasti*, etc. 1883.

   V *Niccolò Spinelli, Antonio del Pollaiuolo*, etc. 1885.

  VI *Sperandio de Mantoue*, etc. 1886.

 VII *Venise et les vénitiens da XVe au XVIIe siècle*, 1887.

VIII *Florence et les florentins du XVe au XVIIe siècle*, première partie, 1891.

  IX *ibid*, deuxième partie, *Florence et la Toscane sous les Médicis 1532–1737*, 1892.

The materials in the first six volumes have been superseded by the *Corpus* of G. F. Hill, but vols. vii–ix contain medals not otherwise illustrated. The ancillary materials given by Heiss in the whole publication remain valuable.

G. F. HILL *A Corpus of the Italian Medals of the Renaissance before Cellini*, 2 vols., London, 1930.

— *A Guide to the exhibition of Medals of the Renaissance in the British Museum*, London, 1923.

— *Select Italian medals of the Renaissance in the British Museum*, London, 1915 (a portfolio of fifty plates of medals to *c*.1600).

— *Portrait Medals of the Italian Artists of the Renaissance*, London, 1912.

— *The medallic portraits of Christ*, etc. Oxford, 1920.

— 'Italian portraits of the Fifteenth Century', *Proceedings of the British Academy* xi, 1925, pp. 331–49.

C. F. KEARY *A Guide to the Exhibition of Italian Medals*, (British Museum) London, 2nd edition, 1893.

H. NUSSBAUM 'Fürstenporträte auf italienischen Münzen des Quattrocento', *Zeitschrift für Numismatik* 35, 1925, pp. 145–92.

J. VON SCHLOSSER 'Die ältesten Medaillen und die Antike', *Jahrbuch der Kunsthistorischen Sammlung des A. H. Kaiserhauses* xviii, Vienna, 1897.

Trésor de numismatique et de glyptique. Médailles coulées et ciselées en Italie aux XVe et XVIe siècles, ed. P. Delaroche, H. Dupont, and C. Lenormant, 2 vols., Paris, 1824, 1826.

R. WEISS 'Le origini franco-bizantine della medaglia italiana del Rinascimento' *Venezia e l'Oriente fra tarde Medioevo e Rinascimento* (ed. A. Pertussi) in the series *Civiltà Europeo e Civiltà Veneziana, Aspetti e Problemi* 4, (Fondazione Giorgio Cini), Venice-Florence, 1966, pp. 339–50.

Public Collections

BERLIN. Königliche Museen. *Sammlung von Renaissance – Kunstwerken gestiftet von Herrn James Simon,* Berlin, 1908.

BRESCIA. P. Rizzini. *Illustrazione dei civici musei di Brescia: parte ii, Medaglie,* Brescia, 1891–3 (including the materials from the Mazzuchelli collection, qv. Gaetani under General Works, above).

FLORENCE. I. B. Supino. *Il medaglieri Mediceo nel R. Museo Nazionale di Firenze,* Florence, 1899.

LONDON. British Museum. G. F. Hill, *A Guide to the exhibition of Medals of the Renaissance in the British Museum,* London, 1923.

G. F. Hill, *Select Italian Medals of the Renaissance,* London, 1915.

C. F. Keary, *A Guide to the Exhibition of Italian Medals,* London, 2nd ed., 1893.

MADRID. F. Alvarez-Ossorio, *Catalogo de las medallas de los siglos xv y xvi conservadas en el Museo Arqueológico Nacional,* Madrid, 1950.

NAPLES, A. De Rinaldis, *Medaglie dei secoli xv e xvi nel Museo Nazionale di Napoli,* Naples, 1913.

SANTA BARBARA, Calif. See MORGENROTH under Private Collections.

WASHINGTON. G. F. Hill and G. Pollard, *Renaissance Medals from the Samuel H. Kress Collection at the National Gallery of Art,* New York, London, 1967 (The collection was formerly that of Gustave Dreyfus, and the catalogue is a revised and enlarged version of the Dreyfus catalogue by G. F. Hill of 1930).

F. PANVINI ROSATI, *Medaglie e Placchette italiane dal Rinascimento al xviii secolo,* Rome 1968 (based on the catalogue of an exhibition held in Germany and Belgium of medals and plaquettes from fourteen Italian public collections).

Private Collections

CIECHONOWIECKI   J. Fischer, *Sculpture in miniature. The Andrew S. Ciechanowiecki collection of gilt and gold medals and plaquettes,* exhibition catalogue, the J. B. Speed Art Museum, Louisville, Kentucky, October-November 1969. (A remarkable collection of European medals, of which 86 are Italian).

DREYFUS   See WASHINGTON, under Public Collections, above.

MORGENROTH   U. Middeldorf and O. Goetz, *Medals and Plaquettes from the Sigmund Morgenroth Collection,* Chicago, 1944. (Now in the University Art Gallery, Santa Barbara, Calif.)

SALTON M. and L. Salton, *The Salton Collection, Renaissance and Baroque medals and plaquettes.* Brunswick, Maine. (Bowdoin College Museum of Art), 2nd ed. 1969. (A loan exhibition.)

Auction Catalogues

GREENE, T. W.   The T. Whitcombe Greene collection, Sotheby, London 30 October 1933 (the catalogue also appears dated 1932, the Auction having been postponed for one year).

LANNA   *Sammlung des Freiherrn Adalbert von Lanna, Prag, dritter Teil, Medaillen und Münzen* (by K. Regling). Lepke, Berlin, 16–19 May 1911.

LÖBBECKE   *Sammlung Arthur Löbbecke, Braunschweig. Kunstmedaillen und Plaketten des xv. bis xvii. Jahrhunderts,* Hirsch, Munich (catalogue no. xxiii) 26 November, 1908.

OPPENHEIMER   *The Henry Oppenheimer collection,* Christie, Manson and Woods, London, 27–29 July, 1936.

ROSENHEIM   *Max and Maurice Rosenheim collection,* Sotheby, London 30 April–4 May 1923. (The British Museum acquired the following lots of Italian medals from the sale: 1, 3, 9, 14, 32–4, 36, 39, 42, 47–9, 52, 59, 60, 64, 66, 67, 85, 87, 91, 92, 97, 100, 104, 105, 107–10, 114, 119–21, 124, 125, 132, 141, 144, 147, 148, 160, 168–70, 172, 177, 178, 184, 189–91, 195, 197, 204, 207, 210–12, 214–16, 221, 226–28, 232, 233.)

WEINZHEIMER   *Medaillen und Plaketten des 15–18 Jahrhunderts. Die Sammlung eines deutschen Künstlers in Italien* (F. W. Weinzheimer). *Auktionskatalog 2,* Münzhandlung, Basel, 8 October, 1934.

Subjects and Schools

BOLOGNA   G. F. Hill, 'Giovanni Zacchi and the Bologna School' *Burlington Magazine* 25, 1914, pp. 335–41.

FLORENCE   A. Heiss, *Les Médailleurs de la Renaissance, viii, Florence et les florentines du xve au xviie siècle*, première partie, Paris, 1891; *ibid.* ix, deuxième partie, *Florence et la Toscane sous les Médicis 1532–1737*, Paris, 1892.

GONZAGA family   see MANTUA below.

MANTUA   A. Magnaguti, *Le medaglie mantovane*, Mantua, 1921.

   A. Magnaguti, *Ex Hummis Historia Parte vii, I. Gonzaga nelle loro monete e nello loro medaglie*, Rome, 1957.

   A. Magnaguti, *Ex Nummis Historia ix, le medaglie dei Gonzaga*, Rome, 1965.

PAPAL MEDALS   see ROME, below.

ROME   C. G. Bulgari, *Argentieri gemmari e orafi d' Italia, Parte Prima, Roma*, 2 vols. Rome, 1958, 1959.

   F. Bartolotti, *La medaglia annuale dei Romani Pontefici da Paolo V a Paolo VI, 1605–1967*, Rimini, 1967.

   F. Bonanni, *Numismata Pontificum Romanorum quae a tempore Martini V usque ad annum MDCXCIX* . . . Rome, 2 vols., 1699.

   G. F. Hill, 'The medals of Paul II', *Numismatic Chronicle* 1910, pp. 340–69.

   G. F. Hill, 'The Roman medallists of the Renaissance to the time of Leo X,' *Papers of the British School at Rome*, 9, 1920, pp. 16–66.

   Messrs W. S. Lincoln, *A descriptive catalogue of papal medals, to which is added papal bullae and medals of cardinals and other church dignitaries*, London, 1898. (The part concerning papal medals was reissued by Messrs Spink, London, 1962, titled *Catalogue of Papal Medals.*)

   E. Martinori, *Annali della Zecca di Roma. Serie papale*, 24 fascicules, Rome (Istituto Italiano di Numismatica). 1917–22.

   Trésor de numismatique et de glyptique (ed. P. Delaroche, H. Dupont, & C. Lenormant) *Choix historique des médailles des papes*, Paris, 1839.

   R. Weiss, *The medals of Pope Sixtus IV (1471–1484)*, Rome, 1961.

   R. Weiss, 'Un umanista veneziano – Papa Paolo II', *Civiltà Veneziana, Saggi 4*, Venice (Fondazioni Cini), 1958.

   R. Weiss, 'The medals of Julius II (1503–13)', *Journal of the Warburg and Courtauld Institutes* 28, 1965, pp. 163–82.

VENICE   A. Heiss, *Les Médailleurs de la Renaissance. VII Venise et les Vénitiens du xve au xviie siècle*, Paris, 1887.

   J. de Foville, 'L'élève vénitien de Riccio,' *Archiv für Medaillen-und Plaketten-Kunde*, i, 1913/14, pp. 73–81.

   G. F. Hill, 'A Group of Venetian Medals', *Archiv für Medaillen-und Plaketten-Kunde*, i, 1913/14, pp. 122–6.

   R. Weiss, 'La medaglia veneziana del Rinascimento e l'umanesimo', *Umanesimo Europeo e Umanesimo Veneziano* (ed. V. Branca), *Civiltà Europea e Civiltà Veneziana, Aspetti e Problemi 2*, Venice/Florence, (Fondazione Cini), 1963, pp. 337–48.

   R. Weiss, 'Vittore Camelio e la medaglia veneziana del Rinascimento' *Rinascimento Europeo e Rinascimento Veneziano* (ed. V. Branca), *Civiltà Europea e Civiltà Veneziana, Aspetti e Problemi 3*, Venice/Florence 1967 (Fondazione Cini), pp. 327–37.

   R, Weiss, 'Un umanista veneziano – Papa Paolo II', *Civiltà Veneziana, saggi 4*, Venice (Fondazione Cini), 1958.

GERMAN MEDALS

M. BERNHART   *Die Bildnismedaillen Karls V*, Munich, 1919.

—— 'Augsburger Medailleure und Bildnisse augsburger Kunsthandwerker auf Schaumünzen des 16 Jahrhunderts', *Mitteilungen der Bayerischen Numismatischen Gessellschaft* 55, 1937, pp. 41–98.

—— 'Kunst und Künstler der nurnberger Schaumünzen des 16. Jahrhunderts', *ibid.*, 54, 1936, pp. 1–61.

K. DOMANIG   *Porträtmedaillen der Erzhauses Oesterreich*, Vienna, 1896.

K. DOMANIG   *Die deutsche Medaille in Kunst-und Kulturhistorischer Hinsicht nach dem Bestande der Medaillensammlung der A. H. Kaiserhauses*, Vienna, 1907.

A. ERMAN   'Deutsche Medailleure des sechszehnten und siebzehnten Jahrhundert', *in Zeitschrift für Numismatik* 12, 1885, pp. 14–102 (also as a book).

G. HABICH 'Studien zur deutschen Renaissance-medaille', *Jahrbuch der Königlich preussischen Kunstsammlungen*, vols. 27, 1906, pp. 13–69; 28, 1907, pp. 181–98, 230–272; 34, 1913, pp. 1–35.

G. HABICH *Die deutschen Medailleure des XVI. Jahrhunderts*, Halle, 1916.

— *Die deutschen Schaumünzen des XVI. Jahrhunderts*, 2 vols. (in 4), Munich, 1929–34.

V. KATZ *Die Erzgebirgische Prägemedaille des XVI. Jahrhunderts*, Prague, 1931.

F. J. STOPP *The Emblems of the Altdorf Academy. Medals and Orations 1577–1626*. London, 1976.

A. SUHLE *Die deutsche Renaissance-Medaille*, Leipzig, 1950. (Principally concerning the work of Schwarz, Weiditz, Hagenauer and Gebel.)

Trésor de numismatique et de glyptique (ed. P. Delaroche, H. Dupont & C. Lenormant) *Choix de médailles exécutées en Allemagne aux xvie et xviie siècles*, Paris, 1841.

MEDALS OF THE NETHERLANDS

J. W. FREDERIKS *Penningen*, Amsterdam, 1947.

PARIS EXHIBITION, 1956 Musée Monetaire, *Médailles des anciens Pays-Bas, contribution numismatique à l'Histoire du Protestantisme*.

A. PINCHART *Histoire de la gravure des médailles en Belgique, Mémoires couronnés par l'Académie* xxxv, Brussels, 1870.

J. SIMONIS *L'Art du Médailleur en Belgique*, Brussels, Jemeppe, 2 vols., 1900, 1904.

J. WELLENS-DE DONDER *Médailleurs et Numismates de la Renaissance aux Pays-Bas*, exhibition catalogue, Bibliothèque Royale, Brussels, 1959 (full bibliography).

F. VAN MIERIS *Historie der nederlandsche vorsten*, 3 vols., The Hague, 1732–5 (medals down to the abdication of Charles V, 1555).

G. VAN LOON *Historie métallique des xvii provinces des Pays-Bas*, 5 vols., The Hague, 1732–7 (continuation of van Mieris to 1716. First published in Dutch, 4 vols., The Hague, 1723–31).

FRENCH MEDALS

J. BABELON *La médaille en France*, Paris, 1948.

J. BABELON *Germain Pilon*, Paris, 1927.

F. MAZEROLLE *Les médailleurs francais, du xve au milieu du xviie siècle*, 2 vols. and album of plates, Paris, 1902–4.

F. MAZEROLLE *Jean Varin*, Paris, 1932.

A. MICHEL (ed.) *Histoire de l'Art*: E. Babelon, 'Les origines de l'art du médailleur', vol. III pt. 2, pp. 897–924, Paris, 1908. J. de Foville, 'La médaille française au temps de Henri IV', vol. V, pt. 2, pp. 758–76, Paris, 1913.

N. RONDOT *Les médailleurs et les graveurs des monnaies, jetons et médailles en France*, Paris, 1904.

Trésor du Numismatique et de Glyptique (ed. P. Delaroche, H. Dupont, C. Lenormant) *Médailles françaises depuis la règne de Charles VII jusqu'à celui de Louis XVI*. Paris, I^e Partie, 1836; IIe Partie, 1834.

J. TRICOU *Médailles lyonnaises du xve au xviiie siècle*, Paris, 1958.

R. WEISS, 'The medieval medals of Constantine and Heraclius', *Numismatic Chronicle* 1963, pp. 129–44.

— 'Le origini franco-bizantine della medaglia italiana del Rinascimento' in *Venezia e l'Oriente fra tardo Medioevo e Rinascimento* (ed. A. Pertussi) in the series *Civiltà Europea e Civiltà Veneziana. Aspetti e Problemi* 4 (Fondazione Giorgio Cini), Venice/Florence, 1966, pp. 339–50.

MEDALS OF ENGLAND AND SCOTLAND

G. C. BROOKE AND G. F. HILL *Guide to the exhibition of historical medals in the British Museum*, London, 1924.

R. W. COCHRAN-PATRICK *Catalogue of the medals of Scotland*, Edinburgh, 1884.

E. HAWKINS *Medallic illustrations of the history of Great Britain and Ireland to the death of George II* (ed. A. W. Franks and H. A. Grueber) 2 vols., London, 1885 (text reprinted, London, 1969). The work is a British Museum publication. The plates were published in 19 folio fascicules, London 1904–11.

MARQUESS OF MILFORD HAVEN *British Naval Medals*, London, 1919.

George Francis Hill
A Biographical Note

George Hill was born on 22 December 1867, at the London Missionary Society's station at Berhampur in India. The station had been founded by his grandfather Micaiah Hill, and his father, Samuel John Hill was also a missionary. Hill was the youngest of four brothers and was sent to the school for the sons of missionaries at Blackheath, and afterwards to University College School, University College, London, and Merton College, Oxford. He took first classes in Classical Moderations and in Greats, his main subject being ancient history. He was a pupil of Professor Percy Gardner, from whom he acquired the special interest in numismatics which determined his career. In 1893 he entered the British Museum as an Assistant in the Department of Coins and Medals. At that time the Department was a world centre for the study of Greek numismatics. The series of catalogues of Greek coins begun by R. S. Poole was being continued by B. V. Head, and Hill joined this labour and published in 1897 the first of the six volumes which he added to the series. Hill was Keeper of the Department from 1912 to 1930. In 1897 he had married Mary Paul, daughter of D. J. D. Paul of Leicester, and Hill spent his long vacations with his parents-in-law who were settled in Rome. Mary Hill died in 1924. The expeditions to Italy stimulated Hill's interest in Italian history and art, he published in 1905 an excellent book on Pisanello, and in 1930 the monumental *Corpus* of Italian Renaissance medals, the product of more than twenty years of work.

Hill was appointed Director and Principal Librarian of the British Museum, 1931–36, and created K.C.B. in 1933. In his retirement he completed a history of Cyprus of which volume one appeared in 1940, volumes two and three in 1948, and volume four in 1952. To celebrate Hill's eightieth birthday a bibliography of his writings in ancient history and archaeology, in numismatics, in history and in Italian art was prepared and presented to him. Its lists forty-five books and pamphlets and some 280 articles in various journals. Hill died on 18 October 1948. (*Who's Who*; *The Times*, 20 October 1948).

A Bibliography of
Sir George Hill's Writings on Medals

The greater part of Hill's publications on medals concerned Italian material. The following bibliography derives, with additions and corrections, from *A Tribute to Sir George Hill on his eightieth Birthday, 1867–1947*, Oxford, 1948. That pamphlet bibliography was privately printed and has remained difficult to find, it seemed therefore appropriate to annex to this re-issue of Hill's only extensive general work on medals, a bibliography of his other writings in the field.

The materials are arranged in the following manner:

1 Books
2 General essays
3 Essays on Italian medals, including contributions to the Thieme-Becker *Kunstler Lexikon*
4 'Notes on Italian Medals', the series of articles in *The Burlington Magazine*
5 Essays on non-Italian medals
6 Reviews and prefaces

In Sections 3–5 of this bibliography the names of medallists are printed in SMALL CAPITALS.

1 BOOKS

Pisanello, London, 1905.

Drawings by Pisanello, a selection with introduction and notes, Paris/Brussels, 1929 (Reprinted, New York, 1965).

Portrait medals of Italian Artists of the Renaissance, London, 1912.

Select Italian medals of the Renaissance in the British Museum, London, 1915 (a portfolio of fifty plates of medals to *c.* 1600).

On Medals (Civic Arts Association), London, 1917.

Medals of the Renaissance, Oxford, 1920.

The Medallic Portraits of Christ; the False Shekels; the Thirty Pieces of Silver, Oxford, 1920.

A Guide to the Exhibition of Medals of the Renaissance in the British Museum, London, 1923.

A Guide to the Exhibition of Historical Medals in the British Museum (with G. C. Brooke), London, 1924.

A Corpus of Italian Medals before Cellini, 2 vols., London, 1930.

The Gustave Dreyfus Collection, Renaissance Medals, Oxford, 1931.

2 GENERAL ESSAYS

'Italian Medals', *Knowledge* xix, 1896, pp. 17–19.

'English Medals', *Knowledge* xx, 1897, pp. 82–4, 184–7.

'Coins and Medals', Hasting's *Encyclopedia of Religion and Ethics*, 1910.

'Numismatics', *Encyclopedia Britannica*, XIth edition, vol. 19, 1911.

'Numismatics: Technique and Art', *Encyclopedia Britannica*, XIVth edition, vol. 16, 1928.

'Medallic Portraits of Christ in the Fifteenth Century', *The Reliquary*, N.S. x, 1904, pp. 173–93.

'Medallic Portraits of Christ in the Sixteenth Century', I, *The Reliquary*, N.S. x, 1904, pp. 260–9; II, *ibid.* xi, 1905, pp. 38–52.

'Renaissance Medals with the Heads of Christ', *The Reliquary*, N.S. xi, 1905, pp. 238–48.

'Coronation Medals', *Apollo* xxv, no. 149, 1937, pp. 255–60.

'Commemorative Medals', *The Times Literary Supplement*, 13 July 1916.

'The Medal: its place in Art', *Proceedings of the British Academy* xxvii, 1941, pp. 225–46.

'Italian Portraiture in the Fifteenth Century', in *Proceedings of the British Academy* xi, 1925, pp. 331–49.

3 ESSAYS ON ITALIAN MEDALS

This section is arranged in alphabetical order of subject, and it includes Hill's contributions to Thieme-Becker, *Kunstler Lexikon*. The names of medallists are printed in SMALL CAPITALS.

A

'Frate ANTONIO DA BRESCIA', *Miscellanea di Storia dell'Arte in onore di Igino Benvenuto Supino, a cura della Rivista d'Arte*, Florence, 1933, pp. 483–4.

'Not in Armand', *Archiv für Medaillen-und Plakettenkunde*, ii, 1920/21, pp. 10–28; 45–54.

B

'Medals of the Bolzanio Family', *Archiv für Medaillen-und Plakettenkunde*, i, 1913/14, pp. 1–6.

C

CANDIDA, Giovanni, Thieme-Becker 5, 1911.

CARADOSSO, Cristofano, Thieme-Becker 5, 1911.

'Chaffrey Carles', *Numismatic Chronicle* 1926, pp. 93–8, (concerning *Corpus* no. 698).

'The Medals of Gianbattista Castaldi', *Numismatic Chronicle* 1917, pp. 166–8 (The medals are by ANIB . . . and by GALEOTTI).

'NICOLO CAVALLERINO et ANTONIO DA VICENZA', *Revue Numismatique* 1915, pp. 243–55.

CAVALLI, Giambattista, Thieme-Becker 6, 1912.

CAVALLI, Giam Marco, Thieme-Becker 6, 1912.

CAVINO, Giovanni, Thieme-Becker 6, 1912.

CESATI, Alessandro, Thieme-Becker 6, 1912.

'Classical Influence on the Italian Medal', *Burlington Magazine* 18, 1911, pp. 259–268.

COMPAGNI, Domenico de', Thieme-Becker 7, 1912.

CORRADINO, Lodovico, Thieme-Becker 7, 1912.

COSTANZO da Ferrara, Thieme-Becker 7, 1912.

'Edward Courtenay', *Numismatic Chronicle* 1925, pp. 265–7 (a medal by PASTORINO).

CRISTOFORO di Ieremia, Thieme-Becker 8, 1913.

D

'Andrea and Gianettino Doria', *Pantheon* iv, 1929, pp. 500–1.

E

ENZOLA, Gian Francesco, Thieme-Becker 10, 1914.

G

'Francesco Girardenghi', *The Library* (Transactions of the Bibliographical Society), vi, 1925, p. 90 (concerning *Corpus* no. 700).

'The Protonotary Giuliano', *Burlington Magazine* 29, 1916, p. 245.

'Francesco Gonzaga and Bartolommeo Montagna', *Burlington Magazine* 60, 1932, pp. 197–8.

'Italian Medals from the Whitcombe Greene Collection', *British Museum Quarterly*, viii, 1934, pp. 115–16.

GUAZZALOTTI, Andrea, Thieme-Becker 15, 1922.

I

'Italian Medals', *Knowledge* xix, 1896, pp. 17–19.

'The Italian Medals in the Salting Collection', *Burlington Magazine* 20, 1912, pp. 18–24.

'Italian Medals from the Whitcombe Greene Collection', *British Museum Quarterly*, viii, 1934, pp. 115–16.

Section on 'Medals' in *Catalogue of Italian Sculpture and other Plastic Arts*, Burlington Fine Arts Club, London, 1913.

'Some Italian Medals of the Sixteenth Century', *Georg Habich zum 60. Geburtstag*, Munich, 1928, pp. 10–15. (Giuseppe Colloredo by Fra GIULIO da Brescia; Princess Isabella of Poland by Giov. Maria MOSCA; unknown woman by Antonio ABONDIO; Titian by Agostino ARDENTI; unknown woman by BOSIO(?); Orazio Tigrino de Marii by T.R.; anonymous medal of Eufrasia Placidi.

'Quelques médailles italiennes', *Arethuse*, fasc. 30, 1931, pp. 27–30. (Mahomet II; Vincenzo Albaresano by PASTORINO; Georges André de Haberstein by Lodovico LEONI, with a table of the other medals by Leoni; three medals by PRIMAVERA, of François d'Aydie, Jules de Guersans, Charles de Lorraine).

'Some lead Italian medals', *Archiv für Medaillen-und Plakettenkunde* v, 1925/26, pp. 20–5. (Onofrio Bartolini de'Medici by Giovanni ZACCHI; four medals by PASTORINO, of Michel Vialar, Caterina Sacrata, Violante Pigna, Francisco de Alava; anonymous medal of Camilla Pallavicina).

'Two Italian medals of Englishmen', *Numismatic Chronicle* 1909, pp. 292–6. (Medals of Sir John Cheke, perhaps by MARTINO DA BERGAMO, and of Richard White by Lodovico LEONI).

'Two medals of Englishmen', *Numismatic Chronicle* 1919, pp. 61–3. (William Villiers, Earl of Jersey, by SOLDANI).

L

LEONI, Leone, Thieme-Becker 23, 1929.

LIXIGNOLO, Giacomo, Thieme-Becker 23, 1929.

M

Malatesta, *see* 'Il Pandolfaccio', below.

'A Maltese medal of 1679', *Numismatic Chronicle* 1938, pp. 198–202 (a foundation medal for the Choir of the Cathedral).

'L'École des Médailleurs de Mantoue', *Arethuse*, fasc. 1, 1923, 12–21: fasc. 2, 1924, pp. 61–6.

MARESCOTTI, Antonio, Thieme-Becker 24, 1930.

'Gold Medal of Queen Mary Tudor', *British Museum Quarterly* ii, 1928, pp. 37–8 (medal by DA TREZZO).

'The portraits of Giuliano de'Medici', *Burlington Magazine* 25, 1914, pp. 117–18.

MELON, Giovanni, Thieme-Becker 24, 1930.

'Milanese Armourers' Marks', *Burlington Magazine* 36, 1920, pp. 49–50. (Marks on medals by PISANELLO, *Corpus* 36, and GUACIALOTI, *Corpus* 745).

O

'Medals of Niccolo Orsini, Count of Pitigliano and Nola', *Numismatic Chronicle* 1925, pp. 380–4.

P

'La Pace della Chiesa', *Atti e Memorie dell'Istituto Italiano di Numismatica*, ii, 1915, pp. 257–61 (concerning *Corpus* no. 755).

'Il Pandolfaccio', *Cronache d'Arte* ii, 1925, p. 20 (medal of Pandolfo IV di Roberto Malatesta, *Corpus* no. 1130).

'The Medals of Matteo de' PASTI', *Numismatic Chronicle* 1917, pp. 298–312.

PASTI, Matteo de', Thieme-Becker 26, 1932.

PASTORINO, Thieme-Becker 26, 1932.

'The medals of Paul II', *Numismatic Chronicle* 1910, pp. 340–69.

'Tre Medaglie di Girolamo di Benedetto Pesaro, Podestà di Padova', in *Boll. del Mus. Civ. di Padova*, N.S. i, 1925, pp. 71–4.

'PISANELLO's Portrait of a Princess', *Burlington Magazine* 5, 1904, pp. 408–13.

'New Light on PISANELLO', *Burlington Magazine* 13, 1908, p. 288.

'Recent Research on PISANELLO', *Burlington Magazine* 17, 1910, pp. 361–2.

'On some dates in the career of PISANELLO', *Numismatic Chronicle* 1931, pp. 181–96.

'A Lost Medal by PISANELLO, *Pantheon*, viii, 1931, pp. 487–8.

'Some Drawings from the Antique attributed to PISANELLO', *Papers of the British School at Rome*, iii, 1906, pp. 295–324.

'Giovanni Pietro de POMIS', *Archiv für Medaillen-und Plakettenkunde*, iv, 1923/24, p. 82.

PRIMAVERA, Thieme-Becker 27, 1933.

R

'Timotheus REFATUS of Mantua and the Medallist 'T.R.', *Numismatic Chronicle* 1902, pp. 55–61 (showing that Refatus is not the medallist 'T.R.').

198

REFATUS, Timotheus, Thieme-Becker 28, 1934.

'The Roman Medallists of the Renaissance to the time of Leo X', *Papers of the British School at Rome* ix, 1920, pp. 16–66.

S

'The Italian Medals in the Salting Collection', *Burlington Magazine* 20, 1912, pp. 18–24.

'La Medaglia di Sebastiano Salvini di proprietà della Società Columbaria', *Atti della Soc. Columb. di Firenze, 1909–10*, 1912, pp. 347–8 (concerning *Corpus* no. 1086).

'Two medals of Englishmen', *Numismatic Chronicle* 1919, pp. 61–3 (medal of William Villiers, Earl of Jersey, by SOLDANI).

SPERANDIO, Thieme-Becker 31, 1937.

SPINELLI, Niccolo, Thieme-Becker 31, 1937.

T

TALPA, Bartolo, Thieme-Becker 32, 1938.

TEGNIZA, Thieme-Becker 32, 1938.

'A Medal of Gian Giacomo Trivulzio', *Per il iv° Centenario della morte di Leonardo da Vinci* (Istituto di Studi Vinciani in Roma), 1915, p. 319.

'Medals of Turkish Sultans', *Numismatic Chronicle* 1926, pp. 287–98.

V

'A group of Venetian Medals', *Archiv für Medaillen- und Plakettenkunde* i, 1913/14, pp. 122–6.

4 NOTES ON ITALIAN MEDALS

Between 1906 and 1923 Hill published a series of articles in the *Burlington Magazine* under the general title 'Notes on Italian Medals'. They are listed below, with their sub-titles where given, and with a note of the respective contents other than materials re-published in Hill's *Corpus of Italian Medals*, 1930. The names of medallists are printed in SMALL CAPITALS.

I 'Some medals by PASTORINO da Siena', in vol. 9, 1906, pp. 408–12.

II 'Some Italian medals in the British Museum', in vol. 10, 1907, pp. 384–7 (medals by PASTORINO; medal of Onofrio Bartholini de'Medici by Giovanni ZACCHI).

III (with Max Rosenheim), in vol. 12, 1907, pp. 141–54 (medals by Antonio ABONDIO and the medallist A.A.; medal of Sir John Cheke).

IV 'The medallist LYPSIPPUS', in vol. 13, 1908, pp. 274–86.

V 'Eight Italian Medals', in vol. 14, 1909, pp. 210–17 (medals of Narcissus Vertunnus; Vettor Grimani; Giovanni Alvise Gonfalonieri by GALEOTTI; Francesco da Ragogna; Baldassare Baldi).

VI 'Three Wax Models', in vol. 15, 1909, pp. 31–5 (models of Giacomo Negroboni; Barbara Romana; Antonio Galateo).

VII in vol. 15, 1909, pp. 94–8 (medal of Charles V by Leone LEONI).

VIII in vol. 16, 1909, pp. 24–31 (a group of fabrications).

IX 'FRANCESCO di Giorgio and Federigo of Urbino', in vol. 17, 1910, pp. 143–6.

X in vol. 18, 1911, pp. 13–21 (some medals by CELLINI).

XI in vol. 19, 1911, pp. 138–44.

XII in vol. 20, 1912, pp. 200–8 (medal of Lelio Torelli by Francesco da SANGALLO; the medallist Giovanni Battista CAPOCACCIA).

XIII 'Some Florentine Medals', in vol. 22, 1912, pp. 131–8 (medals of Count Panico and Pompeo Ludovisi, Gabriele Taddini, by CAVINO; Girolamo Vida by TEGNIZA).

XIV in vol. 23, 1913, pp. 17–22 (a group of Venetian sixteenth century medals depicting Elia and Rica de Lattes; Girolamo and Elena Cornaro; Ludovico and Giampaolo Podocataro; Elisabetta Quirini; Paolo Rannusio; Cecilia Vitali. A medal of Giovanni Fondati).

XV in vol. 24, 1913, pp. 36–40 (medals from the T. W. Greene collection of Niccolo Madruzzo by Antonio ABONDIO; Ottavio Farnese by PASTORINO; Ottaviano Pallavicini; Giulio della Rovere).

XVI in vol. 24, 1914, pp. 211–17 (medal of Francesco Firmi by Leone LEONI; two wax models for medals of Ferdinando I de'Medici by MAZZAFIRRI, and of Sigismund III King of Poland, anonymous).

XVII   in vol. 25, 1914, pp. 221–7.

XVIII   'Giovanni ZACCHI and the Bolognese School', in vol. 25, 1914, pp. 335–41.

XIX   'Scipione Clusona', in vol. 27, 1915, pp. 65–6, 168.

XX   in vol. 27, 1915, pp. 235–42 (anonymous portrait medals, including the Emilian School of the sixteenth century).

XXI   in vol. 29, 1916, pp. 56–9 (anonymous and unidentified sixteenth century portraits. Giovanni Battista Pigna by BOMBARDA).

XXII   in vol. 29, 1916, pp. 251–8 (the medallist T.P.; medals by RUSPAGIARI and BOMBARDA).

XXIII   in vol. 30, 1917, pp. 190–8 (anonymous medals of Pietro Lauro and Federigo de'Negri; Alfonso II d'Este by PASTORINO; Francesco Maria del Monte Santa Maria by Lodovico LEONI; Helen of Troy by Domenico POGGINI).

XXIV   in vol. 31, 1917, pp. 99–105.

XXV–   'On the technique of the Renaissance
XXVI   Medal', in vol. 31, 1917, pp. 178–83, 211–17 (including an account and illustrations of the wax models for coinage by MOLA or MORONE-MOLA, from the T. W. Greene Collection).

XXVII   in vol. 42, 1923, pp. 38–47 (an account of acquisitions by the British Museum. Consalvo da Cordoba signed ANNIB . . . ; Cornelia Siciliana by PASTORINO; Giovanni Battista Giustini Villanova by GALEOTTI; Paolo Regio degli Orseoli by Antonio CANTILENA; Daniele Centurione, signed MARTS. SASO).

5 ESSAYS ON NON-ITALIAN MEDALS

The names of medallists are in SMALL CAPITALS.

'ALEXANDER OF BRUCHSAL', Numismatic Chronicle, 1924, pp. 254–60.

'Note on the medieval medals of Constantine and Heraclius', Numismatic Chronicle 1910, pp. 110–16.

'Medal of Henry VIII as Supreme Head of the Church', Numismatic Chronicle 1916, pp. 194–5.

'The Technique of Simon van der PASSE', Numismatic Chronicle 1915, pp. 230–42.

(with Maurice Rosenheim) 'A Medal of Lorenz Staiber', Numismatic Chronicle 1919, pp. 244–52.

'STEVEN H., Medallist and Painter', Burlington Magazine 12, 1908, pp. 355–63.

'Recent Acquisitions for Public Collections IV: British Museum; STEVEN H', Burlington Magazine 33, 1918, pp. 54–9.

'Two Netherlandish Artists in England. STEVEN VAN HERWIJCK and Steven van der Meulen', The Walpole Society xi, 1923, pp. 29–32.

'A New Medal by Claude WARIN', Numismatic Chronicle 1913, pp. 422–6. (Medal of John Prideaux.)

'Two Medals of Englishmen', Numismatic Chronicle 1919, pp. 61–3 (medals of Tanfield Vachell by B. RICHTER; William Villiers, Earl of Jersey, by SOLDANI).

The Commemorative Medal in the Service of Germany, London, 1917.

Les Médailles Commémoratives Comme Instruments de Propagande Allemande, London, 1917.

Åminnelsemedaljen i Tysklands Tjänst, London, 1918.

Médailles de Guerre Allemandes, Paris/Neuchatel, 1918.

Deutsche Kriegsmedaillen, Bern, 1918.

'French Medals of the Great War', British Museum Quarterly, i, 1927, p. 52.

6 REVIEWS AND PREFACES

Review of J. Babelon, La Médaille et les Médailleurs, Numismatic Chronicle 1926, pp. 478–80.

Review of J. Babelon, Jacopo da Trezzo, Numismatic Chronicle, 1923, pp. 164–6.

Review of M. Bernhart, Die Bildnismedaillen Karls des Fünften, Numismatic Chronicle, 1921, pp. 158–60.

Review of M. Bernhart and K. Roll, Die Münzen und Medaillen des Erzstiftes Salzburg, Numismatic Chronicle 1929, p. 180.

Review of A. Calabi and G. Cornaggia, Matteo dei Pasti, Numismatic Chronicle 1926, pp. 481–2.

Review of C. von Fabriczy, Medaillen der italienischen Renaissance, Numismatic Chronicle 1903, pp. 190–2.

Preface to Mrs G. W. Hamilton's translation of C. von Fabriczy's *Italian Medals*, London, 1904.

Review of G. Habich, *Medaillen der italienischen Renaissance, Numismatic Chronicle* 1924, pp. 121–6.

Introductory Note to Ethel A. C. Harris, *Portrait Medals of a Generation*, London, 1928.

Preface to T. Spicer-Simson, *Medals of Men of Letters of the British Isles*, New York, 1924.

'The Portraits of Michelangelo', *Burlington Magazine* 25, 1914, pp. 345–6 (review of Steinmann).

Review of V. Tourneur, *Jehan de Candida, Numismatic Chronicle* 1920, pp. 90–3.

Key to the Plates

When not otherwise described, the medals are of bronze or some other alloy of copper. The following abbreviations are used for collections.

B.	Berlin Museum.	M.R.	The former collection of Max and Maurice Rosenheim, sold by Sotheby, London, 30 April 1923.
B.M.	British Museum.		
H.O.	The former collection of Henry Oppenheimer, sold by Christie, London, 27 July 1936.	P.	Paris, Bibliothèque Nationale.
		V.A.M.	Victoria and Albert Museum.

1

Alfonso V of Aragon. 1449. By Pisanello. *Rev.* Eagle and prey. B.M. *Corpus* 41e.

2

1. Wax model of medal of Giacomo Negroboni. *Rev.* Lion of St. Mark. H.O. Now in the Metropolitan Museum, New York. *Corpus* 537.

2. Wax model of medal of Barbara Romana. M.R.

3

1. John VIII Palaeologus. 1438. By Pisanello. B.M. *Corpus* 19h.

2. Sigismondo Malatesta, by Pisanello. *Rev.* Sigismondo in armour. B.M. Lead. *Corpus* 33f.

3. *Rev.* of Leonello d'Este, marriage medal. 1444. By Pisanello. Cupid teaching a lion to sing. B.M. *Corpus* 32d.

4. Domenico Malatesta, by Pisanello. *Rev.* Domenico's vow. V.A.M. *Corpus* 35f.

5. *Rev.* of Cecilia Gonzaga. 1447. By Pisanello. Innocence and the unicorn. *Corpus* 37.

6. *Rev.* of Alfonso V of Aragon, by Pisanello. Alfonso hunting a boar. B.M. *Corpus* 42c.

7. John of Tossignano, by Marescotti. B.M. *Corpus* 79.

8. Vittorino da Feltre, by Pisanello. *Rev.* Pelican in her Piety. H.O. *Corpus* 38.

9. Borso d'Este. 1460. By Lixignolo. *Rev.* Unicorn purifying a stream. B.M. *Corpus* 94.

10. Guarino of Verona, by Pasti. B.M. *Corpus* 158.

4

Leonello d'Este, by Pisanello.

1. *Rev.* Youth and age, and impresa of mast and sail. B.M. *Corpus* 26b.

2. *Rev.* Recumbent youth and impresa of the broken vase. B.M. *Corpus* 30b.

3. *Rev.* Blindfolded lynx, symbol of statecraft. B.M. *Corpus* 28b.

5

1. Don Iñigo d'Avalos, by Pisanello. *Rev.* The Shield of Achilles. B.M. *Corpus* 44c.

2. Alfonso V of Aragon, by Paolo da Ragusa. H.O. *Corpus* 45g.

3. Borso d'Este, by Amadeo da Milano. B.M. *Corpus* 69c.

4. Isotta degli Atti, by Pasti. B.M. *Corpus* 189f.

5. Sigismondo Malatesta. 1446. By Pasti. *Rev.* Rocca of Rimini. B.M. *Corpus* 174d.

6

1. L. B. Alberti, by himself (?). Coll. of the late M. Gustave Dreyfus. *Corpus* 16b.

2. Giovanni Cossa, by Laurana. Dresden. *Corpus* 62a.

3. Federigo Gonzaga. 1495. By Talpa. B.M. *Corpus* 204b.

4. Margaret of Anjou, by Pietro da Milano. V.A.M. Bronze gilt. *Corpus* 55a.

5. Degenhart Pfeffinger, by Adriano Fiorentino. Gotha. *Corpus* 347a.

6. *Rev.* of Mohammad II. 1481. By Costanzo. B.M. *Corpus* 322c.

7. Federigo of Urbino, attributed to Francesco di Giorgio. *Rev.* Horseman and dragon. M.R. Now in the British Museum. *Corpus* 307a.

8. Costanzo Sforza of Pesaro. 1475. By Enzola. B.M. *Corpus* 294f.

9. Pasquale Malipieri, Doge of Venice (1457–62), by Guidizani. *Rev.* Concordia group of Senate and Council of Venice. M.R. Now in the British Museum. *Corpus* 414a.

7

1. Francesco Gonzaga, by Melioli. *Rev.* Adolescentia Augusta. B.M. *Corpus* 196e.

2. Giulia Astallia. *Rev.* Phoenix on pyre. B.M. *Corpus* 218e.

3. Giulia Gonzaga (?). By L'Antico. B.M. *Corpus* 214b (Identification rejected).

4. Jacopa Correggia. *Rev.* Captive Cupid. B.M. *Corpus* 234c.

8

1. Bartolommeo della Rovere. 1474. By Sperandio. *Rev.* Arms of della Rovere. B.M. Lead. *Corpus* 375b.

2. Giuliano della Rovere, by Sperandio. *Rev.* Allegory of Life. Lead. B.M. *Corpus* 395d.

9

1. Caracalla, by Boldù. *Rev.* Allegory of Death. B.M. *Corpus* 423g.

2. Gambello, by himself. 1507. *Rev.* Sacrifice. B.M. *Corpus* 446c.

10

1. Nicolò Michiel and Dea Contarini, by Fra Antonio da Brescia. B.M. *Corpus* 471c.

2. Sebastiano Renier, by Maffeo Olivieri. *Rev*. Venice rising from the sea. B.M. *Corpus* 489b.

3. Anonymous Lady, by Pomedelli. *Rev*. Prosperity and Love. B.M. *Corpus* 594c.

11

1. Angelus Marinus Regulus, by Giulio della Torre. *Rev*. Master instructing a bear. B.M. *Corpus* 583.

2. Maximilian I. 1506. By Gian Marco Cavalli. *Rev*. Maximilian on horseback, accompanied by Mars, Justice, and Loyalty. M.R. Now in the British Museum. *Corpus* 248a.

3. Gentile Bellini, by Gambello. B.M. *Corpus* 439a.

4. Gian Maria Pomedelli, by himself. *Rev*. Hercules of Thasos. B. *Corpus* 596a.

5. Pier Maria Rossi of Berceto and Bianca Pellegrini, by Enzola. B. *Corpus* 296a.

6. Giovanni II Bentivoglio, by Francia, commemorating grant of right of coinage. 1494. B.M. *Corpus* 606e.

7. Francesco Alidosi, by a pupil of Francia. *Rev*. Jupiter in eagle-car. B.M. *Corpus* 610f.

12

1. Alfonso, Duke of Calabria. 1481. By Guacialoti. *Rev*. Triumph of Otranto. B.M. *Corpus* 745d.

2. Lodovico Scarampi, by Cristoforo di Geremia. B.M. *Corpus* 756d.

3. Giovanni Candida, by himself(?). Modena. *Corpus* 822a.

4. Lysippus the medallist, by himself. B.M. *Corpus* 796a.

5. Maximilian and Mary of Burgundy, by Candida. M.R. *Corpus* 831.

6. Julius II. 1506. By Caradosso. B.M. *Corpus* 659.

7. Bramante, by Caradosso. *Rev.* Architecture. M.R. Now in the British Museum. Bronze gilt. *Corpus* 657f.

13

1. The Pazzi Conspiracy, escape of Lorenzo and murder of Giuliano de' Medici. 1478. By Bertoldo. B.M. *Corpus* 915h.

2. Jacopo della Sassetta. B.M. *Corpus* 1087a.

3. Pietro Maria. B.M. *Corpus* 999b.

4. John Kendal. B.M. *Corpus* 934b.

14

1. Alfonso I d'Este, by Nicolò Fiorentino. 1492. *Rev.* Alfonso in triumphal car. B.M. *Corpus* 923b.

2. Giovanni Pico della Mirandola. B.M. Lead. *Corpus* 998d.

3. Giovanna Albizzi. *Rev.* The Three Graces. B.M. *Corpus* 1021c.

15

1. Fra Girolamo Savonarola. *Rev.* The Holy Ghost and the Sword of the Lord over Florence. B.M. *Corpus* 1079d.

2. Gioacchino della Torre. *Rev.* Mercury with executioner's sword. B.M. *Corpus* 1089a.

16

1. Pietro Bembo, North Italian. *Rev.* Pegasus. B.M.

2. Lelio Torelli. 1551. By Francesco da Sangallo. B.M.

3. Cosimo I de' Medici, by Domenico Poggini. *Rev.* Victories over French and Turks. B.M. Lead.

4. Hassan the Envoy. 1556. By Pastorino. B.M. Lead.

5. Francesco Taverna, by Galeotti. *Rev.* Dog as symbol of loyalty. B.M.

6. Isabella Rammi d'Este, by Pastorino. B.M. Lead gilt.

7. Benedetto Varchi, by Dom. Poggini. *Rev.* Man reposing under a tree. B.M.

8. Gianpietro Crivelli, by himself. B.M.

9. Girolamo Veralli, by Giovanni Zacchi. *Rev.* Griffin on a palm-tree, attacked by another monster. B.M.

17

1. Clement VII. 1534. By Cellini. *Rev.* Peace burning arms. B.M. Silver.

2. Isabella Spagiari, by Pastorino. B.M. Lead.

3. Giulio Cesare del Grosso, by Pastorino. B.M. Lead.

4. Clement VII, by Giov. Bernardi. *Rev.* Joseph and his Brethren. B.M.

5. Pietro Bembo, by T. P. B.M. Lead.

6. Paul III, by Aless. Cesati. *Rev.* Ganymede watering Farnese lilies. B.M.

7. Andrea Briosco il Riccio. B. *Corpus* p. 140.

8. Pietro Bembo, by Valerio Belli. *Rev.* Bembo beside a spring. P.

9. Elisabetta Quirini. B.M.

10. Reverse of medal of Francesco Comendone. Friendship, double-faced, holding fasces. B.

11. Girolamo Panico and Pompeo Lodovisi, by Cavino. *Rev.* Arms of Panico and Lodovisi. B.M. Silver.

12. The Empress Maria, wife of Maximilian II, by Antonio Abondio. M.R. Now in the British Museum.

18

1. Pietro Aretino, by Vittoria. B.M.

2. Caterina Chieregataa, by Vittoria. B.

3. Jacopo Tatti called Sansovino, by Lodovico Leoni. V.A.M. Lead.

4. Andrea Doria. 1541. By Leone Leoni. *Rev.* Bust of the artist surrounded by fetters. B.M.

5. Martin Hanna, by Leone Leoni. *Rev.* Hope. B.M.

6. Michelangelo Buonarroti. 1561. By Leone Leoni. B.M. Lead.

7. Lodovica Poggi, by Bombarda. B.M. Lead.

8. Reverse of medal of Gianello della Torre, by Jacopo da Trezzo. The Fountain of the Sciences. B.M.

9. Mary Tudor, by Jacopo da Trezzo. B.M. Silver.

10. Nicolò Madruzzo, by Antonio Abondio. *Rev.* The Crises of Fortune. Formerly coll. of Mr. T. W. Greene.

11. Anonymous Lady, by Ruspagiari. B.M. Lead.

19

1. Anonymous woman. 1514. By Albrecht Dürer. B.M. Lead. Habich *Corpus* 15.

2. Otto Henrich Count Palatine. 1527. By Hans Daucher. V.A.M. Habich *Corpus* 54.

3. Conrad Peutinger. 1517–18. By Hans Schwarz. V.A.M. Habich *Corpus* 111.

4. Henry VIII. In the manner of Hans Schwarz. B.M. Lead. Habich *Corpus* 269.

5. Lucia Doerrer. 1522. By Hans Schwarz. B.M. Lead. Habich *Corpus* 239.

6. Urban Labenwolf. 1518. In the manner of Hans Schwarz. V.A.M. Habich *Corpus* 121.

7. Charles V, Ferdinand I, and Maria, Queen of Hungary. 1532. By Peter Flötner. V.A.M. Silver. Habich *Corpus* 1824.

8. Charles V. 1537. By Hans Reinhart. *Rev.* Arms. M.R. Silver. Now in the British Museum. Habich *Corpus* 1926.

9. Hieronymus Paumgartner. 1553. By Joachim Deschler. *Rev.* Arms. M.R. Habich *Corpus* 1611.

20

1. So-called Michael Wolgemuth, by Albrecht Dürer. 1508. M.R. Lead. Now in the British Museum. Habich *Corpus* 13.

2. Lienhard (Lux) Meringer, by Christoph Weiditz. B.M. Lead. Habich *Corpus* 346.

3. Jan Count of Egmont, by Hans Schwarz. B.M. Habich *Corpus* 273.

4. Michael Mercator. 1539. By Hagenauer. B.M. Silver. Habich *Corpus* 627.

5. Agnes Lauchberger. 1532. By Hagenauer. B.M. Silver. Habich *Corpus* 587.

6. Philip Melanchthon, by Hagenauer. B.M. Lead. Habich *Corpus* 652.

7. Sebastian Gienger. 1532. By Hans Kels?. *Rev.* Cupid and skull. M.R. Silver. Habich *Corpus* 1299.

8. Peter Harsdörffer. 1528. By Conrad Meit. *Rev.* Arms and armour. Gotha. Silver. Habich *Corpus* 735.

9. Christoph Kress. 1526. *Rev.* Arms. V.A.M. Silver. Habich *Corpus* 945.

10. Conrad Reutter, Abbot of Kaisersheim. 1527. *Rev.* Arms. V.A.M. Silver. Habich *Corpus* 952.

21

1. Georg von Embs. 1542. By Mathes Gebel. *Rev.* Arms. H.O. Habich *Corpus* 1208.

2. Christoph Tetzel. 1528. By Mathes Gebel. *Rev.* Arms. M.R. Silver. Habich *Corpus* 972.

3. Georg Hermann, Conrad Mair, Heinrich Ribisch. 1531. By Mathes Gebel. *Rev.* Arms. H.O. Silver. Habich *Corpus* 1061.

4. Raimund Fugger. 1530. By Mathes Gebel. *Rev.* Liberality. M.R. Silver. Habich *Corpus* 1014.

5. Leonard von Egk. 1527. By Mathes Gebel?. M.R. Habich *Corpus* 954.

6. Martin Geuder. 1528. By Mathes Gebel. M.R. Now in the British Museum. Habich *Corpus* 973.

7. Wilibolt Gebhart. 1555. By Hans Bolsterer. M.R. Silver. Habich *Corpus* 1797.

8. Sigmund von Nanckenreut. 1551. By Hans Bolsterer. B.M. Lead. Habich *Corpus* 1790.

9. Johann Maslitzer. 1574. By Valentin Maler. B.M. Lead. Habich *Corpus* 2463.

10. Heinrich von Bobenhausen, by Tobias Wolff?. *Rev.* Arms. B.M. Silver.

11. Charles V. 1542. By Ludwig Neufarer. *Rev.* Imperial eagle and Columns of Hercules. V.A.M. Silver. Habich *Corpus* 1404.

22

1. William Schevez, Archbishop of St. Andrews. 1491. *Rev.* Arms. B.M.

2. Erasmus of Rotterdam. 1519. By Quentin Metsys. *Rev.* Terminus. B.M. Lead.

3. Antonis de Taxis. 1552. By Jan Symons. *Rev.* Arms. M.R.

4. Margaret of Austria, Governess of the Netherlands. 1567. By Jonghelinck. *Rev.* Allegory of Firm Government. B.M. Silver.

5. Floris Allewyn. 1559. By Steven van Herwijck. M.R.

6. Engelken Tols. 1558. By Steven van Herwijck. B.M. Lead.

7. Jacobus Fabius. 1559. By Steven van Herwijck. B.M. Lead.

23

1. Julia, mistress of Jean Second, by him. 1528–9. B.M. Lead.

2. Philip II. 1557. By Jonghelinck. *Rev.* St. Quentin. B.M. Silver.

3. Levinus Bloccenus de Burgh. 1566. By Zagar. B.M. Lead.

4. Mary Dimock. 1562. By Steven van Herwijck. *Rev.* Diana and stag. B.M. Silver.

5. Antonis van Stralen. 1565. By Jonghelinck. *Rev.* Fortune. B.M. Silver.

6. Richard and Dorcas Martin. 1562. By Steven van Herwijck. B.M. Silver.

7. Charity, by Steven van Herwijck. (*Rev.* of medal of Hans van den Broeck. 1559). B.M. Lead.

8. Pomponne de Bellièvre. 1598. By Coenrad Bloc. *Rev.* Sun dispelling clouds. B.M. Silver gilt.

24

1. Constantine the Great. *Rev.* The Church and Paganism?. B.M. Silver.

2. Philibert and Margaret of Savoy, by Jean Marende. 1502. *Rev.* Arms. Mazerolle 30.

3. Louis XII and Anne of Brittany. 1500. By Nicolas Le Clerc and Jean de Saint-Priest. B.M. Mazerolle 27.

4. Anne of Brittany and the Dauphin Charles-Orland. 1494. *Rev.* Arms of France and Dauphiné quartered. B.M. Mazerolle 25.

5. Henri II. 1559. By Germain Pilon. B.M. Mazerolle 232.

6. Marie de Vignon, Marquise de Treffort. 1613. By J. Richier. B.M. Lead. Mazerolle 759.

7. Jean Salian, Augustinian preacher. By Claude Warin. B.M. Lead.

25

1. Charles, Cardinal Bourbon. 1486. *Rev.* St. John Baptist. B.M.

2. Charles VIII and Anne of Brittany. 1493 (O.S.). By Louis Lepère, Nicolas de Florence and Jean Lepère. B.M. Silver. Mazerolle 22.

3. Louis XII. 1499. By Nichel Colombe. *Rev.* Porcupine. P. Gold. Mazerolle 26.

4. Marguerite de Foix, Marquise de Saluces. 1516. *Rev.* Arms. B.M. Silver. *Corpus* 711.

5. François I, by Matteo dal Nassaro. *Rev.* Mars and Victory crowning the king. B.M. Silver.

6. Henri II. 1552. By Étienne de Laune. *Rev.* Fame. B.M. Silver. Mazerolle 97.

7. Antoine, King of Navarre, by Étienne de Laune. *Rev.* Sun dispelling clouds. B.M. Silver. Mazerolle 104/376.

8. *Rev.* of Charles IX, by Alex. Olivier, 1572; the king triumphant over Huguenots. B.M. Silver. Mazerolle 164.

9. Henri II, Charles V, Caesar and Lucretia, by Rouaire. *Rev.* Fame. B.M. Silver. Mazerolle 297.

26

1. Regnault Danet and his wife Marguerite. By R. Danet. B.M. Lead.

2. Jacques de Vitry, by the Medallist of 1518. B.M. Lead. Mazerolle 41.

3. Jacques Gauvain, by himself. B.M. Lead. Mazerolle 51.

4. Elizabeth, Queen of England, by Primavera. B.M. Lead. Mazerolle 305.

5. Mary, Queen of Scots, by Primavera. B.M. Mazerolle 300.

6. Philippe Desportes, by Germain Pilon. B.M. Lead. Cp. Mazerolle 249.

7. Cardinal Richelieu. 1630. By Jean Warin. B.M.

8. Henri IV as Hercules. 1602. By Philippe Danfrie. B.M. Silver.

9. Jean de Caylar de Saint Bonnet, Marquis de Toyras. 1634. By G. Dupré. B.M. Silver.

10. Marcantonio Memmo, Doge of Venice. 1612. By G. Dupré. B.M. Silver.

11. Marie de Médicis. 1624. By G. Dupré. B.M. Silver.

27

1. Henry VIII. *Rev.* Tudor Rose. B.M. Silver. M.I.30 15: pl. 2 5.

2. Henry VIII. B.M. Lead. M.I.50 48: pl. 3 8.

3. Henry VIII. *Rev.* Lion and orb. B.M. Silver. M.I.44 38: pl. 3 3.

4. Elizabeth, Recovery from small-pox. 1572. *Rev.* St. Paul's hand and the serpent. B.M. Silver. M.I.116 48: pl. 8 1.

5. Elizabeth. *Rev.* Phoenix. B.M. Copper. M.I.91 3: pl. 6 9.

6. Elizabeth. 1602. *Rev.* Minerva. B.M. Silver. M.I.181 184: pl. 13 15.

7. Henry, Prince of Wales. Jeton. B.M. Gold. M.I.200 29: pl. 15 7.

8. Anne of Denmark. Jeton. B.M. Silver. M.I.192 12: pl. 14 12.

9. Charles I, Scottish Coronation. 1633. By Nicolas Briot. B.M. Gold. M.I. 265 59: pl. 22 1.

10. James I, by Simon Passe; *Rev.* Arms. B.M. Engraved silver plate. M.I.215 62: pl. 16 2.

11. Charles I and Prince Charles. The so-called Forlorn Hope medal. 1643. By Thomas Rawlins. B.M. Silver gilt. M.I.301 122: pl. 26 8.

12. Prince Rupert. 1645. B.M. Silver. M.I.323 159: pl. 28 7.

28

1. Henry VIII as Supreme Head of the Church. 1545. By Henry Basse. B.M. Gold. M.I.47 44: pl. 3 6.

2. Thomas Cromwell. 1538. *Rev.* Arms. B.M. Silver gilt. M.I.39 32: pl. 2 10.

3. Edward VI, Coronation. 1547. By Henry Basse. B.M. Silver. M.I.54 2: pl. 3 11.

4. Elizabeth. Phoenix Badge. B.M. Silver. M.I.124 70: pl. 8 17.

5. Robert Dudley, Earl of Leicester, Departure from Netherlands 1587. *Rev.* Sheep dog leaving flock. B.M. Silver. M.I.140 100: pl. 10 6.

6. Elizabeth. B.M. Silver. M.I.183 186: pl. 13 17.

7. Elizabeth, destruction of the Armada. 1588. *Rev.* Bay-tree on island. B.M. Gold. M.I.154 129: pl. 11 9.

8. Elizabeth, destruction of the Armada. 1588. *Rev.* Ark in a storm. B.M. Silver. M.I.148 119: pl. 11 2.

9. James I, offering-besant. 1603. B.M. Silver. M.I.187 2: pl. 14 2.

10. Nicholas and Dorothy Wadham, 1618. B.M. Silver. M.I.220 73: pl. 17 4.

29

1. Charles I, Dominion of the Sea. 1630. By Nicolas Briot. *Rev.* Ship in full sail. B.M. Gold. M.I. 256 41: pl. 21 1.

2. Henry VIII. B.M. Lead. M.I.48 45: pl. 3 7.

3. Théodore de Mayerne. 1625. By Nicolas Briot. *Rev.* Hermetic symbols. B.M. Lead. M.I.241 8: pl. 19 14.

4. Edward VI. B.M. Lead. M.I.56 7: pl. 4 1.

5. William Blake. 1634. By Warin. B.M. Silver. M.I.270 70: pl. 22 11.

6. Anne Blake. 1634. By Warin. B.M. Silver. M.I.272 71: pl. 22 12.

7. Thomas Cary. 1633. By Warin. B.M. M.I.269 67: pl. 22 9.

8. James VI of Scotland and Anne of Denmark. Marriage. 1590. Coll. of the Duke of Atholl. Gold. M.I.157 136: pl. 11 13.

30

1. Sir Sidenham Pointz. 1646. By Abraham Simon. B.M. Silver. M.I.325 163: pl. 28 12.

2. Dorcas Brabazon, Lady Lane. 1662. By Abraham and Thomas Simon. B.M. Silver. M.I.479 89: pl. 30 2.

3. George Monk, Duke of Albemarle. 1660. By Abraham Simon. B.M. Gold. M.I. 465 63: pl. 44 11.

4. Thomas Wriothesley, Earl of Southampton. 1664. By Abraham and Thomas Simon. B.M. Gold. M.I.502 137: pl. 48 9.

5. Naval Reward. 1653. By Thomas Simon. (Later reproduction. This reproduction, inadvertently substituted for the original in the Plate, is exact, save in some details of the border). Shields of England, Scotland, and Ireland on an anchor. *Rev.* Sea fight. B.M. Silver. M.I.398 26: pl. 35 14.

6. Charles II, Coronation. 1661. By Thomas Simon. B.M. Gold. M.I.472 76: pl 45 7.

7. Oliver Cromwell, Battle of Dunbar. 1650. By Thomas Simon. *Rev.* Parliament in session in one house. B.M. Silver. M.I.392 14: pl. 35 5.

8. John, Duke of Albany. Jeton. 1524. Arms and Phoenix. Hunterian Coll., Glasgow. Gold. M.I.28 11: pl. 2 3.

9. Mary, Queen of Scots, Pattern half-testoon. 1553. By John Acheson?. *Rev.* Arms. B.M. Silver. M.I.65 4: pl. 4 5.

10. George Lord Seton and his wife, Isabella. 1562. Jeton. By Michael Gilbert. B.M. Gold. M.I.102 27: pl. 7 4.

11. Mary, Queen of Scots. 1560. Claim to the English throne. *Rev.* Two worldly and one celestial crowns. B.M. M.I.96 15: pl. 6 14.

31

1. Pietro Bembo, by Valerio Belli, the *obv.* and *rev.* Dies. The *rev.* shows Bembo reclining by a stream. Bargello, Florence. See note 245.

2. a. Pope Clement VII, by Cellini. b. *rev.* Moses striking the rock. c. *rev.* Peace. Bargello, Florence. See note p. 85; note 217.

3. Cardinal d'Armagnac, 1554. Pastorino. Fitzwilliam Museum. Uniface lead. From the Whitcombe Greene Collection, the specimen is unique. See p. 86.

4. Cleopatra, by Camelio. *Rev.* Seated Pan. Birmingham City Museum and Art Gallery. (The medal identifies as Cleopatra the piece published by Schwabacher at note 128.) See p. 58; notes 128, 240.

5. François I, by Cellini. Fitzwilliam Museum. Uniface struck lead. See p. 85; note 127.

6. Jan van Gorp. By Steven van Herwijck. *Rev.* Harpocrates. Fitzwilliam Museum. See note 338.

32

1. Edward Courtenay, Earl of Devon, 1556. By Pastorino. Fitzwilliam Museum. Uniface lead. The medal was made at Ferrara in March 1556. (Hill in *Numismatic Chronicle* 1925, pp. 265–7.) See pp. 85–6.

2. Elizabeth I. By Steven van Herwijck. *Rev.* Faith at the Divine Fountain of the Realm. National Portrait Gallery. Lead. See note 383.

3. Unknown man, 1647. By Abraham Simon. Fitzwilliam Museum. Silver. See note 405.

4. Unknown man, by Simon Van De Passe. *Rev.* (not shown) Arms of Ramsey. British Museum. Engraved silver. See p. 155.

5. Robert, Earl of Leicester. By Hubert Goltzius. Birmingham City Museum and Art Gallery. Engraved gold. M.I.134 90: pl. 9 12. See note 388.

6. Edward Wray of Barlings, Lincs., 1657. By Thomas Rawlins. Fitzwilliam Museum. Silver, uniface. See note 403.

7. Obverse of an engraved silver map of Drake's voyages, dated 1589. By Michael Mercator. H. P. Kraus Collection, New York (reproduced from an electrotype copy in the British Museum). See pp. 149–50; note 387.

8. Cromwell. Anonymous Dutch satirical medal of probably 1654/5, on England's treaties with Portugal and France. Engraved silver. Jacques Schulman BV Amsterdam. *Obv.* Equestrian figure of Cromwell. The legend calls him a relation of the Sultan of Turkey. (The *rev.*, not shown, depicts a Turk and a monk conversing, in the background an army.) See note 399.

Index

1. Alfonso V of Aragon by Pisanello. (Actual size)

2. Giacomo Negroboni and Barbara Romana. Wax models (actual size)

3. By Pisanello, Pasti, and Lixignolo. (Half actual size)

4. Leonello d'Este by Pisanello. (Actual size)

5. By Pisanello, Paolo da Ragusa, Amadeo and Pasti. (Actual size)

6. By Laurana, Alberti, Costanzo and others. (Half actual size)

7. Medals of the Mantuan School. (Actual size)

8. Bartolommeo and Giuliano della Rovere by Sperandio. (Actual size)

9. Caracalla by Boldù. Gambello by himself. (Actual size)

10. By Fra Antonio da Brescia, Maffeo Olivieri and Pomedelli. (Actual size)

11. By Giulio della Torre, Gambello, Enzola, Francia and others. (Actual size)

12. Medals of the Roman School. (Actual size)

13. Medals of the Florentine School. (Actual size)

14. Medals of the Florentine School. (Actual size)

15. Florentine School: Savonarola and Gioacchino della Torre. (Actual size)

16. Florentine, Roman and Bolognese Schools. (Two-thirds actual size)

17. Various Italian Schools of the sixteenth century. (Actual size)

18. North Italian Schools of the sixteenth century. (Two-thirds actual size)

1

2

3

4

5

6

7

8

7

9

8

9

19. By Dürer, Hans Schwarz, Reinhardt and others. (Two-thirds actual size)

20. By Dürer, Weiditz, Hagenauer and others. (Actual size)

21. By Mattes Gebel, Bolsterer, Neufarer and others. (Actual size)

22. By Quentin Matsys, Jonghelinck, Van Herwijck and others. (Approx. two-thirds actual size)

23. By Jean Second, Jonghelinck, Van Herwijck and others. (Actual size)

24. French School. (Half actual size)

25. French School. (Actual size)

26. French School. (Two-thirds actual size)

27. English Medals. (Actual size)

28. English Medals. (Three-quarters actual size)

29. English and Scottish Medals. (Two-thirds actual size)

30. English and Scottish Medals. (Actual size)

1a

2a

2b

1b

2c

4a

3

5

4b

6a

6b

31. Supplementary Plate. (Actual size)

32. Supplementary Plate. (Actual size)